Approaches
to Media
LITERACY

Approaches to Media LITERACY

A Handbook

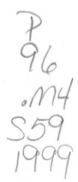

Art Silverblatt

Jane Ferry

Barbara Finan

M.E. Sharpe
Armonk, New York
London, England

Library of Congress Cataloging-in-Publication Data

Silverblatt, Art. 1949– .
Approaches to media literacy : a handbook / Art Silverblatt, Jane Ferry, Barbara Finan.
p. cm.
Includes bibliographical references and index.
ISBN 0–7656–0184–2 (hc. : alk. paper). ISBN 0–7656–0185–0 (pbk. : alk. paper)
1. Media literacy—Handbooks, manuals, etc. I. Ferry, Jane, 1941– .
II. Finan, Barbara, 1937– . III. Title.
P96.M4S59   1999
302.23—dc21
98–47331
CIP

Printed in the United States of America

The paper used in this publication meets the minimum requirements of
American National Standard for Information Sciences—
Permanence of Paper for Printed Library Materials,
ANSI Z 39.48-1984.

⊗

MV (c)   10   9   8   7   6   5   4   3   2
MV (p)   10   9   8   7   6   5   4   3

To Monkey, with love:
"If you remember, I remember, good old Eddie Stanky."
—Art

In memory of Dick
For Megan, Maureen, and Sean
—Jane

To the Coach and our sons, Tony, Mike, and Tom
—Barb

CONTENTS

LIST OF FIGURES

PREFACE

When one of the co-authors was a doctoral student, his final course was a required Shakespeare class. On the first day, the elderly professor addressed the class: "There is one Truth to Shakespeare," he intoned. "And I know what that Truth is." Having set the ground rules, the game became clear. We, as graduate students, were to climb into the professor's dusty brain and extract that Truth.

Our intrepid co-author then raised his hand and mentioned that the university library was filled with books that offered different perspectives ("truths") about the Great Bard. This apparently was unwelcome news to the professor. It was not a pleasant semester.

With this in mind, *Approaches to Media Literacy* offers a range of approaches to the study of media literacy (in that regard, the book is expansive rather than reductive). Our discussion of these various approaches is intended to provide students with strategies to make media content accessible and understandable. Ideally, these approaches will enable you to see media content from different perspectives. And, depending on the specific area of study, one approach may be more useful than others. The old professor not withstanding, there is no one truth to media content. The key is to be able to select critical approaches that provide fresh insight into media content. In that regard, critical approaches serve as tools for a systematic analysis of media content.

It should be emphasized that these critical approaches that appear in the text are not the only approaches to media literacy analysis. Others include narratology, dramatological approaches, and keys to interpreting media literacy (Silverblatt). The more critical tools that you have at your command, the better.

The authors are indebted to research assistants Deborah Allen, Darlene Diel, and Janis Valdes, and contributing photographers Jamie Clark and Aaron Mednick, for their support and contributions to the text. Many thanks for your professionalism and patience in the face of chaos.

Approaches
to Media
LITERACY

CHAPTER 1

IDEOLOGICAL ANALYSIS

Overview

The ideological approach to the study of media is designed to help people become more sensitive to the relationship between ideology and culture. Culture refers to the customary beliefs, social forms, and material character of a social group. Ideology is the system of beliefs or ideas that help determine the thinking and behavior of that culture.

Although ideology typically refers to a particular political orientation, Raymond Williams observes that ideology may involve a "more general way of seeing the world, human nature, and relationships."[1] However, even this expanded notion of ideology has political implications, containing assumptions about how the world should operate, who should oversee this world, and the proper and appropriate relationships among its inhabitants.

Cultural Studies

Ideological analysis has its roots in the discipline of cultural studies. The focus of cultural studies is not on aesthetic aspects of text, but rather what these texts reveal in terms of the social system. The fundamental principles of cultural studies are as follows: (1) there is inequitable distribution of power in our culture, hence it is possible to detect race, gender, and class power profiles; (2) forces of domination and subordination are central in our social system; and (3) the same ideology is repeated in a variety of texts; audiences bring this cumulative information to new material, which reinforces this dominant ideology. Linda Holtzman characterizes the dominant class as follows: "Dominant groups have greater access to privileges, resources and power because of their membership in a particular group. . . . For example, in the United States, men traditionally have had greater access to positions of power (e.g., Senators, CEOs of corporations). . . . Conversely, women have had less access to positions of power."[2] Rather than imposing their will on the subordinate class through force, members of the dominant class represent their own interests as being aligned with the welfare of society as a whole. The subordinate class, in adopting this world view, willingly consents to the continued preeminence of the dominant class.

The media have emerged as a principal means by which ideology is introduced and reinforced within contemporary culture. One of the central principles of cultural studies is that the world view presented through the media does not merely reflect or reinforce culture but in fact shapes thinking by promoting the dominant ideology of a culture through *cultural hegemony;* that is, the ability of the dominant classes to exercise social and cultural leadership in order to maintain economic and political control over the subordinate classes.

As a product (and beneficiary) of the prevailing system, the media generally reflect the predominant ideology within a culture. Nikolai Zlobin observes that even seemingly innocuous media programming promotes the dominant ideology of the culture: "Take a textbook on history—U.S., Russian, French, and German—and read a chapter about World War II. It will be like reading about four different wars. Why? Because we construct different ideas about world history and our own histories, and the media supports this."[3]

The dominant ideology frequently assumes a disarming "naturalness" within a text, which makes it particularly effective in promoting and reinforcing the prevailing ideology.[4] Media presentations begin with unquestioned assumptions about the correctness of this order. For example, in police dramas like "NYPD Blue," basic assumptions about the origin and nature of crime and criminals are adopted by actors with whom we identify. While a media program may be open to several interpretations, the text often dictates a *preferred reading,* based on the social position/orientation of the media communicator, so that the sympathies of the audience are aligned with the values and beliefs of the dominant culture. The preferred reading asks the audience to assume the role, perspective, and orientation of the primary figure. Within this construct, the audience assumes a passive role in the communications process.

Ideological Approach to Media Literacy

Ideology is integral to all aspects of media production, distribution, exchange, and consumption. A primary objective of the ideological approach, then, is to move beyond the description of a media production into a discussion of the values implicit within the presentation, as well as whose interests are served by such ideas. The objectives of ideological analysis include:

- examining media text as a way to identify its prevailing ideology;
- enabling the audience to become more sensitive to the impact of ideology on content;
- understanding media content as a vehicle which shapes, reflects, and reinforces ideology within a culture;
- broadening the public's exposure to the unique experience and contributions of subcultures in society;
- identifying ideological shifts within the culture;
- encouraging a healthy skepticism toward ideologically based explanations of the world by challenging the media's representations of culture.

A Cautionary Note

Identifying the ideology of a media presentation is a far more complex matter than the discussion thus far would suggest, for several reasons. First, the audience may assume a far more active role in interpreting media content, based on their own personal experience, than the preferred reading model discussed above (for further discussion, see the discussion of *reception theory* in chapter 2).

In addition, the very notion of "the media" implies that there is one collective entity with a single mentality. Despite the conglomeratization of the media, numerous small media outlets, such as alternative community newspapers, represent a variety of ideological perspectives. New technologies such as desktop publishing, affordable at-home audio studios, camcorders, and the interactive media make it affordable for individuals to develop relatively sophisticated media outlets. At the same time, the Internet introduces a means of directly distributing information and entertainment to the public without corporate middlemen.

Further, the media industry is not always the mirror image of dominant ideology. Len Masterman observes,

> We do need to recognize that the credibility of the media within democratic societies rests upon their ability to demonstrate some independence from government, big business and powerful interest groups. Media institutions, that is, possess their own ideologies—their own philosophies, imperatives, conventions and practices—which will not always be entirely congruent with dominant ideologies. That is the source of any strength they possess.[5]

The competition between different media (e.g., newspapers and television), as well as the rivalry between different organizations in the same medium (e.g., two TV news operations), also creates an opportunity for different outlets to present divergent points of view. Thus, the situation comedy "Ellen" (shown on ABC, which is owned by Disney) provided a protrait of a lesbian character who faced issues about her sexual identity. The network played up this "new" angle as a way to "break through the clutter" of programming and promote the series. (However, the series was soon canceled by the network.)

The media industry's shift from *broadcasting* to *narrowcasting* has introduced some multicultural perspectives into programming. In the early days of American media, the overall audience was limited. Consequently, the mass communicator had to appeal to the broadest possible audience to generate a profit. Over time, the media market has become so large that it is now profitable to direct messages at specialized interests, tastes, and groups. For example, if you turn your radio dial, you will find AM stations geared to African Americans, young people, and country music lovers. The emergence of media produced by members of subcultures offers other alternatives to the single voice of dominant culture. Filmmaker Spike Lee has found commercial success by appealing directly to the interests and concerns of the African-American community, while building a white, mainstream audience as well.

Finally, Masterman raises the prospect that in some cases the interests of the dominant culture and subgroups may coincide: "The idea that ruling groups impose a dominant ideology upon subordinate groups does less than justice to the fact that dominant ideas are often not simply imposed but often appear to be acceptable, and even to speak to the interests of subordinate classes."[6]

But while the premises and assumptions behind the ideological approach may not account for all media patterns, issues, and cumulative messages, this perspective provides considerable insight into media content, as well as the behaviors, attitudes, values, and preoccupations of media audiences and the culture.

Theoretical Framework: Approaches to Ideological Analysis

Organizational Analysis

The ownership patterns of the media industry influence (1) what information appears in the media, and (2) how it is presented. Ben Bagdikian has identified a disturbing trend involving the narrowing of control in the American media industry. In 1981, forty-six corporations owned or controlled the majority of media outlets in the United States. However, by 1996 that number had shrunk to ten: Time Warner, Disney, Viacom, News Corporation Limited (Murdoch), Sony, Telecommunications, Inc., Seagram (TV, movies, cable, books, music), Westinghouse, Gannett, and General Electric.[7]

The ownership of media companies affects content in several ways. As a major beneficiary of the current system, media ownership in the United States generally supports the status quo. Bagdikian argues that as major industry, the corporate world view has become prevalent in media programming:

> No sacred cow has been so protected and has left more generous residues in the news than the American corporation. . . . (At the same time), large classes of people are ignored in the news, are reported as exotic fads, or appear only at their worst—minorities, blue-collar workers, the lower middle class, the poor. They become publicized mainly when they are in spectacular accidents, go on strike, or are arrested. . . . But since World War I, hardly a mainstream American news medium has failed to grant its most favored treatment to corporate life.[8]

Consequently, the changes that the media advocate are generally refinements of the current system, rather than any radical overhaul of structure or policy. The reason behind this status quo position is that the media ownership is never going to advocate its own overthrow.

As part of the corporate community, media companies may be susceptible to conflicts of interest. Consequently, owners have occasionally censored content. For example, CNN president Rick Kaplan instructed his staffers to "limit their use of the word 'scandal' in reporting on President Clinton's campaign fund-raising woes. A longtime Clinton supporter, Kaplan has stayed in the Lincoln Bedroom."[9]

Another example of direct ownership interference due to conflict of interest occurred in February 1998, when the HarperCollins Publishing company dropped plans to publish a book by Chris Patten, the last British governor of Hong Kong, because of complaints from the company's owner, Rupert Murdoch, that it took too negative a view of China. Warren Hoge explains,

> Murdoch, the international media executive, has extensive holdings in China and ambitious plans to expand them. In a similar move in 1994 to avoid irritating the Chinese government, he removed the BBC news service from his Hong Kong–based satellite service, Star TV, after Beijing protested its documentaries on China and its coverage of Chinese dissidents. . . . HarperCollins declined all comment. The News Corporation, Murdoch's holding company, said in a statement on Friday: "Rupert Murdoch did not agree with many of Patten's positions in Hong Kong, which he thought abrogated promises made by the previous government." It added that from

the start, Murdoch had been dissatisfied that HarperCollins had decided to publish the book.

. . . Friday's (London) *Daily Telegraph* printed a "private and confidential" HarperCollins memo acknowledging Murdoch's assessment of the "negative aspect of publication" of the Patten book and setting out a strategy for disguising the real reason publication was being abandoned.[10]

Hoge adds that the dispute had received broad coverage in British newspapers but had been ignored by the *London Times* and the *Sun,* both owned by Murdoch.[11]

Media mergers also contribute to the homogenization of content by reducing the number of voices that are available to the public. According to Bagdikian, fourteen companies currently own half or more of the daily newspaper business in the United States.[12] As a result, the newspaper that a person might pick up in one city may be strikingly similar in layout, design, and editorial content to what appears in another city.

At times, a media program has been used to promote other company subsidiaries. Columnist Frank Rich declares,

Nowhere has this problem been more acute than at . . . ABC News, where *Good Morning America* on-camera were enlisted to promote a theme park of the network's parent company, Disney, and where Diane Sawyer all but turned the selling of *Ellen* into a full-time news magazine beat last season. But you can also find this incessant product-plugging in almost every local news show, as fake stories are dreamed up at 11 o'clock to promote network movies, series and specials. My enterprising local NBC affiliate in New York . . . has gone so far as to hyperventilate about previously little-known Nazi activity in World War II–era Long Island as a tie-in to its network's airing of *Schindler's List.*[13]

Wally Bowen recalls another occasion in which a local television news station selected a news item which promoted the program following the newscast:

About four or five years ago, ABC broadcast a made-for-TV movie entitled *Murder in the Heartland* about a serial killer and his girlfriend in Kansas in the 1950s (apparently based on a real incident). The night before the broadcast, I tuned into my local ABC affiliate for the local news and was treated to a reprise of a late 1970s serial murder here in Western North Carolina. Unaware of the upcoming movie, I was puzzled about why my local news was dredging up this old news story. . . . I then called a friend who had just gone to work in the TV station's marketing department. She said she had seen a memo "from the network" encouraging local affiliates to create tie-ins during their local newscasts.[14]

In this corporate environment, programming decisions are often made for economic reasons rather than because of any commitment to the media project or concern for the audience. For instance, after Westinghouse Electric Corporation bought CBS radio, they issued a mandate that members of its network had to bring in a 40 percent profit in order to ensure "local programming autonomy." Consequently, KMOX radio in St. Louis, Missouri, which had brought in a 22 percent profit the previous year, was forced to cut ten members of its news staff. In addition, the station added the syndicated Rush Limbaugh talk show to its programming lineup, saving the station the expense of a live local radio personality and an engineer. Thus, ironically, in order to ensure "programming autonomy," the station purchased a packaged, nationally syndicated program heard in markets throughout the country.[15]

Some media operations have simply adopted a corporate mentality, without thought of their responsibilities as mass communicators. The management of the Minneapolis-based *Star Tribune* sent a memo to its staff announcing that "the goal is to change Minnesotans' perception of the *Star Tribune* from that of a newspaper to 'the brand of choice for information products.' "[16] Jeremy Iggers declares,

> Many observers worry about the impact that this state of affairs will have on our democratic future. Will corporate-owned media twist the news to promote their own narrow economic interests? But an even more vexing question is what happens to the story journalists when, under the thumb of corporate ownership, news is reconceived and repackaged as a product instead of being allowed to remain the complex process of informing citizens.[17]

Because of its corporate sensibility, U.S. media companies are extraordinarily responsive to the objections and concerns of their primary sources of revenue—the advertisers. Ronald K.L. Collins cites instances in which reporters have been called off of stories involving advertisers: "In a confidential survey of 42 real-estate editors by the *Washington Journalism Review,* nearly half said publishers and senior editors had prohibited critical coverage of the industry for fear of offending advertisers."[18] A related phenomenon is self-censorship, in which the industry alters content for fear of antagonizing advertisers. Bob Herbert recalls,

> In March 1997, the *San Francisco Examiner* killed a column by Stephanie Salter that was highly critical of Nike. No good reason was ever advanced for not running the column. But at the time there was concern at the paper about

Nike's cosponsorship of the *Examiner*'s big annual promotion, known as the "Bay to Breakers" race.
Ms. Salter's protests were futile. She was no match for Nike's looming presence. The column eventually ran on the op-ed page of the *Miami Herald*.[19]

As media outlets frantically woo advertisers, the line between editorial copy and advertising can become blurred. Julie Grippo, copywriter at Brown Shoe Company in St. Louis, Missouri, recalls,

> A popular magazine contacted the company to inform us that they planned to run an article on our product and asked if we were interested in placing an ad in that issue. We agreed, and the next issue contained a nice article about our product. Ten pages later, our ad appeared. The article that appeared on the same page with our shoe ad was a fashion piece, in keeping with the theme of our ad. They also picked up the exact same colors that were in our ad. The pictures and gradated tones and type of the article matched our ad exactly.[20]

In their haste to attract the largest possible audience, newspapers, television stations, and radio stations frequently cater to the whims of the audience—to a fault. In order to attract the largest possible audience, the old news imperative of providing what the public needs to know has been replaced by what the audience wants to know. Michiko Kakutani declares, "The sales imperative—be popular, be accessible, be liked—is . . . threatening to turn writing into another capitalist tool. In an effort to raise circulation, newspapers like the *Miami Herald* and the *Boca Raton News* have used reader preference surveys to determine their 'coverage priorities.'"[21] (Consequently, entertainment is being presented as news and news content must be entertaining.)

The internal structure of a media organization also has an enormous impact on content. The available resources of the media operation (e.g., the size of the staff, available technological support) influence programming quality. And although local news operations continue to reap large profits, they are not investing in additional reporters and equipment. News editors are asking their staffs to do more with fewer resources. As a result, these professionals may not be able to research stories thoroughly. At times, they are forced to rely on "expert" sources whose backgrounds and motives for talking may be unclear. Often, the salaries of TV reporters (apart from the high-visibility anchors in large markets) are frightfully small, so that the news staff consists largely of young reporters who lack experience, contacts, and savvy.

At times, corporate interests are able to get their message across because they offer cost-efficient programming for news operations. Media consultant Tripp Frohlichstein explains,

> Corporate America routinely provides free video to television stations for newscasts that are actually commercials for their products or services, but since television has so much time to fill, they are using the video as if it is their own. Given budget cutbacks, skeletal news staffs, etc., using these videos as news saves time and money.[22]

Frohlichstein recalls an incident in which General Mills sent out a video "news" release announcing a university study which cited the health benefits of whole oat grains. As the voice-over discussed the study, the visuals depicted a well-dressed woman who poured Cheerios into her crystal bowl—clearly not news footage but a staged shot. The video was included in news broadcasts around the country. Frohlichstein declares, "Viewers are subtly being influenced by these commercials without knowing it, because they think it's news."[23]

The composition of the staff also reflects the ideology of dominant culture. In 1994, women made up 36.2 percent of all news persons at stations. Minorities accounted for 18 percent of all news staff in 1994 (down one-half of a percent from 1993).[24] The problem is not so much that news rooms are made up of hostile, active sexists or racists, but rather that they may be guilty of a "benign" racism. That is, because white male editors are limited by their own experience, they may not be sensitive to the use of words or images that might be clearly offensive to a member of a subculture.

Art Silverblatt recalls an incident that occurred during a seminar on press coverage of people with disabilities:

> One of the panelists displayed a series of headlines appearing in newspapers and clarified the meaning behind these labels, including the following:
>
> • "Disabled person" suggests less than a whole person as a result of his/her disability;
> • "People with disabilities" (the preferred term) refers to an individual who has a disability.
>
> After the seminar, Bob, a photojournalist, complained to me, "All this is a lot of bull. The operative principle in journalism is economy. If we can say something in fewer words, this leaves more space for additional ideas."
>
> I said, "Bob, what is your ethnic background? Where are your ancestors from?"
>
> He replied, "Italy."
>
> I responded, "Well, I know a shorter word than Italian" (thinking of the derogatory term for Italians, "wop").
>
> Bob immediately protested, "Heyyyy . . ."
>
> I said, "See, Bob, it depends on whose ox is being gored, doesn't it?"

A culturally diverse news staff is more likely to pick up these types of unintended slights against minority groups and women.

Ownership and the Internet

The Internet represents a significant battleground with regard to ownership. Supreme Court Justice Paul Stevens praises the "democratic forum" of the Internet, which he describes as "the most mass participatory medium yet invented, . . . as diverse as human thought."[25] Kim Gordon, an international interactive technology producer and consultant, explains, "The Internet offers a decentralized source of information and interchange. Traditional mass media requires a press or operating license or significant capital investment. However, with the Internet, anyone with a little hardware can be an electronic publisher, as it were."[26]

The Internet has emerged as a virtual community in which people throughout the globe communicate with others who share common interests. It is an almost limitless source of information, providing access to a wide range of information, from areas of academic interest to pornography. The Internet also provides a forum for individuals representing a range of views, from pro-democracy unionists in Hong Kong to members of separatist hate groups.

A good case in point is the emergence of film reviews on the web, written by movie fans. Joe Baltake reports that the proliferation of film critics poses a threat to the Hollywood establishment:

> Hollywood is probably without peer in terms of controlling its product at every stage and managing what information is made available to the public. However, while the studios have their ways of dealing with the press, the public is something else. If a newspaper reporter or TV personality gets feisty and out of hand, asking the wrong question or saying the wrong thing, a film company can retaliate by threatening to drop its advertising (although they rarely do), ostracizing the reporter from movie functions, or harassing his or her boss. . . . Hollywood always counted on the testimonials of average movie fans, but the fans don't think they're so average anymore. . . . Everybody is a movie expert now. Everybody is a critic. . . . How do you keep the audience from going on the Web to gripe about what they saw? You can't.[27]

Consequently, the Internet is challenging the established distribution systems for goods and services—including the media industry. The music business, for example, has been dominated by two powerful organizations, ASCAP and BMI. These organizations have a vested interest in the distribution of music in all forms: performance, physical (CDs, records, tapes, etc.), and broadcast (radio, television, public usage, etc.). But thanks to interactive technology, enterprising musicians now can bypass the established distribution channels entirely by posting, or "publishing," their CDs on the Internet. Consumers can make purchases directly from the artists/producers.

According to Kim Gordon, the Internet has the potential to alter the established compensation system as well:

> For example, in a broadcast model, a radio station plays a particular piece regardless of whether or not anyone is actually tuned into the station at that particular 2–3 minute interval. Odds are you do have an audience, but there is no feedback mechanism to confirm this. In an interactive model . . . we can tell *exactly* how many people requested a particular piece of music. We can tell how many people are tuned to that piece of music at that time. With feedback radio systems, I can "watch" you jump stations from your car until you settle on a piece of music. In these cases, the distributor would not pay compensation unless you as an individual were actually tuned in. Take this logically to its next level: why not actually charge you as an individual (micro-cents) when you listen in?[28]

In the face of this unwieldy, egalitarian media system, corporations and entrepreneurs are scrambling to identify strategies to seize control of the Internet for commercial purposes. When analyzed from an ideological perspective, a 1996 television ad for Lotus Software can be seen as a declaration of rights by the dominant class to assume control of the Internet.

In the beginning of this highly stylized, quirky commercial spot, the camera follows a waitress who is serving people in a courtyard. The camera looks down at an Asian woman who is working on her laptop. The camera then shifts to comedian Denis Leary, who assumes the same camera angle and motion as the original shot. The point of view of Leary and the audience merge, so that his interests and ours are presumably now one and the same.

Leary, a blond, blue-eyed male, strolls through the courtyard. Everyone else is seated, so that Leary occupies the upper, dominant spatial position. In contrast with the Aryan look of our protagonist, the people occupying the courtyard are all members of subcultures: the Asian female, an African-American woman, an elderly female, a punk teenager, and an elderly man. The protagonist is in control, with the freedom to roam around the courtyard. In contrast, the others are chained to their seats. Leary bursts into the personal space of these characters, checking on what they are doing, uninvited, unannounced— but with a confidence that makes it clear that he considers it his right.

Leary is frowning, serious . . . and angry. The camera shoots up at him, investing him with power.

Leary: "Do you know what I'm sick of hearing about?
Young girl: "The internet."
Older female: "The internet."
Young male (punk): "The internet."
Leary leans over the shoulder of the punk: "Hey, what are you doing?"
Punk: "Surfing the internet."
Leary assumes a look of contempt: "Nice hair."
Leary leans over the shoulder of Asian-American female and announces: "Solarized pictures of dead fat rock stars."
Leary then peers over the shoulder of the old man. Leary looks up at camera (at us) and sneers: "UFOs."
Leary leans over the African-American woman: "A gazillion dollars of technology and what are we doing with it?"
The African-American woman (looks up): "Browsing."

At this point, Leary begins to launch a series of statements, commenting on what he considers to be a frivolous use of the Internet by these marginal members of society. Each statement is accompanied by a closer shot of Leary, as he confronts the audience.

Leary looks up at camera: "Here's an idea. Use the internet for something useful."
(Closer shot) "Like running a business."
(Closer shot) "No kids. No chat rooms. No smiley faces."
(EX Close shot) "Just raw, naked, in your face capitalism."
At this point, the commercial shifts to black. Then a graphic appears (one word at a time): "Work the Web."
The final shot is of Leary leaving the courtyard, who then turns his attention to us: "You wanna surf? Move to Maui."

In shifting his point of view, Leary once again is in our faces, making us feel uncomfortable. In order to resolve this tension, the audience is faced with two choices: either acquiesce to his challenge (in effect, move to Maui, to leave the field open for the corporations to move in) or join him and his capitalist colleagues in the taming of this new, virtual frontier.

Media and Government

The relationship between the government and its media system plays an enormous role in the ideology of media content. Every country maintains a policy on the content and dissemination of information through the channels of mass communication. This relationship between a media system and government regulations helps shape the quality and diversity of media messages. Each country has its own policy regarding the kinds of information that can be conveyed through its channels of mass communication. In the

United States, the First Amendment to the Constitution declares, "Congress shall make no laws abridging the freedom of speech, or of the press." Over the years, the term has been expanded to include any governmental body, local or federal. The First Amendment was established on the premise that the United States is a marketplace of ideas. All forms of ideas should be expressed, and each individual must be able to make his/her own decision about what is right and appropriate.

In contrast, in an authoritarian country like China, the media are regarded as instruments of the state. Information, including criticism of the government, is tightly controlled. The Communist Party regards the media as a tool to guide the people toward their social, political, and economic destiny. News and editorial duties are performed by professionals committed to the goals of the Communist Party. Content is selected which assists in the ongoing social processes. To illustrate, when the Chinese government shut down many state enterprises, the Chinese media helped the public adjust to the loss of millions of jobs. Newspapers published stories of workers who found happiness and success after losing their state jobs.[29] However, with the technological advances in communications, it is increasingly difficult for governments to control the flow of information. Despite government efforts, millions of Chinese are now reading *Tunnel,* an indigenous on-line, anti-communist magazine.[30]

Every country has policies regarding not only *what* can be covered by the media but *who* can be covered. In the United States, people can be subjected to media scrutiny as "public figures" if they have met the following criteria:

- voluntarily stepped into the spotlight;
- assumed an important role in the resolution of important public issues;
- had an impact on a public issue;
- become a public figure through means other than simply media attention.[31]

In recent years, journalists have abused this journalistic license to intrude into the personal affairs of celebrities. A tragic example can be found in the death of Princess Diana. On August 30, 1997, a car carrying the princess was pursued by seven paparazzi on motorcycles along the streets of Paris, France. The Mercedes lurched out of control and crashed, killing Diana and her companion, Dodi Fayed. Ironically, the week before her death, Princess Di had commented on the toll that fame had taken on her personal life: "The press is ferocious, it pardons nothing. It only hunts for mistakes. Every motive is twisted, every gesture criticized. . . . I think that in my place, any sane person would have left [Britain] long ago. But I cannot. I have my sons."[32]

The paparazzi who were pursuing Diana were attempting to cash in on a lucrative market for photos of the princess' personal life. Photographs taken by telephoto lenses of Diana and Fayed relaxing on vacation had sold to the tabloid press for $200,000. A veteran reporter who covered the royalty beat for the *Daily Mirror* suggested that as a "public figure," Diana had somehow brought this attention on herself by engaging in everyday activities: "She walked on the beach. She stood talking to people. She got on a Jet Ski. She got on a motorboat. Why shouldn't she do this? I'm not saying she shouldn't. But that was definitely a virtuoso performance for us to get photographs and a story."[33]

However, freedom of speech is not solely determined by governmental regulation. Although the U.S. media system maintains a strict independence from government, it struggles with *freedom from market forces* that shape the coverage of issues. Seth Faison comments,

> When will the news media stop reporting so much about celebrities, sex, and violence, all that silly stuff none of us should want to read? Consider China, one of the few nations where the sudden death of Diana, Princess of Wales, was not big news. . . . The day after Diana died, China's most influential newspaper, *People's Daily*, ran a small item on page 7, giving it less prominence than an adjacent article about problems in the Malaysian economy and a piece on the Tibetan artistic troupe visiting Greece.
>
> Although Chinese society is much more open each day, firm principles still guide what can and cannot be printed in newspapers. As a result, there is no real danger of the privacy of movie stars or other celebrities being invaded by the Chinese media, nor of anything offensive or distasteful being published. The state, not the market, still rules the media in China. . . .
>
> For those who tire of all the violence and tragedy in the American media, domestic coverage in China might seem better at first, too; newspapers are dominated by good news. Of course, that ultimately means it cannot be balanced: reports are carefully filtered to praise the achievements of the authorities and, on some occasions, to point out problems that officials have decided should be addressed.[34]

As a result, American media outlets are forced to operate according to a *double negative* syndrome. To illustrate, in the Monica Lewinsky/Bill Clinton matter, television networks did not necessarily want to saturate the airwaves with meaningless updates and unsubstantiated innuendo; however, they could not afford to not cover the story, for fear of losing their audience to a competing station that did carry the story.

With technological communications advances, governments now are limited in their ability to regulate information. The Internet eliminates borders, challenging governments' ability to impose tax systems and commerce regulations on individual entrepreneurs. Gordon raises this revolutionary scenario:

- I live in the United States.
- I open a new business.
- I do not manufacture a product—but provide an information service.
- It is entirely online.
- I deal in milli-cents for use of my service—the monetary transactions are credited to my account in the Netherlands.
- I bypass the local tax structure.
- I bypass the national tax structure.
- I bypass the international tax structure.
- In fact, I don't pay taxes anywhere.
- Does this mean the government (and which one?) has the right to monitor what I do on my own machine in my own home/business?
- How can the U.S. government require me to pay taxes if the machine and information and accounting transaction systems are physically located in South Africa?
- What if I am paying taxes there because they are lower?[35]

Media and Political Proselytization

Governments commonly employ the media as a propagandist device to promote ideology, both internally and in the global arena. Harold D. Laswell identified the following functions of wartime propaganda: (1) to mobilize hatred against the enemy; (2) to preserve the friendship of allies; (3) to preserve the friendship and, if possible, to procure the cooperation of neutrals; (4) to demoralize the enemy. In peacetime, propaganda serves the purposes of expansion, trade, tourism, and investment.[36]

Critics argue that the media is an instrument of elite control: the domination of international media for political purposes. Clearly, the overwhelming amount of information circulated throughout the globe is Western (primarily from the United States). Four of the five major news agencies are Western, and these agencies account for 90 percent of the global news flow.[37] Defenders of international news coverage maintain that the current system reflects the principles of free speech. Countries are free to develop their communications systems to the best of their abilities. And finally, no one is forcing Third World countries to consume the American-generated media content.

In the twentieth century, the United States has relied on the news media as a propagandist device, using such channels as Radio Free Europe to achieve its political agenda. However, the entertainment media are an *indirect,* but far more effective, means of promoting the American way of life. American media programming saturates the international market.

"Baywatch" has been shown in 144 countries and seen by more people than any other entertainment show in history. In 1995, *Die Hard 3* was the top-grossing film in Hungary and Japan. And although Michael Jackson's album "HIStory" enjoyed only modest success in the United States (3 million sold in 1995), 9 million copies were bought in the international market.[38] Josef Joffe declares,

> One has to go back to the Roman Empire for a similar instance of cultural hegemony. Actually, there is no comparison. The cultural sway of Greece and Rome, or France in the age of Louis XIV and Napoleon, or Germany between 1871 and 1933 reached much beyond the economic and educational elites of the world. But America's writ encircles the globe, penetrating all lay-society.[39]

Joffe contends that even if citizens of other countries object to our politics, they remain friendly to America, largely because of the cumulative cultural messages contained in the entertainment media:

> Not so long ago, young Europeans used to burn the American flag. Now they wear it—like that big brash replica of Old Glory knit into a line of pricey Ralph Lauren sweaters. . . . Unconsciously, they might be making more than just a fashion statement—like the mullah in Teheran who had just completed a two-hour tirade against "Am'rikah" in front of the former United States Embassy on the anniversary of the takeover. Grabbing a Western journalist by the arm, he smiled and said, "We don't really hate you Americans." Drawing close, the crowd that had just been screaming "Death to America" nodded vigorously. And the cleric pulled a pair of Ray-Bans out of his robes, as if to say, "Look, man, I'm cool, too."[40]

The American media saturate the globe with *cumulative* messages about American culture. Cumulative messages occur with such frequency over time that they form meanings independent of any individual production. These messages are reinforced through the countless hours of media that repeat the cultural script. While there are a multitude of messages (indeed, conflicting cumulative messages may exist at the same time), the ultimate test of a cumulative message is its universality; that is, the degree to which an audience is able to recognize a cumulative message that is conveyed through a variety of media channels and programs.

The cumulative messages found in media promote the following attributes of the American system:

Freedom of Expression. Films and music discuss personal angst, societal taboos, and even poke fun at politicians. Although Dan Quayle and Bob

Dole rail against the "Hollywood elites" who are polluting American culture, this freedom of expression is very attractive to members of other cultures. Panrawee Pantumchinda, a Thai graduate student at Webster University, conducted an analysis of *Cosmopolitan* magazine. She observes that the publication enjoys phenomenal success in Thailand:

> The content [of *Cosmopolitan*] emphasizes women's strengths, ways to be successful in relationships and their careers. . . . This content is attractive to Thai readers because the magazine is like their representative to speak about women's issues and sexuality, which are things [Thai women] want to do but cannot because of Thai customs. Moreover, they learn to express their feelings to others from the magazine.[41]

Personal Empowerment. American media programming sends messages about freedom of choice. Audiences can decide what they want to watch from a growing menu of programming. In many programs, characters are faced with making a choice between several alternatives. Heroes and heroines are in control of their destinies, so that they make decisions that are in their best interests. Joffe notes that many ads present their products within the context of personal freedom:

> Why did Big Mac blanket the world? Not just because [it] is convenient, cheap and timesaving. It also promises a bit of individual freedom, as certified by an angry Hamburg parent: "My kids don't have to be at the dinner table anymore when they can stay out and wolf down a couple of Quarter Pounders."[42]

Individualism. Entertainment programming like the film *Rocky* (1976) focuses on the underdog who triumphs despite great odds. Although he is written off by other characters, he (and the audience) know that he is a special individual who can meet whatever challenges that present themselves.

Celebration of Life. American media programs are characterized by an infectious energy. Popular music is a celebration of youth and revives the youthful spirit in us, regardless of age. This high-intensity vigor and enthusiasm also reinforce the message that the United States is a young country—both in terms of its history and its veneration of youth culture.

World View

In producing a media presentation, media communicators construct a complete world based on certain fundamental assumptions about how this world operates. Consequently, films and television programs establish who and what are important within the world view of the program. The following questions related to the world view are useful in identifying the ideology of a media presentation:

- What culture or cultures populate this world?
- What do we know about the people who populate this world?
  1. What kinds of people populate this world?
  2. Are characters presented in a stereotypical manner?
  3. What does this tell us about the cultural stereotype of this group?
- Does this world present an optimistic or pessimistic view of life?
  1. Are the characters in the presentation happy?
  2. Do the characters have a chance to be happy?
- Are people in control of their own destinies?
  1. Is there a supernatural presence in this world?
  2. Are the characters under the influence of other people?
- What does it mean to be a success in this world?
  1. How does a person succeed in this world?
  2. What kinds of behavior are rewarded in this world?[43]

While news, entertainment, and advertising programming generally avoid specific mention of political issues, they do comment on political life in a broader sense. Media programs convey cumulative messages about the sources of power and authority in American culture and the value of political activism. Embedded in these types of programming are depictions of an established social order, the role of government and laws, portraits of the class system, and images of success.

Cumulative ideological messages conveyed in the media include the following:

A World Preoccupied with the Self Rather than the Collective Good

In the narcissistic world of media programming, audiences are encouraged to indulge their own needs. Ads convince us that "we deserve a break today," so that the greater good has been reduced to our individual satisfaction. A hierarchy of values is established in which personal amusement is valued over societal well-being. Even films set within a social-political context such as *First Knight* (1995), *Braveheart* (1995), and *Rob Roy*

(1995) focus on how historical events affect the characters on a personal level.

Because political issues are reduced to personal experience, the appearance of successful minority members in entertainment programs and advertising tends to negate the existence of social problems. Sut Jhally and Justin Lewis have argued that the depiction the Huxtable family in "The Bill Cosby Show" conveys the message that there is no lingering impact from a history of racism, that there are no institutional barriers to success, and no class divisions—only individual failures. The success of "The Bill Cosby Show," then, contributed to the belief that racism is no longer a problem in this country, and that African Americans who do not succeed are simply individually inadequate.[44]

Clearly, media programming does not encourage audiences to look beyond their immediate needs to consider the public good.

A World of Immediate Gratification

In media programming, the solution to a problem is never far off. To revise an old adage, nothing worth having is worth waiting for. One explanation for the swift resolution to problems can be found in the competitive nature of the media industry. Entertainment programs, in competition for ratings, must attract audiences by holding nothing back. There is no value in patience or subtly. The preponderance of violence in media programming gives viewers greater doses of instant stimulation to maintain their interest. One clear cumulative message is that violence is indeed an effective solution to problems. Change is swift, immediate, and dramatic.

The instant gratification syndrome in media programming is also a response to the audience's longing for resolution. People enjoy clarity and certainty in their entertainment programming, possibly in reaction to the uncertainty in their own lives. A film like *Sleepless in Seattle* (1993) plays on the audience's desire for resolution by postponing the inevitable meeting of the couple. The momentary delays add an edge to the anticipated meeting. However, this had to be handled delicately by the filmmaker; keeping the audience waiting too long would lose them altogether.

The time constraints of media programs further contribute to this sense of urgency. In TV situation comedies, as many as three subplots (all involving some conflict or predicament) must be resolved within a half hour. In film, one must wait for up to two hours for a resolution.

Advertising accelerates this push toward immediate gratification. Advertising measures its success by its ability to influence the consumer to buy a product as soon as possible. Some ads actually command the consumer to act and act quickly by using directive words such as "hurry" and "now."

Television commercials operate according to a formulaic plot that reinforces this notion of instant satisfaction. First, a person is introduced who has a particular problem, need, or desire. Within seconds, a product is presented as the solution to this problem. Finally, the viewer can see that the character is entirely transformed by the acquisition of the product. Print ads are even more streamlined, eliminating the establishment of the problem. We see the model, beaming with delight, showing the product. The audience is left to infer the problem by seeing how fulfilled the consumer is with the problem solved.

In contrast, political life is deliberative. Lawmakers study issues and discuss nuances before taking action. The process can seem endless to a public used to an action-oriented sensibility. Columnist Edwin Yoder declares, "The sluggish character of the American political system ... was designed for delay and obstruction (otherwise known as checks and balances). Action is slow to come even when there is ample understanding of what needs to be done. Even when it is working relatively well, the system is slow to process and resolve conflict; and that does make people cynical."[45] It is not surprising, then, that the cumbersome nature of the American political process contributes to the feeling that political decisions have little impact on the lives of its citizens. To illustrate, the 1994 election saw a shift in congressional power and the legislative agenda. The impact of these changes would be indirect, over time, in the form of welfare reform, student aid opportunities, and environmental protection. However, the day after the election, people carried on with their everyday lives with no apparent change. They woke up, went to work, and waxed their cars without any noticeable difference in their lives.

Indeed, some of the initial disillusionment with the Clinton presidency was a reaction to his 1992 campaign theme of "change." Many people were convinced that Clinton's election would instantly change their lives. Consequently, they were disappointed when this did not materialize. The mainstream press reflected this impatience. On November 6, three days after the November election, liberal columnist Richard Cohen declared, "The clock is already ticking on the [Clinton] honeymoon."[46] Three days later, conservative columnist William Safire repeated this same sentiment: "OK, that's it—the honeymoon is over."[47] These statements are striking, given that the traditional "honeymoon period" accorded a new president is 100 days. In addition, although Clinton was elected in November, he did not assume office for two months—until the following January.

A World That Expects Simple Solutions
to Complex Problems

Media programming offers simple solutions to complex problems. Given America's market-driven media system, media communicators are compelled to present a world that is easy to identify and understand. Consequently, the world of entertainment programs and ads are populated by uncomplicated characters who personify a particular value or point of view in the story. Popular films and television programs generally deal in absolutes—good vs. evil, and right vs. wrong. Heroes are virtuous without fault, and villains are simply evil. There is no room for subjectivity or ambiguity. No one does the wrong thing for the right reason, or vice versa.

To be sure, some programs focus on complex problems that relate to the personal experiences of the audience: relationship issues, socialization pressures, and obstacles to success and happiness. However, the time constraints of media presentations require a swift, tidy resolution to these issues—so that the conclusion is often simplistic and illogical.

In this climate, it is not surprising that people grow impatient and frustrated with the complexities of political life. This sensibility is not limited to the public but applies to the press as well. After President Clinton's 1995 State of the Union Address, an NBC analyst panned the speech, complaining that there was "no definitive bumper sticker" (i.e., one condensed statement) to be found in Clinton's very detailed address.

Politicians recognize the public's impatience with complexity and consequently select simple campaign themes that people can immediately grasp (e.g., patriotism or "character"). During the 1992 presidential campaign, Clinton's campaign manager James Carville posted a sign at headquarters that read, "It's the economy, stupid." That is, the key to effective "issues management" was reducing the web of issues to one statement, and then basing the campaign strategy on getting this one message across.

A Cynical World That Sees the Political System
as Dysfunctional

In the world of media programming, the political system clearly does not work. To illustrate, in police dramas like "Hill Street Blues," and "NYPD Blue," the law enforcement officers are frustrated by the inadequacy of the legal system. At the beginning of each episode, the audience witnesses criminals committing a crime. However, constitutional rights (the presumed innocence and search and seizure laws) prevent the cops from bringing to justice those characters who the protagonists (and the audience) know are guilty. Significantly, in the *Dirty Harry* films, Detective Harry Callahan (Clint Eastwood) faces two adversaries: the perpetrator of the crime that Harry is trying to crack, and the bureaucracy of his own department, which frustrates Harry's attempts to get the job done. In this world, bureaucracy only gets in the way. This attitude leads to an audience with diminished expectations about the value and purpose of our political system.

A World Operating According to a Romantic Ideal: When You Wish Upon a Star . . .

The romantic ideal presumes the existence of an ordered universe, which is a microcosm of heaven. This world operates according to an absolute value system consisting of Truth, Beauty, Justice, Faith, and Love. These values are fixed and interchangeable. For example, the external beauty of heroes and heroines is a reflection of inner virtue. It is a just world, in which good always wins in the end. Faith is an integral part of the romantic ideal, as epitomized by Disney films. As Jiminy Cricket advised Pinocchio, "When you wish upon a star, your dreams come true." In other words, if you believe hard enough and are deserving, good will be rewarded.

Unfortunately, the realities of political life often fly in the face of this romantic ideal. There is no guarantee that good will prevail over evil, or that justice will be served. Change cannot be achieved simply by believing in your dream. Wanting something badly enough is of limited help if it is not translated into social action.

A World in Which Consumerism Is the Cardinal Ideology

In consumer ideology, success is defined in terms of material acquisition, replacing other sources of fulfillment. Personal problems and metaphysical issues have been transformed into consumer needs. Are you lonely? Have money problems? Are you aging? These issues all find resolution through a wise consumer purchase.

Consumer ideology is now global in scope. In a radio address in December 1997, Russian president Boris Yeltsin commented on the dangers of the emergence of consumerism as the prevailing ideology in the new Russian market-based economy:

> I would like to talk about . . . something I had no chance to discuss amid the daily grind of our work. About spiritual values and civil responsibility. About

how we are living in the new, very material world. About what kind of a generation is forming before our eyes. . . . We overlooked many things when we entered the free market. We have fixed its legal frameworks, but have forgotten about the laws of morality, about such a simple thing as business ethics.[48]

Consumerism has emerged as a principal form of recreation and lifestyle in America. Twelve states rank malls among their top three tourist attractions.[49] The average American shops six hours each week while spending only forty minutes playing with his or her children. By 1987, America had more shopping malls than high schools.[50] As the spokesperson for an ad for Potomac Mills Mall declares, "You can buy happiness. Just don't pay retail for it."[51] However, the evidence suggests that Americans are not as happy as they once were; according to polls, the pinnacle of happiness in America was 1956.[52] Scott Simon reports, "We are working more and saving less. People suffer from chronic stress (the cumulative load of minor, day-to-day stresses), which results in short-term symptoms (headaches and depression), as well as long-term consequences such as heart attacks. And in 90 percent of divorce cases, arguments about finances play a prominent role."[53]

But despite their personal experiences, people are conditioned to participate in the consumer society without questioning its basic assumptions. To illustrate, in the film *Blue Collar* (1978), Jerry (Harvey Keitel), a Detroit auto worker, is in perpetual debt but still has a lots of "stuff" he doesn't really want—motorcycles, cars, elaborate home furnishings. His buddy Smokey (Yaphet Kotto) explains, "Why do you go on the [assembly] line on Friday? Because the finance man will be at your house on Saturday. And that's what the company wants . . . to keep you on the line."

The media are crucial in shaping and reinforcing our involvement in consumer culture, because the media are part of—as well as financed by—the market-driven economy. The system perpetuates itself by cultivating a longing for possessions. Media programming depicts a world in which social problems are resolved through consumerism rather than political action. By purchasing the right products, we can move into another social class (or at least maintain the illusion of upward mobility). We celebrate our democratic (or rather, capitalistic) system by participating in the market economy. As Stuart Ewan has observed, the concept of the "citizen" has been replaced in the American vernacular by the label "consumer."[54] An ad for McDonald's reinforces this notion: A man informs the audience that there is a wide selection of precooked breakfast sandwiches at McDonald's, marveling, "Is this a great country, or what?" Freedom of choice has been reduced to the freedom to *buy*.

Advertising is pervasive; by the age of twenty, the average American has seen 1 million commercial messages. On average, each of us will spend one full year of our lives watching TV commercials. But beyond any specific product promotion, the cumulative message of the advertising industry exhorts the public to adopt a consumer mentality. In advertising, personal problems are transformed into consumer needs. Advertising positions products as keys to emotional well-being and happiness. In the aforementioned TV commercial for Potomac Mills Mall, the spokeswoman whispers seductively that "shopping is therapy"—a way to soothe yourself. Conversely, the latent message is that not buying a product will prevent one from realizing these emotional plateaus.[55]

A derivative strategy used in children's advertising equates the purchase of goods with parental love and approval. Heeding a child's plea for a product is part of being a good parent. This approach pits children against their parents, pressuring the adults to feed into this consumer sensibility.

The consumer ideology has had a direct impact not just on commercials but on entertainment and news programming as well. The mood of television programs must be upbeat or suspenseful at the commercial break in order to make people receptive to the commercial messages (who is in the mood to buy things if they are depressed?). Robin Anderson observes that "often, topics which are antithetical to the product or its image are eliminated."[56] Regardless of its manifest message, the latent message of a media program frequently supports the values of consumer culture. For example, the film *Jerry Maguire* (1996) stars Tom Cruise as a sports agent who goes through a personal reexamination of his goals and priorities and, consequently, is fired from his high-powered agency. He attempts to go off on his own, contacting his old clients and offering to provide services based on loyalty, concern, and personal attention. Unfortunately, none of his previous clients will return his phone calls, with the exception of one player—Rod Tidwell (Cuba Gooding, Jr.), whose battle cry is, "Show me the money."

As the film progresses, Jerry develops a close relationship with his one remaining client, Tidwell. The audience also gains insight into the special relationship that Tidwell enjoys with his wife, and how he struggles to maintain control and dignity in a sports world that seemingly only rewards clowns and showboats. In the final game of the season, Tidwell catches a key touchdown pass but is knocked unconscious. After a moment (presumably bolstered by the faith and support of his family—and Jerry), Tidwell gets to his feet and finally expresses his enthusiasm and passion for the game ironically, (by clowning and showboating). At the conclusion of the film, Jerry's commitment to basic human values pay off—in the form of a $3 million, multiyear deal. This "feel good" ending ultimately reinforces the ideology of consumer culture, as virtue is rewarded by a long-term contract with a no-trade clause.

A World in Which Style Has Become Substance

Before the media boom, the best one could hope for was to make appearance reflect reality. Now, image can be *better* than reality. As Andre Agassi put it so succinctly in his ads for Cannon, "Image is everything." People devote their time and energies to "re-inventing themselves" as more attractive (and marketable) human beings.

Conversely, substance has been reduced to pure image. The media industry undermines grassroots political movements by exploiting the ideological significance behind a program, star, or genre for commercial purposes, leaving only the framework and style intact. In co-opting the image of a movement, the original meaning is lost. To illustrate, when Elvis Presley emerged on the American scene in the 1950s, he was regarded as dangerous by the dominant (white, middle-class) culture. His sound was rooted in black culture; he was a white kid who sounded black. Elvis's hip gyrations and snarling lip emitted a sexuality that threatened the 1950s sexual mores. Following the grassroots success of Elvis, the record industry (with considerable help from Dick Clark) manufactured a series of clean cut rock 'n' roll idols who maintained the image of Elvis, but devoid of ideological substance: Ricky Nelson, Fabian, Bobby Rydell. This pattern was repeated in the 1960s: The Beatles, who sang about revolution, were followed by the creation of the Monkeys, who warbled harmlessly about that last train to Clarksville. This depletion of meaning culminated in a 1995 TV spot, in which Ringo Starr teamed up with members of the Monkees . . . as spokespersons for Pizza Hut.

Similarly, rap music originated in the streets as an expression of the concerns of inner-city African-American youth. This genre of music was co-opted with the marketing of Vanilla Ice, a white kid who was nonthreatening to mainstream culture. The commercialization of rap music is now complete, with clothes and haircuts sold at malls. The familiar trappings of rap music (cadence, dance moves, etc.) are employed in commercials selling potato chips, breakfast cereal—everything but insurance.

Currently, the Rock 'n' Roll Fashion Awards on VH1 promote a connection between rock music and the fashion industry, conveniently forgetting that the nonconformist ideology of popular music was intentionally *unfashionable*.

The consumer culture co-opts individuals as well. For example, nonconformist Dennis Rodman was quickly transformed into a commodity. His rebellious persona has been parlayed into a successful marketing gimmick to sell books, products, and promote his acting career—so that, in reality, he has become the epitome of conformity to the market-driven system. Athletes participating in the Super Bowl are now making tentative arrangements to promote products ("I'm going to Disney World"). Even as they walk off the field, they cannot wait to capitalize on their success and fame.

A Hierarchal (Rather Than Democratic) World

The model society depicted in popular media programs is far from democratic. Only the major characters play a significant decision-making role, leaving the supporting cast with no choice but to follow their leaders. An example of this autocratic social structure recurs throughout the original "Star Trek" series. Search parties typically include some of the main characters (Captain Kirk, Spock, Dr. McCoy), accompanied by conspicuously anonymous crew members. It is clear that these peripheral crew members, the ultimate followers, are doomed. The central characters, having learned about the perils facing the *Enterprise* through the sacrifice of their subordinates, are now prepared to carry out their mission.

A World Satisfied with the Status Quo

A number of factors contribute to the reinforcement of the status quo in media programming. Advertising instructs audiences that success can be achieved through adherence to the system. More than merely selling a product, ads often sell a successful lifestyle. These ads feature models who are young, attractive, and the center of attention. They are beneficiaries of the system who have found happiness through the acquisition of the product being promoted.

Entertainment programs reinforce the status quo by romanticizing the established order. *Gone with the Wind* (1939) represents an idealized vision of the antebellum South, in which slaves and masters lived in harmony. In the film, the slaves regarded the outbreak of the Civil War as an unwelcome disruption of harmonious plantation life rather than as an opportunity to end the institution of slavery.

Entertainment programs also reinforce the class system through their depictions of rulers and those who serve. The world depicted in these programs is predominately populated by members of the dominant stratum. The featured characters in films and television epitomize standards of success. They are in control of their environment and have the freedom to act in their best interests. In contrast, members of subcultures are underrepresented on American television, reflecting their relative powerlessness in society:

	Percentage of characters appearing on prime-time television	Percentage of general population
Senior citizens (over the age of 65)	2.1	12.5
Latino/Hispanic	1.0	9.0
Lower-class	1.3	13.0
African American	10.8	12.4

Source: Gerbner Cultural Indicators study, 1992.

When members of these subgroups *do* appear in television narratives, they experience a lower success rate within the context of the programs than their more mainstream counterparts (this indicator was determined by the characters' ability to achieve their goals). Thus, one of the chief measures of success in the world of entertainment programming is simply being a member of the dominant stratum.

Members of subcultures who appear as media stereotypes often are presented as marginal members of society. When African Americans appear as characters on TV programs, they generally are found in one of the following categories:

• As exceptions (e.g., the one black face in an otherwise all-white cast)
• As extras (part of the background that provides the contrast for the successful protagonists)
• As villains who are threats to the system
• As victims of violence (and of the system)

These stereotypes send the message that it is futile for members of minority groups to overcome their prescribed roles and capabilities. Recently, some prime-time programs featuring African Americans have moved beyond these traditional stereotypes. But, as mentioned earlier, these shows often fall into the trap of denying that race is even an issue in America and suggest that overcoming racism is simply a result of individual effort.

The cumulative messages cited above contribute to an ideology of apathy, cynicism, and lack of connectedness, ultimately discouraging public participation in the political process. This sensibility feeds into the ideology of the dominant culture, leaving major decisions in the hands of those currently holding positions of power.

Historical Context

Looking at the historical context of media programs provides considerable insight into the ideology of the presentation. Media programming is often shaped by historical events. For example, the long-running series of Godzilla films serve as an allegory about Japan's ideological relationship with the United States and, later, with the Soviet Union. On March 1, 1954, as the United States conducted a test of its new hydrogen bomb in the South Pacific, a small Japanese fishing boat, the *Lucky Dragon,* was exposed to the nuclear fallout. However, despite public anguish, the Japanese government conducted a strict code of silence about the incident, fearful about upsetting its delicate relationship with the United States in the post–World War II era. Historian Michael Schaller observes that "the monster's trail stretches back to a time of fear and mistrust in Japan."[57]

> Against this backdrop, *Godzilla: King of the Monsters* was released in late 1954, the first of more than 20 *Godzilla* features from Japan. The horror genre gave the filmmakers the cover they needed to skirt the Government's policy of silence. Appearing only a few months after the Lucky Dragon incident, *Godzilla* opens with an ominous explosion and series of flashes that sink Japanese fishing boats. Moving along an island-hopping route like that of both America's wartime aerial attacks and the Lucky Dragon, Godzilla inflicts burns and carnage that are described in the same terms used by the Japanese press for the war's bombing victims.[58]

During the 1970s, the focus of the films shifted, with the monster representing the emerging threat of the Soviet Union. In these versions, Godzilla swept down from the Arctic Ocean and first attacked the northern Japanese island of Hokkaido—"just as the Soviets might."[59] In one film, the Japanese enlisted the help of King Kong, an American creation who embodied the alliance between Japan and the United States.

Examining a media program from another era can also furnish a perspective into the ideology of the period in which it was produced. For instance, many old films feature women in subservient roles. One striking exception was *City for Conquest* (1940), starring Jimmy Cagney and Ann Sheridan. In this movie, Peggy Nash (Sheridan) is a dancer who is forced to choose between a career and her childhood sweetheart, Danny Kenny (Cagney). Mesmerized by ambition, Peggy deserts Danny and, within the context of the film, betrays herself as well. Although Danny is a gifted amateur boxer, he is satisfied with his situation as a truck driver. But in order to win Peggy back, he agrees to box professionally. Unfortunately, in the title match, Danny is blinded by his opponent. When Peggy meets Danny again, he is selling pencils on the street corner. It is only when she gives up her career and devotes herself to Danny that she again becomes a "whole" woman.

The ideological subtext of the film casts Peggy as a villain whose desire for a career is a betrayal of her duty as a woman. However disturbing to a modern audience, this film provides a useful glimpse into the gender politics of the times.

Point of View

The audiences' response to a media presentation is largely determined by the point of view of the narrative, as established by the media communicator. Point of view refers to the source of information—who tells the story. Point of view has an impact on how a story is told and what information is conveyed, including: (1) what is important; (2) what is included and excluded; and (3) commentary on what is being presented. Consequently, point of view dictates the audience's response to the content. We are directed to see the world in a particular way and to sympathize with the plight of particular characters.

The audience naturally assumes that information is being presented in a truthful, straightforward manner. However, the perspective of narrators (or reporters) may not be reliable, for a variety of reasons. As mentioned earlier, the ownership of media companies may have corporate agendas or conflicts of interest that have an influence on media content. Media communicators may be limited by their personal point of view, background, or experience. Further, media communicators may have an insufficient command of the information to prepare a thorough and balanced presentation. And finally, media communicators may include inaccuracies by mistake.

Film and television generally employ an omniscient point of view, in which the camera moves freely between scenes and characters, suggesting objectivity. However, a critical element in visual media is not always what shot is selected, but rather when the camera focuses on a particular character, what information is included, and what footage is omitted. The simplest way to determine the point of view is to ask: Whose story is this? For instance, in screen romances, a tipoff is, who is facing the camera when the couple embraces? The main character receives the attention from the other character. The audience vicariously assumes the position of the subordinate character.

It is often useful to pay attention to the visual field that is encompassed by the gaze of the protagonist when the camera assumes his or her point of view. Frequently, the protagonist (and audience) sees an imperfect world, in which members of a subculture are the source of the problems in the story.

This depiction serves as the ideological foundation for the film—the need for restoration of order (as defined at the conclusion of the presentation).

Media presentations generally assume the point of view of the dominant culture. Michael Parenti points out that historical dramas typically assume the point of view of the aristocracy.[60] For example, *The Private Lives of Elizabeth and Essex* (1939), starring Bette Davis and Errol Flynn, takes a very sympathetic view of the burdens of rule facing Queen Elizabeth. In another Flynn film, *The Adventures of Robin Hood* (1938), the revolt incited by the Robin's merry band is not intended to install democracy but rather to restore the rightful, benevolent ruler to the throne of England. Indeed, in the course of the film Robin Hood gently rebukes King Richard for having deserted his subjects to join the crusades, which necessitated that the lower classes (led by Robin) fight to restore him to the throne.

Although the manifest (surface) point of view offers sometimes an alternative perspective, the dominant culture often remains the latent (under the surface) point of view. For example, children's programming often appears to be presented from a kid's perspective. Commercials for children feature actors who are slightly older than the target audience. Young audiences are influenced by how "cool" these performers are; consequently, they either "take their word" for the quality of the product or associate the positive qualities of the actors with the quality of the product. However, the point of view in these children's programs is actually adult and corporate. The actual media communicators—the producer, writer, and advertising executive—generally are white, male adults whose interest in the audience extends only to profit margin. An interesting exercise, then, is to show a television ad to children and ask them who is *really* speaking—and why.

One technique that can provide insight into the ideological point of view of a media presentation involves *oppositional interpretation*. Even though media presentations offer a preferred reading, all texts are open to alternative interpretations. Assuming the perspective of a sub-culture in the program furnishes perspective on the operation and impact of the dominant ideology reflected in the text. In addition, this approach can enhance the audiences' sensitivity to the ideology of subcultures that exist within the dominant culture. An oppositional interpretation also provides insight into the dynamics between the dominant ideology and subcultures.

A film that lends itself to oppositional interpretation is *Gunga Din* (1939), starring Cary Grant, Douglas Fairbanks, Jr., Victor McLaglen, and Sam Jaffe as Gunga Din. Based loosely on the poem by Rudyard Kipling, the film takes place in British India during the Thuggee uprising. Within the context of the film (i.e., the preferred reading), the British are the heroes who are faced with the task of bringing civilization to India. Grant, Fairbanks, and McLaglen are three fun-loving sergeants who adopt Gunga Din as an unofficial company mascot. They allow him to hang around the barracks and pretend to be a "real soldier," but his actual duties consist of attending to the sergeants' personal needs.

In the film, the Indian natives mount an insurrection against the British forces. Shot in close-ups, with the lighting coming from below, the natives look unnatural and demonic. Individually, the natives are no match for the heroes, a sign of their physical and spiritual inferiority to the British. In one scene a band of natives pounces on McLaglen, but he shakes them off with ease. These natives are atrocious marksmen; try as they might, they can never hit the British heroes. In contrast, every shot fired by the sergeants seems to find a native target.

The unscrupulous natives lure the British troops into an ambush. However, Gunga Din saves the day by climbing to the top of a tower and blowing his bugle, alerting the oncoming British reinforcements of the impending ambush. Gunga Din is killed in mid-toot, a martyr to the British cause. For his act of selflessness, the British award him a posthumous medal, finally accepting him as a bona fide British soldier.

An oppositional interpretation from the perspective of the subculture (the native Indians) results in a far different reading of the film. Within the context of this alternative reading, the British are the aggressors who have invaded India and, armed with superior weaponry, imposed their way of life on the natives. The three heroes are drunken mercenaries whose interests are confined to fighting, carousing with each other, and plundering the country for gold. Yet they consider themselves morally superior, referring to the non-Christian natives as "savages," "heathens," "fiends," and "apes." In contrast, the insurgents are patriots, committed to resisting the British takeover. According to *this* interpretation, Gunga Din is a traitor who has betrayed his country and his people. The conclusion of the film is hardly a celebration but, instead, a chilling commentary about the forces of colonial imperialism on the sovereignty of a people.

Rhetorical Techniques

Rhetoric refers to the use of language as a means of persuasion. Roger Silverstone observes that rhetoric not only has an aesthetic agenda (to please/appeal) but a political agenda as well (to command/persuade).[61] The following rhetorical devices are used to position ideas in ways that reinforce the dominant ideology of the culture:

A *euphemism* is an inoffensive term that tempers or softens the meaning of an explicit, harsh, or distasteful idea or concept. The derivation of euphe-

Figure 1.1. *Gunga Din* (RKO Radio Pictures, 1939)

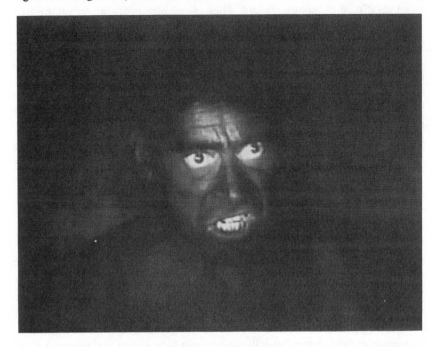

Oppositional interpretation is a technique which furnishes perspective on the ideological point of view of a media presentation. A film that lends itself to oppositional interpretation is *Gunga Din* (1939). Within the context of the film (i.e., the preferred reading), the British are the heroes who are faced with the task of bringing civilization to India. The production values of this shot of the leader of the insurrection reinforces the dominant ideology by emphasizing the dark skin of the villain. In addition, the lighting makes the native look satanic.

mism comes from the Greek word *euphonos,* or sweet-voiced, suggesting that this discourse device can make harsh concepts or ideas "sweeter," or more palatable. To illustrate, William Lutz offers examples of euphemisms used in war:

- *preemptive counterattack:* an invasion where we strike first;
- *predawn vertical insertion:* we strike first, and when it's still dark;
- *collateral damage:* civilian casualties;
- *traumatic amputation:* arms and legs blown off soldiers;

- *special weapon:* atomic bomb;
- *aluminum transfer containers:* temporary coffins;
- *misspoke:* lied;
- *energetic disassemblies:* nuclear explosions;
- *radiation enhancement devices:* nuclear weapons.[62]

Special interest organizations often assume euphemistic titles to conceal their mission, ideology, and sponsorship. Jim Drinkard refers to this phenomenon as "astroturf," in that the names of these organizations suggest grassroots activism.[63] For instance, the Information Council on the Environment, which sounds like a pro-environmental group, is actually an organization formed by the oil and coal lobbies to discourage the establishment of global warming policies. Molly Ivins reports:

> The public relations firm hired to do its bidding frankly stated its mission: "to reposition global warming as theory rather than fact." According to Ross Gelbspan [author of *The Heat Is On*], "Big oil and big coal have successfully created the general perception that climate scientists are sharply divided over the extent and the likely impacts of climate change—and even over whether it is taking place at all."[64]

Other examples of "astroturf" lobbying groups, whose names do not always reflect financial backing or agenda, include:

- *Californians for Statewide Smoking Restrictions:* A group formed in 1994 by tobacco companies in an effort to head off strict new rules on workplace smoking.
- *Coalition for Energy and Economic Revitalization:* Formed by a Roanoke, Virginia, public relations consultant, this organization is pushing for a new 115–mile power line for American Electrical Power Co., which is paying its expenses.
- *Coalition for Vehicle Choice:* In arguing against stricter auto fuel–economy standards, this group has cited police needs for large cruisers, the need for full-sized vans for the disabled, and the safety of big cars. Its money comes from Detroit automakers.[65]

Labels are connotative words or phrases that describe a person or group. Labels such as "oil-rich," "arch-conservative," "liberal," and "special interests" possess connotative meanings that transcend their denotative (or dictionary) definition. Labels often appear with such frequency in the media that they no longer simply describe but, in fact, define the group. To illustrate, in December 1997, Audrey Mullen, executive director of the Conservative Americans for Tax Reform, turned to her arsenal of labels in blasting Vice President Al Gore's efforts to reach a global warming accord: "Al Gore would prefer to stick *working-class* America with a big tax increase and stick America with lost jobs or seek the approval of his *liberal environmentalist tree hugging friends.*"[66] (Emphasis added.)

A *metaphor* is an implied analogy that links one object or concept with another and, in the process, invests the first with qualities associated with the second. Metaphors can shape the audience's attitude toward a subject, as they begin to think about one in terms of the other. The use of metaphors can be confined to a single, isolated comparison or it can be broadened into a *metaphorical concept,* which encompass an entire world view or ideology.[67] Lakoff and Johnson note that a prominent metaphorical concept in the United States is: *time is money.* They cite the following examples of common vernacular deriving from this metaphorical concept:

- "You're wasting my time."
- "This gadget will save you hours."
- "I don't have the time to give you."
- "You're running out of time."
- "He's living on borrowed time."[68]

The ideological assumptions that underlie this metaphorical concept hearken back to the nineteenth-century industrial age, when a worker's productivity was measured in terms of time rather than completed projects. Laborers were paid "by the hour," so that time and, indeed, the lives of workers were considered commodities. A related assumption is that some people's time is more valuable than others'—specifically, those in positions of power and authority. Thus, examining the assumptions that underlie the use of extended metaphors can provide considerable insight into the ideology of much of our public discourse.

Obfuscation occurs when people employ jargon, convoluted sentences, and erudite words to mask ideology and discourage discussion. To illustrate, on June 4, 1996, the Ariane-5 rocket exploded on its first launch. The press release that followed the explosion began as follows: "The first Ariane-5 flight did not result in validation of Europe's new launcher."[69] Because the language is so unintelligible, the audience remained confused about what happened; consequently, they were hardly in a position to consider essential questions, such as *who* was responsible for the catastrophe.

Spin is a rhetorical strategy in which communicators present their particular interpretation, or "spin," on a story in order to shape how information is presented, reported, and received by the public. The objectives of spin control are to: (1) establish the agenda (what is important about the event or issue); (2) influence the public's attitude toward the event or issue; and (3) in cases of negative news, deflect responsibility for the event or issue in another direction.

For example, immediately after the 1996 presidential debates between Bob Dole and Bill Clinton, media consultants and political cronies of both candidates circulated among the press, announcing that their candidate had "won" the debate.

Spin tactics are employed outside the political arena. The Ku Klux Klan has begun to employ spin techniques to influence public attitude toward this extremist organization. Christopher Goodwin notes:

> It is a challenge that would tax the most devious political spindoctor: the Ku Klux Klan (KKK), founded to enforce white supremacy . . . is launching a recruitment drive and claims that it wants to become more respectable. The racist language has been toned down and the organization, founded in 1866, is now more likely to hold coffee mornings than cross burnings as it tries to attract new recruits. The KKK fears it is losing many extremists to America's burgeoning militia movement and so it is trying to edge closer to mainstream American politics by encouraging more young professionals to join its ranks.
>
> This new image was in danger of being jeopardized last week after two Klansmen pleaded guilty to burning down churches in rural southern states, the traditional stronghold of the KKK. More than 70 churches with black congregations have been destroyed in fires since the beginning of last year. However, Thom Robb, the grand wizard of the Klan, dismisses allegations of KKK violence: "We have a long-standing position against violence," he insisted at the Klan's remote headquarters just outside the half-abandoned mining town of Zinc, in the Ozark mountains of north-western Arkansas.
>
> It is Robb, 48, who is seeking to broaden the Klan's appeal, trying to attract middle-class supporters by recasting the Klan as a "civil rights group for whites." . . . Robb is even planning to abandon his own title of grand wizard soon in favor of the blander and more technocratic "national director" and his underlings will no longer be known as grand dragons . . . [Robb] insists that "we don't hate blacks; we just love whites. . . ."[70]

Redirection occurs when a media communicator uses language that shifts the audience's attention from one ideological sphere to a more innocuous or acceptable ideology. An example can be found in the political debate in the United States over the issue of global warming. In November 1997, a UN-sponsored conference of more than 150 countries was held to draw up an international accord that would reduce global emissions and halt global warming. These measures were met with overwhelming approval by the American public: 65 percent of Americans surveyed favored steps to cut U.S. emissions of greenhouse gases "regardless of what other countries do."[71] However, opponents of the plan mounted efforts to reframe the debate within the context of other issues that Americans cherish just as strongly—national sovereignty and economic security. Steve Forbes, a Republican candidate for president in 1996, called the accord "an unprecedented government seizure of American freedom and sovereignty." Jim Nicholson, chairperson of the Republican National Committee, said the pact will "radically change the American lifestyle."[72]

Another example of redirection is the ad campaign for Nike, the ubiquitous shoe empire. In the early 1990s, Nike moved its manufacturing operations from the United States to countries in Asia as a cost-saving measure. The labor abuses of the company have been well-documented. In Vietnam, young women are paid twenty cents an hour to make Nike athletic products. An internal audit of a Vietnamese Nike factory found that the electric ventilation system and natural-air booths at the plant were insufficient to reduce the dust from harmful chemical powders. As many as 77 percent of the workers there suffered from respiratory problems. The chemical solvent toluene was measured at levels of between 6 and 177 times the amount allowed by Vietnamese law. Prolonged exposure to this chemical can cause severe damage to the liver, kidneys, and nervous system.[73]

This level of worker exploitation has contributed to huge profits for the company and its ownership. In 1996, Nike earned $650 million in profits. During that same year, Phil Knight, founder and chairperson of Nike, earned a salary of $1,650,000, and his fortune is estimated at $5.4 billion.[74]

However, the advertising campaign for Nike substitutes an altogether different ideology for its oppressive company policy. The cumulative message of Nike ads is one of empowerment: "*Just do it.*" This pro-social message promotes the athletic accomplishments of women ("Play like a girl") and celebrates the achievements of African Americans ("Thank You, Jackie Robinson"). In December 1997, Nike introduced a new variation of this ideological theme: "I can."

A 1997 Nike ad featuring Michael Jordan offers the ultimate empowerment message. In this commercial, Jordon leaves a basketball game during halftime to tend to his business. As a Nike corporate executive, Jordon sits at his desk inspecting a pile of shoes. In this fantasy, labor has merged with management, and workers have been given a raise—from 20 cents per hour to $34 million per year. Nike's ideology has been redirected back onto itself, so that it promotes the empowerment of the labor movement, while continuing its unfair labor practices abroad.

Another example of redirection occurs in a 1997 ad for Pizza Hut, which is a thinly disguised adaptation of Martin Luther King's apocalyptic sermon, "I see the Promised Land," delivered on the eve of his death on April 3, 1968. Knowing that he was the target of assassins, King concluded his remarks as follows:

> Well, I don't know what will happen now. We've got some difficult days ahead. But it doesn't matter with me now. Because I've been to the mountaintop. And I don't mind. Like anybody, I would like to live a long life. Longevity has its place. But I'm not concerned about that now. I just want to do God's will. And He's allowed me to go up on the mountain. And I've looked over. And I've seen the promised land. I may not get there with you. But I want you to know tonight, that we, as a people will get to the promised land. And I'm happy, tonight. I'm not worried about anything. I'm not fearing any man. Mine eyes have seen the glory of the coming of the Lord.[75]

In the Pizza Hut adaptation, the sermon takes place in a locker room during the halftime of a football game. Using the same ministerial intonation as Dr. King, an African-American coach gives a halftime motivational speech. Rather than going to the mountaintop, the coach has "been to the edge and back." What has he seen, the young men ask with their eyes? "What I've learned is . . . you don't need other crusts!" At Pizza Hut the toppings extend all the way to the edge of the dough. He begins to recite a litany of toppings: "Pepperoni . . . mushrooms." The ad cuts to closeups of the players, who are stunned, amazed, and, finally, converted to Pizza Hut. This ad has reduced Dr. King's vision and, indeed, the civil rights movement, to a pitch for fast food. Once again, ideology has been diverted, and style has triumphed over substance.

Narrative Analysis

Popular media narratives frequently depend upon unquestioned recognition and acceptance on the part of the audience. Examining the narrative can uncover the ideological principles that underlie these assumptions.

One aspect of narrative to consider is the *illogical premise.* Joseph Schuster, professor of communications at Webster University, defines premise as the central idea of a story, which answers the question, "what is this program about?"[76] Many fictional narratives call for the willing suspension of disbelief, in which the audience is asked to accept, without question, the basic premise of the program: Bugs Bunny can talk, Rambo can run and fight for hours without getting tired, and using Head and Shoulders shampoo will get you a girlfriend and a role on Broadway. Once the premise has been accepted, the remainder of the narrative progresses logically.

In some cases, the audience accepts, without question, premises with ideological overtones. For example, the animated feature film *Anastasia* (1997) is a romantic tale about a beautiful young princess who has become separated from her family, and then orphaned, during the fall of the Romanov monarchy in Russia. She meets a young Russian boy and, together, they set off for Paris to find her true identity. In the process, they must contend with Rasputin and his minions, who try to bring about her demise. At the conclusion, Anastasia reclaims her birthright, including the royal jewels to which she was entitled.

The premise of the film assumes the following: (1) that the fall of the czar was a result of a magical spell by "the evil sorcerer" Rasputin; (2) that the toppling of the monarchy caused a sense of loss among the people; (3) that the masses suffered more after the revolution; and (4) that the people longed for the restoration of the monarchy. However, Nikolai Zlobin, Russian historian and editor of *Demokratizatsiya,* disputes these assumptions:

> March 2, 1917, was a very mystical moment in Russian history, when Nikolas II signed his resignation decree and abdicated the throne. It was mystical because one of the strongest European monarchies disappeared peacefully (the Romanov family came to the throne in 1613). The Russian monarchy fell like the leaves from a dead tree. Everyone saw the fall as inevitable. Nobody supported Nikolas II, and nobody asked him to keep the throne. Even more, the people who came to him with the draft of the Resignation Act were members of the monarchy party. People were surprisingly indifferent to the dissolution of the monarchy, and they certainly weren't nostalgic about the royalty after they were gone. Even many who disagreed with communism were interested in a constitutional republic—there was no place for a Czar in the system anymore.
>
> Rasputin was hardly involved in state business, was unknown outside of the circle of nobility, and was killed in December 1916, before the fall of the monarchy.
>
> Regarding the condition of the people, any kind of reform brings some instability to society. But we must remember that most people suffered under the Czars, and that revolution brought them, at least, the hope that the majority of society would have a better life. People were prepared for hardship in the wake of the revolution. And the communist system did raise the standard of living for the masses, within a very few years. Only a very few people who had prospered under the Czars longed for the return of the Romanovs.
>
> Finally, the jewels were not the private property of the Romanov family but were national property, which were [*sic*] taken out of the country illegally.[77]

Identifying *illogical conclusions* in media presentations can also furnish perspective into ideological messages. The conclusions of many media programs are illogical, confused, or simply implausible when considered within the flow of the program. Given the ideology of the program, a happy ending requires the "divine" intervention of a scriptwriter and director. The illogical conclusions of media presentations resolve the inequities of the narrative, reinforcing the dominant ideology. For instance, *Pretty Woman* (1990) is a modern fairy tale involving corporate executive Edward Lewis (Richard Gere) and a hooker, Vivian Ward (Julia Roberts). The promo for the film announces, "She walked off of the street, into his life, and stole his heart."[78] While the film clearly is a romance, it is also a story about class differences. Although it is unlikely that Vivian could adapt to Edward's world, and even more unlikely that Edward would accept Vivian into his world, the two parade off at the end of the film, undermining a central message of the movie: that class separates people and defines their expectations, aspirations, and vision. The movie dismisses these issues with a romantic (but false) ending, in which love renders class differences meaningless.

Characterization in media presentations also sends ideological messages. According to Daniel Chandler, characters can be considered embodiments of ideological positions, based upon whose interests they represent.[79] Examples of these ideological oppositions include:

Nature/Culture	Animal/Human	Mind/Body	Art/Science
Male/Female	Old/Young	Us/Them	Rich/Poor
Old/New	Freedom/Constraint		Knower/Known
Inner/Outer	Individual/Society	Private/Public	Gay/Straight
West/East	Insider/Outsider	Inclusion/Exclusion	Black/White	Weak/Strong
Dominant/Subordinate	Producer/Consumer		

Henry A. Murray observes that heroes and heroines epitomize those qualities that society considers admirable and thus generally reflect the values of dominant culture: "The forces that are aligned with the group's welfare, with its hopes for the future, being beneficent in direction, are exalted as the good powers. The opposing and hence maleficent forces are portrayed as evil."[80]

Thus, in *Pretty Woman,* the character of Edward Lewis represents several ideological positions in Chandler's paradigm that support the dominant culture: male, white, dominant, rich, exclusive, producer, insider.

The triumph of good over evil generally is dependent on the characters' adherence to the values and goals of dominant culture. In "Gunsmoke" Matt Dillon complied with the code of law and order: never draw first or shoot a man in the back. Despite these disadvantages, the marshal's adherence to the rules gave him the strength to defeat his adversaries. The triumph of the hero at the conclusion of the program, therefore, reinforces the ideology of the dominant culture. Chandler declares, "The structure of the text works to position the reader to 'privilege one set of values and meanings over the other.'"[81]

Significantly, many contemporary programs depict the hero cheating a bit or going outside of the law. For instance, in episodes of "ER," Doug Ross, Mark Green, and Carol Hathaway continually violate hospital policy in the interest of patient care. This behavior reflects a more complex and subjective sense of ethics within the culture. But in addition, this attitude coalesces with the corporate ideology of "doing what it takes" and demonstrating free-enterprise initiative to achieve your goals.

Heroes in media programs always enjoy the benefits of a material world, surrounded by comforts. In cop shows (e.g., "Miami Vice" or the *Lethal Weapon* films), the protagonists do not have to dress in uniform like their peers but instead wear fashionable clothing and drive expensive, high-speed cars. In the sitcom "Friends," the characters live in expensive apartments in New York City, although most of them have no apparent means to support themselves in that style.

Characterization in media programming also sends message about the value of conformity to the system. Heroes epitomize conformity. For example, with his normal, all-American good-looks, Tom Cruise looks like everyone else—only better. Conversely, characters who are too different are objects of ridicule or scorn. In this sense, there is a suspicion of difference and fear of change. However, many programs offer the illusion of the hero-as-rebel. In the series of *Lethal Weapon* films, Mel Gibson plays nonconformist cop Martin Riggs. However, Riggs's rebellious persona is only cosmetic; despite his long hair and jeans, Riggs remains an agent of the establishment, eradicating crime without questioning the conditions that contribute to these situations.

Conversely, characters who do not buy into the basic assumptions of the culture are depicted as misfits, exceptions, and buffoons. Villains represent negative values that threaten the established world view. They are not bound by the moral constraints to which heroes must adhere. Villains are free to draw first, lie, and cheat. However, these momentary advantages are not powerful enough to contest the moral order of the universe. They are inevitably brought to justice—for their crimes and, in a broader sense, for their transgressions against the system.

Genre Analysis

A genre is a type, class, or category of artistic work, featuring a standardized narrative format that is distinctive and easily recognizable. Examples include horror films, romances, science fiction, situation comedies, westerns, and the evening news. Each genre is distinctive and readily identifiable, regardless of time or place of composition, author, or subject matter. A genre is not confined to one medium. For instance, at one time or another, westerns have appeared in print, on radio, television, and film.

A genre contains a recognizable narrative format, including patterns in plot, structure, characteristic conventions or devices (such as horses, characters, and outfits found in westerns), and stylistic similarities. Individual programs generally conform to a clear formula of the genre. As John Cawelti observes, "Individual works are ephemeral, but the formula lingers on, evolving and changing with time, yet still basically recognizable."[82]

There are many ways to study genre. One approach that is useful for our purposes is to consider the *shared ideological orientation* of a particular genre. A genre shapes the audience's interpretation of content by framing the action within a particular world view and set of expectations with respect to the culture or cultures that populate this world, definitions of success, and whether or not people are in control of their own destinies.

The ideology of the *action drama* is essentially conservative, in that the central focus of each program is a return to the status quo. The conventional plot operates according to the formula of order/chaos/order. Initially, the world exists in a state of harmony. However, almost immediately some problem (i.e., a troublemaker or natural disaster) disrupts this initial tranquility. Most of the plot focuses on the restoration of order, which is achieved at the conclusion. Thus, this world is reactionary; it does not require change but changing back.

The population of this world (and by extension, the audience) longs for some form of authoritarianism—either a more efficient law enforcement system or a protector who goes outside the system to punish wrongdoers. The striking amount of violence in action dramas is also an instrument of the status quo. According to George Gerbner, violence teaches lessons about the exercise of power: who can impose his/her will on whom. Action dramas therefore create a climate in which audience members value protection, often at the expense of individual civil liberties.

At the same time, the social issues facing the characters in action dramas are trivialized as simply personal problems or individual choices.

Stephen Brookfield declares: "The mass media socialize adults to view political issues, disputes, and events in an excessively simple, unidimensional manner. Issues rooted in ideological conflict are presented as personality differences."[83] In action dramas, street hoods deal drugs because they are inherently evil or because they have made a personal, conscious choice, without the social context that might provide insight into this type of behavior.

The *horror* genre conveys ideological messages about the powerlessness of human beings. In some presentations, the characters are victims of supernatural forces (e.g., ghosts, monsters, Satan, Dracula). In the story of Frankenstein, the inventor is a victim of his own hubris—failing to understand his limits as a human being. In other contemporary programs, the horror originates *within* human beings. Slasher movies depict a world in which we are the monsters; human nature is bestial, wicked, and corrupt. In this Darwinian world, the weak (usually women characters) are preyed upon and brutalized by the strong.

According to Douglas Kellner, the horror genre often reflects the uncertainty posed by threats, or perceived threats, to the system. During periods in which people feel a loss of control in their lives, there is a resurgence of occult horror films. Consequently, the escalation of Cold War tensions in the 1950s was accompanied by a wave of horror films.[84]

The *gangster genre* presents conflicting ideological messages, as reflected in the rise and fall of the hero. The beginning of the film typically focuses on the spectacular success of the young gangster, who epitomizes the American ideology of hard work, initiative, and free enterprise. But at some point in the narrative, the gangster typically crosses a moral line, and he is punished for his violation of the social order. This stage of the plot sends the message that individuals must obey the law and conform to the system.

However, the initial ascension of the gangster is often the most glamorous and memorable part of the narrative. Jimmy Cagney's performance as a "rising" mobster in the first phase of *Public Enemy* (1931) was so mesmerizing that the studio was compelled to include a prologue and epilogue emphasizing that the film should serve as a lesson *against* criminal behavior.

The ideological orientation of *situation comedies* focuses on the satisfaction of personal needs. Sitcoms concentrate on the small problems facing the major characters (e.g., Seinfeld gets a haircut or Frasier enrolls the family dog in obedience school). Sitcoms often deal with the travails of relationships. Much of the confusion or plot conflict results from dishonesty or poor communication (e.g., mistaken identity). In that regard, success is measured purely in terms of personal gratification. Values such as communication, loyalty, and honesty are rewarded at the conclusion of each episode. To be sure, in "Seinfeld," traditional values of the genre often serve as a source of humor—Jerry, George, Elaine, and Kramer are hardly loyal, caring, or honest. However, this seeming departure is an implicit acknowledgment of the sitcom values system. The audience would not laugh at the selfish antics of the Seinfeld characters unless they were familiar with the traditional values of the genre.

In sitcoms, the concept of community is limited to members of the immediate cast. Thus, in programs like "Cheers," "Seinfeld," or "Friends," society is a place "where everybody knows your name." When the primary characters do think beyond their own needs, they focus only on the well-being of the other characters in the program. Hence, social activism is reduced to taking care of one's own immediate network.

Increasingly, situation comedies are becoming vehicles for the ideology of consumer culture. Although "Seinfeld" proudly promoted itself as a show "about nothing," this description is only half accurate: the series was about nothing of *substance*. Instead, the episodes focused on an empty world, devoid of meaning. Jerry, George, Elaine, and Kramer are shallow, self-absorbed characters who are incapable of sustaining relationships. What meaning there is in the world of Seinfeld—and what constitutes the plot of each program—consists of acts of consumerism. Characters spend their time engaged in diversions, such as going to the movies, shopping, or hanging out at the coffee shop. Life consists of small pleasures—a cup of soup, Junior mints—which can be purchased.

Musicals present an ideology that moves people away from the consideration of societal or political concerns. James M. Collins notes that musicals present "dance as the only viable alternative to despair (financial or otherwise) . . ."[85] or as the solution to problems.

> One finds in this depiction of "life in the streets" the central ideological tensions of these early Warner musicals, perhaps best illustrated by the opening and closing numbers of *Gold Diggers of 1933*. In the opening, assembled chorus girls are clad in giant coins as they sing "We're in the Money," a scene which is surely one of the most preposterously optimistic reflections on the Depression in film history. Here the Hollywood musical offers the viewer a saccharine alternative to economic hard times outside the confines of the movie theater.[86]

Some musicals, such as *There's No Business Like Show Business* (1954), revolve around the backstage workings of show business. In the backstage musical, the *central metaphorical concept* is that "Life is a show." The title song declares that even though life is full of disappointments, you must "go on with the show"—that is, put the best face on your situation and perform as though you are satisfied.

Other musicals incorporate music and dance into the narrative, so that people spontaneously burst into song. For instance, in *Meet Me in St. Louis* (1944), Judy Garland launches into "The Trolley Song" as she is riding around St. Louis. Collins points out that in this category of musical, life itself becomes a musical: "The shift from day-to-day life to musical life appears completely natural, the distinctions purposely blurred—life is not like a song, it is a song."[87] The message is that, although there may be nothing that we can do about the inadequacies and injustices in society, we can control our attitude toward these conditions. Keeping a song in our hearts keeps alive the possibility of personal redemption.

Perhaps more than any other genre, the *science fiction* genre is distinctly ideological in nature, offering a range of commentary on the present and future condition of society. One subgenre consists of invasion films, in which some foreign element threatens our current system. In the invasion films, the outside threat often brings out the best in the prevailing system. In *Independence Day* (1997), people of all nationalities work together (under American leadership) to defeat the forces of evil who are trying to conquer the earth.

Another subcategory of science fiction consists of allegories that are set in the future but comment on present conditions. *Blade Runner* (1982) is a film that takes place in 2019 but makes a statement about alienation in contemporary culture. Human beings have lost their humanity and turned into machines. At the same time, technology (in the form of robotic "replicants") has assumed a life of its own and, in the process, become more human than its creators.

A derivative category of utopian science fiction programs alert the audience to societal possibilities by offering a glimpse into a world that is superior to our own. In *Contact* (1997), after a great deal of political infighting, scientist Ellie Arroway (Jodie Foster) embarks on a space voyage. She discovers a highly evolved civilization that has transcended many of the limitations plaguing contemporary earthlings (exemplified by the petty bickering and shortsighted thinking which nearly sabotage the space expedition). In this way, the film extends hope to a world that has become corrupt and self-absorbed.

Other genres such as westerns, quiz shows, news programs, tabloid talk shows, spy programs, and sports programming also possess distinctive ideological orientations and send messages about what life is and what life ought to be. Examining the ideological underpinnings of these genres can provide insight into ways in which genres shape audiences' expectations and understanding with their content.

Production Elements

Another way to approach the study of ideology is through consideration of production elements. Production elements, which refer to the style and attributes of a media presentation, shape the interpretation placed on the information by the media communicator. Elements such as color, shape, and movement convey ideological messages by affecting our way of seeing, attributing meaning, and understanding social relationships within a program. (For a more comprehensive discussion of production elements, see chapter 5.)

Production choices frequently signify *approval* or *disapproval,* which reinforces the interests of dominant culture. Through the choice of editing, lighting, or color, the ideology of a program simply may "feel right" to the audience. On the other hand, the production values used to depict an alternative ideological world view may trigger feelings of discomfort or antagonism. Consequently, a fruitful area of investigation involves examining production elements as a way to uncover the ideological subtext in the media production.

Production elements frequently work in combination to convey a message. Research assistant Darlene Diel observes,

> *Titanic* (1997) contains a scene in which Rose DeWitt Bukater (Kate Winslet) reunites with Jack Dawson (Leonardo DiCaprio) after telling him earlier that day that she no longer wanted to see him. Rose finds Jack overlooking the sea at the forefront of the ship. All is still—the ocean, the serenity of the music and lighting. Jack asks Rose to step up onto the railing that overlooks the front of the ship. While the two embrace, a rush of romantic music, combined with dark, dramatic lighting, underscores the significance of the moment.[88]

Recurrences of certain production elements also may signal approval or disapproval. The appearance of a villain may be accompanied by a distinctive discordant musical theme throughout the narrative, so that the audience learns to associate his appearance with something disagreeable. Analysis of production elements can be a useful tool in uncovering ideological messages in media presentations. Warm *colors,* like red, orange, and yellow, tend to make us feel happy, secure, positive, and intensely involved. Dead colors, like gray or black, make us feel sad, alone, or uncomfortable. For example, the most common background colors employed in American politics are red, white, and blue. In addition to their patriotic connotation, these bold, uplifting colors evoke positive feelings in the audience. Bright colors are also common in positive political ads. In contrast, dark colors are frequently employed to send negative messages.

Costumes can also signify ideology. In John Singleton's *Boyz N the Hood* (1991), clothing is used to chart the complex issues of racial identity and alienation facing a black youth moving into maturity in South Central Los Angeles. Concerned about her son Tre (Cuba Gooding, Jr.), his mother Reva (Angela Basset) sends him to live with his father Furious (Larry Fishburne). Furious works as a mortgage broker in the neighborhood. Furious's clothes (chinos, striped shirts, knitted tops, and glasses) exhibit the conventional insignia of a black male socialized into a white middle-class culture. Conversely, the "gansta" style of Tre's best friend Doughboy (Ice Cube) make a political statement against the established social order. His clothes convey a message of aggression and defiance against dominant white male hegemony. In addition, the clothes represent black masculinity and imply toughness and independence.

Thus, the costumes in *Boyz N the Hood* represent fundamental choices facing the African-American male in American culture. If Tre chooses the conventional, banal style of the white middle class, he merits acceptance into the dominant white culture but becomes alienated from his own sense of self by repressing his black, masculine identity. Donning the street uniform, Tre assumes "hood" affinity and masculine identity, but suffers alienation from the mainstream American community and is relegated to the life of the streets.

Lighting is another production element that can convey ideological messages by manipulating the emotions of audience members. A brightly lit photograph evokes feelings of security and happiness. In contrast, a dark picture filled with shadow creates a mysterious atmosphere or arouses fear and apprehension. Dim lighting also can trigger a sense of powerlessness, as the viewer must struggle to grasp clear visual control of the environment.

Relative position refers to where a character or object appears on the screen (or page). Objects appearing toward the front attract immediate attention, whereas things in the background are generally considered of secondary importance. The upper portion of the page or screen connotes positive messages, so that people who appear on the upper portion of the page or screen display power, dominance, importance, happiness, control, enlightenment, health, prosperity, status, virtue, and reason. Conversely, people positioned on the lower portion reflect positions of powerlessness, subordination, unimportance, sadness, lack of control, unconsciousness, illness, poverty, lack of status, wickedness, and emotional distress.[89] People appearing off-center of the screen are marginalized.

A print advertisement for Tommy Hilfiger Fragrance provides an example of how relative position discloses ideology. On the surface, the photograph of six young people appearing in the ad represents a multicultural society (the photo contains a balance of four men and two women, three Caucasians and three African Americans). However, as graduate student Angela Rollins observes, a closer examination of relative position reveals that the subgroups are marginalized in the ad:

> The white members of the ad are squarely in the center, reflecting their status within the group. The African Americans are off to both sides. . . . At the same time, the female is far below where the men appear, indicating a subordinate position. The message seems to be that differences appear to be acceptable, it is still the mainstream (white males) who are the center of power. This juxtaposition of diversity and conformity sends a conflicting message to the audience.[90]

In film and television, relative position is also used in the sequencing of programming. Although a news broadcast may contain a number of separate reports, the flow of segments has a powerful tendency to merge contents together, sending unintended (or intentional) messages. Jane Caputi observes that the sequencing of messages work together: (1) to emphasize a political meaning of the primary text; (2) to undercut, defuse, or mock a political meaning of the primary text; or (3) to create an explicit political significance that otherwise would be absent from any of the segments taken singly.[91]

To illustrate, a CNN segment "News from Medicine" aired a report on the beneficial effects of aspirin in preventing heart attacks. Immediately following the segment, a tag line appeared, "'News From Medicine' is brought to you by Bristol-Meyers Squibb, makers of Bayer Aspirin," followed by a commercial for Bayer aspirin. This sequence conveys the message that not simply aspirin, but Bayer aspirin, will reduce heart attacks.[92]

The direction of *movement* also has distinct ideological properties. Movement directed toward the audience can either be friendly (e.g., an invitation or sign of intimacy), aggressive, or menacing. Movement directed away from the audience can signal either abandonment, retreat, avoidance, or resolution. Movement directed upward often is a positive sign (something going to heaven or, perhaps, outer space). Movement directed downward often is a negative sign (e.g., crashes or fights), possibly signaling defeat.

Angle refers to the level at which the camera is shooting in relation to the subject. A person filmed from a high angle looks small, weak, frightened, or vulnerable. In contrast, a person filmed from a low angle appears larger, important, and powerful. In political ads, the camera is often tilted up at candidates, which evokes feelings of respect and associations of competence.

Figure 1.2. **Tommy Hilfiger**

Relative position can convey ideological messages. This photograph simulates the composition and arrangement of an advertisement for Tommy Hilfiger Fragrance. On the
surface, the photograph of six young people appearing in the ad represents a multicultural society. However, a closer examination of relative position reveals that the members
of subcultures are marginalized in the ad. The males assume the dominant (upper) position in the North-South corridor. At the same time, members of minority groups appear
on the edges of the East-West corridor, so that the white models occupy the center.
Thus, although the manifest message of the ad is that differences appear to be acceptable, the latent message of this arrangement is that white males remain the center of
power. Photo by Aaron Mednick.

The use of *images* is intimately connected to the perpetuation of ideology by shaping how we think about our world. Bill Nichols explains,

> Images ... contribute to our sense of who we are and to our everyday engagement with the world around us. What these signs never announce is that they are most fundamentally the signifiers of ideology. ... After all, seeing is believing, and how we see ourselves and the world around us is often how we believe ourselves and the world to be.[93]

There are several different types of ideological imaging:

The *juxtaposition of images* can produce a third, distinct meaning (described by the equation A + B = C). This fusion of images operates on humans' *gestalt,* or predisposition to order, so that the audience naturally makes a connection between the two disparate images. The media communicator can use the juxtaposition of images to comment on the relationship between objects and events. For example, an American Express ad juxtaposes images of the Greek Parthenon with an American Express card, linking the power, stability, and wealth of the ancient Greek temple and American Express. On another level, the idea of sacredness of the temple is transferred to the credit card, sanctifying the power of wealth.

Another example of the juxtaposition of images occurred during CBS's coverage of the 1998 Winter Olympics in Nagano, Japan. Nike, a major sponsor of CBS's Winter Olympics coverage, provided sports clothes, complete with Nike's signature "swoosh" for the entire CBS crew, including news correspondents Harry Smith, Bill Geist, Mark McEwen, and Bob Simon. On one side, the blue jackets carried a CBS-eye logo, while on the opposite breast was the curve-logo of Nike. The juxtaposed images undermined the credibility of the broadcast journalists and the CBS news operation. Steve Rendell of the media watchdog group FAIR commented, "You couldn't have a better symbol of the corporatization of the news than seeing the Nike swoosh on the chest of CBS correspondents. There is a big difference between running ads for a product and having your correspondents themselves become advertisements."[94]

Imagistic layering occurs when one image is inserted into the primary representation, sending latent ideological messages. An example of imagistic layering can be found in the first film version of *Dracula* (1931). As part of his attire, Bela Lugosi wore a medallion around his neck, consisting of a star with six points—the Jewish Star of David. This combination of images attaches a vicious anti-Semitic meaning to the vampire tale. The anti-Semitic subtext of the film hearkens back to the views of the nine-

Figure 1.3. **American Express**

The juxtaposition of images can be used to construct a separate, discrete meaning. This American Express ad juxtaposes images of the Greek Parthenon with an American Express card, connecting the power, stability, and wealth of the ancient Greek temple with American Express. Copyright © American Express TRS Inc. Reprinted by Permission.

teenth-century author of the novel, Bram Stoker, who was a member of several anti-Semitic organizations.

As the embodiment of the stereotypes, misconceptions, and superstitions that formed the basis of the persecution of the Jews, Dracula is a figure to be dreaded. Dracula is of dark Eastern European descent, of unknown origin. The Count is wealthy; yet the source of his wealth is unknown. At the beginning of the film, he is cast out of his country and is buying an estate in the richest area of London. The problems in the film stem from his unwanted intrusion into British aristocratic society.

Dracula is "undead," meaning that he has no hope for salvation through acceptance of Christ. Dracula cannot bear to behold the Cross, reflecting his state of damnation as an enemy of Christ. This "prince of darkness" has a strange hypnotic power that can seduce people to his way of life if they are not vigilant.

Vampires live by taking the blood from young innocents; this echoes tales of Jews kidnapping Christian children and using their blood in the making of the Passover meal. An anonymous author on the Internet has contributed this insight into the victims of Dracula:

> The victims of Dracula fall into two classes: Those whom he drains of their blood (or money) and immediately destroys, and those who he attacks and contaminates by mixing his blood with theirs. . . . This has two meanings: The proselytes the vampire wins (seduces) become like him and prey on others while he preys on them. Also, those women of different races with whom he mingles his blood, he forever separates from their people and makes them Jews like himself.[95]

Another example of imagistic layering can be found in a documentary photography project entitled *Neighborhood: A State of Mind,* by Linda G. Rich, Joan Clark Netherwood, and Elinor B. Cahn, which captured the tensions among the longtime residents of East Baltimore in the face of changes in their neighborhood. As new groups moved in, the residents struggled to preserve the old way of life, while faced with the reality that their neighborhood was changing before their eyes. As part of the exhibit, Elinor Cahn photographed Doc Price in his drugstore on O'Donnell Street. The nonverbal elements in the photograph present mixed messages, reflecting the difficult transition facing the incumbent citizens of the community of East Baltimore.

Doc Price stands behind his soda fountain, where he has been the proprietor for forty-five years. The elements in the photograph send a visual invitation to enter the store. A line of stools encourages guests to take a seat at the counter; indeed, the stools come equipped with footrests, so that the

Figure 1.4. **Dracula** (Universal Pictures, 1931)

In this example of imagistic layering from the film *Dracula* (1931), Count Dracula is wearing the Jewish Star of David. This combination of images attaches an anti-semitic perspective to the vampire story.

guests can put their feet up and be comfortable. An old sign above the counter advertises "Family Treat" packages, with a picture of two teenagers enjoying a snack together. A Coke sign invites us to "Pause . . . Refresh" ourselves at the drugstore. Doc's store is a repository of convenience items, including film, razors, cigarettes, sunglasses, and disposable diapers, encouraging customers to browse.

However, a handwritten sign over the cash register announces, "This Store Is No Hang Out For The Teen-Age. Please Make Your Purchases And Leave. Thank You." This notice undermines the inviting environment of the soda fountain. The layering of this image sends a mixed visual message which comments on the tension that accompanies change within the traditional social structure of East Baltimore.[96]

Imagistic layering occurs routinely in the advertising practice of *product placement.* The appearance of specific products in media presentations is hardly accidental; companies pay a hefty fee to ensure that their products are displayed in the narrative. These brands are cleverly embedded in the narrative, so that the audience accepts the appearance of the product within the context of the story. For example, eight companies paid in excess of $100 million to place their products in the James Bond film *Tomorrow Never Dies* (1997), including Visa, BMW of North America, Heineken, Smirnoff, Omega watches, and Swedish telecommunications giant Ericsson Corporation. During a key action sequence, Bond uses a futuristic Ericsson's mobile phone to get out of a jam—a testament to the value of the product: "Ericsson is using placement in the movie to craft an edgy, sci-fi image for its phones, which play a crucial part in the storyline. For instance . . . in the movie, Ericsson's phones do more than just phone home. They also are remote-control devices of destruction, navigation and surveillance."[97]

A different ideological use of product placement occurred on "Melrose Place," the popular television nighttime soap opera. Artist Mel Chen led a two-year project entitled "In the Name of the Place," which used "Melrose Place" as a public art space. The project was designed as a comment on the influence of television, using the layering of images in the set to make political and artistic statements.

Chen placed props into the show's set design which commented on violence, misogyny, abortion, AIDS, and other social issues. A promiscuous lover's bed sheets contained images of condoms and red AIDS ribbons. Boxes of Chinese takeout food included Chinese phrases alluding to human rights violations. Jeff Daniel declares, "Background props become political statements, wardrobe design turned into cultural critique—anything and everything was now grist for satirical send up or self-reflexive pun. Suddenly, quintessentially superficial Melrose Place burst at the seams with cutting edge commentary."[98] In one scene, a quilt decorated with the molecular structure of RU-148 (the abortion pill), was wrapped around the body of Allison, a character who was debating what to do about her pregnancy. A bar was stocked with bottles with labels itemizing the turbulent history of alcohol. Finally, on the pool table an eight ball was stamped with an outline of Africa—a commentary on the linkage of blackness and negativity.[99]

Although the props blend into the production framework of the show, this imagistic layering has attracted audience attention, resulting in the construction of a special website and a touring art exhibit.

Transmutation of symbols occurs when an image assumes a symbolic meaning that supports the dominant ideology. Images of violence like the Magnum symbolize economic dominance, power, and control. Sexual images are also transformed into symbols that support the system. Ads commonly employ

Figure 1.5. **East Baltimore**

Doc Price in his drugstore on O'Donnell Street. In this example of imagistic layering, photographer Elinor B. Cahn captured the tensions among the longtime residents in the face of changes in a neighborhood in East Baltimore. The overwhelming majority of visual images in the photograph, such as the counter and various impulse items, invite browsers. However, the handwritten sign above the Salem cigarette ad (see insert) clearly contradicts the invitation, reflecting the attitude of longtime residents in response to changes in the neighborhood. Photo by Elinor B. Cahn. Used with permission.

images of sexy women with automobiles to draw attention. But through the continued use of sexual imagery, the consumer is conditioned to associate the automobile with sexual desire. We buy cars as an expression of our sexuality. Indeed, we learn to see the cars themselves as sexy.

The diamond industry has been successful in positioning its product as a symbol of eternal love. Media programs contain countless images of men giving diamonds as tangible evidence of their love—to the point that *not* giving a diamond is regarded as a lack of devotion. A diamond declares that love will be permanent, and that the couple will live happily ever after. An ad for the American Gem Society asks the question, "The diamond engagement ring. Is two month's salary too much for something that lasts forever?" Given what the diamond represents (eternal love), "only two months salary" represents quite a bargain.

Product packaging frequently symbolizes prestige. Jose Cuervo is marketing a brand of tequila for $1,000 a bottle (far in excess of the standard $16 bottle of Cuervo Gold). Frank J. Prial asks, "It must be good, but, then again, how good can tequila get?" The answer is that customers are purchasing the status associated with the expensive brand through packaging and advertising. Prial adds, "As the Cuervo people readily acknowledge, half the price is in the package: a bottle made of Belgian crystal, trimmed in pewter and served up in a suede and leather case."[100] The tequila becomes a symbol of status which, for some, is worth the inflated price tag. Indeed, the extraordinary cost of the product reinforces its image of opulence and prosperity.

Masking images conceal inequities of the system by presenting a world view that reframes how we think about our experience under the existing system. Bill Nichols declares, "Ideology seeks to mask contradictions and paradox inherent in a given historical situation."[101] For instance, Visa commercials depict a world in which debt is presented as freedom. And ads for gambling boats show everyday citizens hitting it rich, masking the reality that the big winners ultimately always are the owners of the casinos. Consequently, despite their personal experiences, people are conditioned to participate in a system without questioning its basic assumptions.

In film and television, the *sequence of images* often sends ideological messages. Through thematic editing, or *montage,* the media communicator selects a succession of images which, in turn, establishes conceptual relationships, based upon what these images represent. The Odessa Steps sequence in Soviet filmmaker Sergei M. Eisenstein's film *Potemkin* (1925) offers a classic example of montage. Based on the historical events, the movie tells the story of a riot at the battleship *Potemkin.* The incident begins as a protest strike by the sailors over inedible food and then escalates to rebellion against the officers. The citizens of Odessa join the revolt. Cossacks then intervene and slaughter the helpless citizens on the steps leading to the harbor, effectively ending the revolt in Odessa. One of the most famous scenes of the film contains a sequence of images consisting of soldiers, a woman crying, and a baby carriage bouncing down the steps out of control. This juxtaposition of shots drew conceptual connections between the authoritarian power of the Cossacks, the suffering of the people, and the devastation of the town.

Another example of imagistic sequencing occurred in a television news story about a Hepatitis B outbreak in the St. Louis region in 1992. The report featured interviews with African-American families who had contracted the disease. The reporter's voiceover then explained that the way to prevent the disease is to be certain to wash your hands after bathroom use. In the course of this voiceover, the visuals cut from shots of African Americans to an image of a pair white hands washing with soap and water. Students found the following disturbing ideological messages in the succession of visuals: (1) only African Americans contract the disease; (2) African Americans are responsible for transmitting the disease; (3) African Americans do not practice safe hygiene.[102]

Finally, *music* can enhance our moods or distract us from our immediate concerns. In film, advertising, and television, music is more than merely background for the visuals. Music can work in conjunction with the visuals to "punctuate" or emphasize the major points of the presentation. Ideological meaning can be transferred to music, signaling approval or disapproval. Music elicits an affective response in the audience, arousing feelings of excitement, tension, drama, or romance in the audience that can be used to reinforce media messages. For instance, in *Jaws* (1975), the approach of the shark was accompanied by the ominous theme music, so that the music itself began to evoke feelings of fear and dread.

Essay: Ideological Analysis of *The English Patient*

Media programs often reflect shifts in cultural ideology. The late twentieth century is an intense period of conflicts and shifting boundaries. With these changes, the culture's ideologies begin to restructure themselves, which in turn influences the public attitudes and values. To illustrate, America's legal, religious, political, and medical institutions currently are struggling with the crucial issue of assisted suicide.

Mass media, both a public and popular forum accessible to most people, is a place where these important cultural debates take place. Anthony Minghella's *The English Patient* (1996) presents a coherent, elaborate construct of a changing ideology. The assisted death of the "English patient,"

Figures 1.6, 1.7, and 1.8. *Potemkin* (Goskino Production Co., 1925)

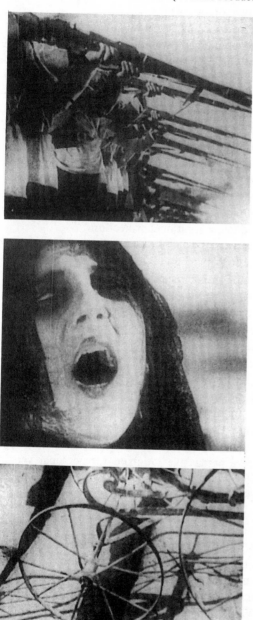

The *sequence of images* in film and television often sends ideological messages. The famous Odessa Steps scene in Sergei M. Eisenstein's film *Potemkin* (1925) contains a sequence of images consisting of: 1) soldiers; 2) a woman crying; and 3) a baby carriage bouncing down the steps. This montage established thematic connections between the authoritarian power of the Cossacks, the suffering of the people, and the devastation of the town.

Count Laszlo Almasy (Ralph Fiennes), not only dramatizes the debate but shapes attitudes through the course of the narrative.

To better understand the significance of the film, it would be helpful to summarize America's heated legal, medical, and religious battles surrounding the issue of "how" terminally ill people will die. On June 26, 1997, the Supreme Court unanimously held that physician-assisted death is not a fundamental interest protected by the Fourteenth Amendment of the Constitution. In writing his opinion, Chief Justice William H. Rehnquist invited the American people to consider the issue themselves. "Throughout the nation, Americans are engaged in an earnest and profound debate about the morality, legality and practicality of physician-assisted suicide. Our [ruling] permits this debate to continue, as it should in a democratic society." Notably, five other members of the Court wrote separate opinions suggesting that in the future there will be "situations in which an interest in hastening death is legitimate [and] entitled to constitutional protection."[103]

On November 1997, Oregon voters tested the strength of their Constitution when they passed a "Death With Dignity Act" for the second time. Although this act permits doctor-assisted suicide, the Drug Enforcement Agency (DEA) warned that a physician who helps a patient commit suicide could lose his or her license to write prescriptions. The Act has launched a heated battle within the state for repeal and has paved the way for other state-by-state battles surrounding the controversial medical practice.

In the midst of this wrenching social and political battle, *The English Patient* entered the debate by crystallizing the issue of assisted suicide into a coherent narrative. The characters in the film cross a range of boundaries: marital, international, cultural, class distinctions, and life-and-death. Unlike the novel, which makes the nurse Hanna the central figure, the film's story unfolds from the viewpoint of the dying Count Laszlo Almasy. Within Almasy's account lies a persuasive rationale for personal versus medical control over one's life.

In the opening scene, a biplane is flying over the vast undulating terrain of the Sahara Desert. Almasy is a mapmaker employed by the Royal Geographical Society to chart the vast expanses of this North African desert. The symbolism is significant: Maps orient us. Maps use symbols to lay out a territory, and these serve as guideposts for those embarking on the terrain. The symbols on maps represent features or objects within the environmental terrain; however, they are not the terrain itself. Almasy alludes to this when he tells Madox (Julian Wadham), "[Y]ou can't explore from the air. If you could explore from the air life would be very simple." Aerial maps flatten the contour. Only the experience of physically navigating the shifting terrain furnishes a true understanding of the territory. In the same way, only through personal experience (or indirectly, by watching the film) can a person truly understand the value of life—and death.

In the film, maps and cartography serve as metaphors for contemporary culture in which people are struggling to chart the boundaries between life and death. Medical technology has reconfigured the entire scope of health care and, consequently, the contextual environment in which we live and die. Katharine (Kristin Scott-Thomas) tells Almasy, "This is a different world is what I tell myself—different life." New cultural maps are needed to navigate this new terra incognita.

In the beginning of the film, Almasy's plane is shot down in a ball of fire. His badly charred body is rescued by a band of Bedouins, and he is taken to a monastery under the care of Hanna (Juliette Binoche), a nurse. The monastery is a spiritual place rather than a secular site, where Almasy can "die well." "The little bit of air in my lungs, each day, gets less and less, which is all right, quite all right," Almasy tells Hanna. Removed from the fray outside where thousands of people are brutally being killed with the technology of guns or land mines, Almasy prepares himself to die in a humane fashion. Within the spiritual environment of the monastery, Almasy is permitted to recover his memories, grieve his loss, and hope for eternal happiness with his beloved Katharine. Even Garavaggio (William Dafoe), a thief who comes to the monastery to kill Almasy, decides not to rob him of his spiritual journey to death.

Hanna's physical and spiritual care of Almasy signifies respect for the dying process. This presents a contrasting image of dying alone in a depersonalized environment surrounded by technology and strangers. (Medical care is often framed in war metaphors, like the battle for life being fought on the front of medical technology.) The film illustrates these disparate environments—the difference between "killing" and "letting die."

As Almasy lies dying, Hanna reads from Herodotus's *History*. It is not by accident that *The English Patient* chooses the Greek historian Herodotus as its *leitmotif*. Herodotus described cultures and shifting boundaries, which are reconfigured in the film's representation of World War II. Herodotus's criticism of Athenian tradition reflects another interesting parallel to the contemporary social struggle. Currently, many medical professionals who oppose active euthanasia turn to the ancient and venerable Greek Hippocratic tradition.

At the end of the film, Hanna is preparing Almasy's morphine injection when Almasy's hand knocks over the box of morphine vials and pushes them toward her. He looks pleadingly at her. They stare at each other. She twists her lips, bends her head, and cries. As she prepares the six vials for injection, Almasy looks up at her and says, "thank you." He then asks her to read to him. She opens the book and begins reading a letter Katharine wrote while waiting for Almasy to return for her. "We die, We die rich with lovers and tripes, tastes we have swallowed . . . fears we have hidden in. . . . I know you'll come and carry me out into the palace of winds . . . an earth without maps." In keeping with the words of Herodotus, 440 B.C., "call no man happy until he is dead," Almasy died with the hope of finding happiness in his death.

Recent television programs, including episodes of "Millennium," "The Promised Land," and "ER," have also raised the issue of assisted suicide as a viable option. Thus, the media are contributing to the cultural debate by reflecting a growing acceptance of this ideology, providing reinforcement to people who hold these beliefs, and shaping opinions on the issue.

Summary: Approaches to Ideological Analysis

The ideological approach to the study of media is designed to help people become more sensitive to the prevailing ideology in a media presentation. The objectives of ideological analysis include:

- examining media text as a way to identify its prevailing ideology;
- enabling the audience to become more sensitive to the impact of ideology on content;
- understanding the ways in which media content shapes, reflects, and reinforces ideology wihtin a culture;
- broadening the public's exposure to the unique experience and contributions of subcultures in society;
- identifying ideological shifts within the culture;
- encouraging an *ideological detoxification*, that is, a healthy skepticism toward ideologically based explanations of the world by challenging the media's representations of culture.

Theoretical Framework: Approaches to Ideological Analysis

I.   Organizational Analysis

    A. What are the ownership patterns within the media industry? How do these ownership patterns affect media content?

    B. What are the ownership patterns within the particular media system you are examining? (e.g., television, film, radio)?

    C. Who owns the production company that has produced the presentation you are examining (e.g., television station, newspaper, film company)?

D. How is the media industry regulated? How does government regulation affect media messages?

E. What is the internal structure of the media organization responsible for producing the media presentation? How does this internal structure influence content?

   1. What are the resources of the production company?
   2. What is the organizational framework of the production company?
   3. What is the process of decision making in the production company?

II. World View

What is the prevailing ideological world view in the media presentation?

A. What culture or cultures populate this world?
   1. What kinds of people populate this world?
   2. What is the ideology of this culture?

B. What do we know about the people who populate this world?
   1. Are characters presented in a stereotypical manner?
   2. What does this tell us about the cultural stereotype of this group?

C. Does this world present an optimistic or pessimistic view of life?
   1. Are the characters in the presentation happy?
   2. Do the characters have a chance to be happy?

D. Are people in control of their own destinies?
   1. Is there a supernatural presence in this world?
   2. Are the characters under the influence of other people?

E. What does it mean to be a success in this world?
   1. How does a person succeed in this world?
   2. What kinds of behavior are rewarded in this world?

III. Historical Context

A. In what ways has the media presentation been influenced by the events of the day?
   1. When was this media production first presented?
   2. What prior events led to the climate in which this media presentation was produced?
   3. How did people react to the production when it was first presented? Why?
      a. How do people react to the production today?
      b. How do you account for any differences in reaction?

      c. In what ways does an understanding of thehistorical context provide insight into the ideological messages contained in the presentation?

    B. What does the media production tell us about the ideology of the period in which it was produced?

    C. What can be learned about shifts in cultural ideology by contrasting past and present media presentations?

IV. Point of View: Oppositional Interpretation

    A. What point of view is employed in the media presentation?

    B. Oppositional Interpretation

      1. Does an alternative reading furnish perspective on the operation and impact of the dominant ideology reflected in the text?

      2. What are the ideologies of the subcultures that exist within the dominant culture in the program?

      3. What does the oppositional interpretation reveal about the dynamics between the dominant ideology and subcultures?

V.   Rhetorical Techniques

Are any of the following rhetorical devices used to position ideas in ways that reinforce the ideological perspective of the media presentation? Explain.

    A. Euphemisms

    B. Labels

    C. Metaphors

    D. Obfuscation

    E. Spin

    F. Redirection

VI. Narrative Analysis

Does analysis of the narrative structure provide insight into the ideology of the media presentation? Examine the following:

    A. Illogical premise

    B. Illogical conclusion

    C. Characterization

VII. Genre Analysis

Examine a presentation within the context of genre.

    A. What is the genre's ideological orientation?

    B. How does the program reinforce this ideological orientation?

VIII. Production Elements

What do the following production elements disclose about the ideological subtext in the media production?

A. Color
B. Lighting
C. Relative position
D. Scale
E. Movement
F. Angle
G. Music
H. Images
    1. The juxtaposition of images
    2. Imagistic layering
    3. Transmutation of symbols
    4. Masking images
    5. Sequence of images

CHAPTER 2

AUTOBIOGRAPHICAL ANALYSIS

Overview

Autobiographical analysis is an approach which investigates media content as a way to promote personal discovery and growth. This framework offers a reference point of personal experience, though which individuals can examine the impact of the media on their attitudes, values, lifestyles, and personal decisions. At the same time, analyzing media presentations within the context of one's own experiences can furnish insight into media content, including characterization, plot conventions, world view, and messages regarding success and violence.

The autobiographical approach is audience driven; that is, the individual uses his/her own experience as a springboard for analysis. This approach emphasizes process and exploration—ways of looking at media content—rather than set answers.

The first step in developing critical autonomy is recognizing that media programming represents only one version of reality. The combination of sight, sound, and motion in film and television creates the illusion that what appears on screen is real. However, production techniques like editing can create a reality that never existed.

Politicians often stage media events that appear authentic. During Dan Quayle's 1992 vice-presidential campaign, his media advisers arranged for his plane to land at military bases on the outskirts of several medium-sized cities. Quayle would appear at the open door and wave enthusiastically—not to an audience, but into empty fields off in the distance. In this production set-up, viewers are led to believe that Quayle was in their city, being greeted by throngs of people.[1]

Journalist Michael Lewis describes the orchestrating of a *tableau vivant* during the 1996 presidential campaign which created the illusion that Bob Dole and his wife Elizabeth were ordinary folks who shared the everyday experiences and concerns of most Americans. With their tickets already paid for, the Dole entourage of staffers, secret service men, and journalists marched into the movies. The Doles, on the other hand, with cameras rolling, stepped up to the ticket counter and purchased their tickets for the film *Independence Day.*[2]

The *personas* of media performers have become so ingrained in the public consciousness that people often are unable to distinguish between the person and the character. In August 1997, Autumn Jackson was found guilty of attempting to extort $40 million from Bill Cosby by threatening to go public with the news that Cosby was her father. After the verdict, Jackson's attorney, Robert Baum, expressed hope that Cosby would ask the court for leniency, saying, "I know Dr. Huxtable would come forward." A journalist picked up on Baum's mass-mediated reality, declaring, "Reality check, please; the good doctor (probably too good to be true) was a fictional TV character—and nobody ever tried to blackmail him for millions."[3]

Because of the verisimilitude of media content, recognizing media as a construction of reality can be especially difficult—even for members of the media. To illustrate, an article about "rich and famous" couples who remained married cited the following examples: Abraham and Mary Todd Lincoln, Paul Newman and Joanne Woodward, Paul and Linda McCartney, Jimmy and Rosalyn Carter, Ossie Davis and Ruby Dee, Cliff and Clair Huxtable, and Rob and Laura Petrie.[4] Of course, the Huxtables and the Petries are fictitious television characters, played by actors. This merging of fiction and reality establishes an unrealistic standard of behavior, as well an unfair basis of comparison. For the Huxtables and Petries, remaining faithful involves little commitment, other than a decision on the part of the scriptwriters.

Not only is the media a construction (or version) of reality, but the presence of the media often alters the reality it intends to capture. For example, wedding photographs are never an accurate record of the occasion. The photographer marches the couple through a formulaic series of shots (holding a rose, posing stiffly with various relatives), rather than concentrating on more candid shots of the couple and their well-wishers. Without these media constraints, newlyweds doubtless would have more opportunity to mingle with the guests and enjoy their day.

Audience Interpretation of Media Content

Understanding the role of the audience in the interpretation of media content is critical to autobiographical analysis. The autobiographical approach is based on the *reception theory,* which maintains that the audience assumes a more active role in interpreting information than preferred reading model, which is the basis of the Ideological Approach (see explanatory note at the end of the chapter). The Ontario Ministry of Education declares that audience members *negotiate* their own meaning as they encounter media messages:

> Basic to an understanding of media is an awareness of how we interact with media texts. When we look at any media text, each of us finds meaning through a wide variety of factors: personal needs and anxieties, the pleasures or troubles of the day, racial and sexual attitudes, family and cultural background. All of these have a bearing on how we process information. For example, the way in which two students respond to a television situation comedy (sitcom) depends on what each brings to that text. In short, each of us finds or "negotiates" meaning in different ways. Media teachers, therefore, have to be open to the ways in which students have individually experienced the text with which they are dealing.[5]

Consequently, audiences negotiate a meaning that may be entirely different than the "preferred" reading dictated by the media communicator.

Individuals use several processes to filter information they receive through the media. *Selective exposure* is a process in which individuals choose what to watch and listen to, based on their personal values and interests. If a person has an aversion to horror movies, he or she will avoid these types of programs. *Selective perception* occurs when a person's interpretation of content is colored by his/her predispositions and opinions. For example, audiences at political debates tend to think that their candidate "won" the debate. *Selective retention* occurs when individuals remember (or forget) information based upon their interest level and attitudes toward the topic. We have all been cornered by a person who insists on talking at us about a subject we know (or care) little about. In these situations, we tend to tune the person out, waiting for an appropriate moment to escape to a more rewarding conversation.

A number of factors may influence how a person responds to media programming:

Stage of Development

An individual's stage of development affects how they interpret content. Byron Reeves found that younger children were more attuned to external characteristics (e.g., strength, beauty) than older children. On the other hand, older children were more likely to use internal descriptors, such as motivational and personality characteristics.[6] A person's stage of development can also affect the frame of reference, which defines content. Adults who were asked to interpret the title of Olivia Newton-John's popular single, "Let's Get Physical" said that the song was about sex. Teenagers thought that the song was talking about exercise.[7]

Psychological Disposition of the Individual

A person's emotional disposition also affects their interpretation of content. Some studies suggest that aggressive children may be attracted to media violence, which causes them to be even more aggressive.[8] Other personality variables that influence response to media-carried violence include whether the individual is an introvert or extrovert, stable or unstable, and tender or tough-minded.[9]

Social Context

Seeing a program with friends can be a very different experience from watching it by yourself. For instance, watching a comedy in an empty movie theater is a vastly different experience than seeing the film in a full house, with everyone laughing. David Buckingham found that children often engaged in a secondary response in groups—expressive or dramatic displays such as crying or hugging, in reaction to (or for the benefit of) others in the group.[10] In some cases, social context inhibits behavior. For instance, boys may feel uncomfortable crying in front of others during poignant points of a film.

At other times, the social context can be distracting. Is someone sitting directly in front of you in the movie theater, blocking your view? Are kids running up and down the aisles? Can you hear the dialogue in the film? People talking behind you in the movie theater or a particularly tall person seated in front of you can affect the way you react to a film.

Content Attributes

The specific qualities of a media program have a bearing on how people respond to media content. One factor is the quality of the presentation. A program with a solid script, fine performances, and skillful direction can elicit intended reactions in the audience. Conversely, a program that lacks these qualities can generate an unintended response—laughter instead of fear—or, worse yet, elicit no response whatsoever.

Another content attribute is the *verisimilitude* of the program—how real the program appears to be. Barry Gunter found that children are more disturbed by realistic depictions of violence than similar acts presented in fictional entertainment genres, such as westerns, science fiction, or cartoons.[11]

Sometimes the situation depicted in a program may be similar to circumstances facing a member of the audience. This *psychological proximity* can also occur when the characters resemble someone with whom the audience member has been involved. An anecdote by one of the authors may illustrate this point. In the early days of television, Jimmy Durante hosted a weekly variety program. The end of each episode featured the same formula. The set darkened, except for a series of spotlights on the floor. Durante would walk away from the camera; as he moved from one spotlight to the next, the circle of light he had occupied faded. Durante then would turn to the camera and wave, calling, "Good night, Mrs. Calabash [his pet name for his departed wife]—wherever you are." At the end of each show, the author (then a small child) would become hysterical, bursting into tears. His bewildered parents would explain that Jimmy would return next week—but to no avail.

This rather innocuous program had assumed a personal significance to the youngster, triggering this response. At that time, the author's grandfather (an elderly man who resembled Durante) had suffered a debilitating stroke. Durante's finale was an enactment of death for the boy, triggering feelings of fear and grief in the child. Thus, regardless of the intentions of the media communicator, a presentation may strike a responsive chord within the audience member.

Gender

Gender can be a factor in the negotiation of meaning. Reeves found that children tend to respond most favorably toward characters of their same sex.[12] Perhaps because of cultural expectations and conditioning, boys are attracted to characters high in activity and strength dimensions, while girls are drawn to attractive characters.[13] Different responses to media content by gender also reflect the relative position of men and women in society. Women may respond negatively to a horror film that depicts the victimization of females, whereas the males who view the film may not be sensitive to this behavior on-screen.

Ethnic/Racial/Class Identity

Members of different subcultures (e.g., racial or ethnic groups, social classes) have distinct, identifiable interests and look for specific objectives or gratifications in media programming. Frost and Stoffer found that a sample of inner-city subjects were significantly more aroused by viewing violent programming than a sample of middle-class college students: When media content is generally congruent with the real-life experience of the audience, the result is a marked amplification of the reality of media messages. They concluded that since the environment of the inner-city residents is more violent than that of the college students, the former's significantly higher arousal levels in response to violent stimuli may be connected to their real-life surroundings.[14]

Theoretical Framework: Approaches to Autobiographical Analysis

The following approaches to autobiographical analysis can be applied to the study of media content as a means of making media content more accessible and understandable.

Narrative Reconstruction

In narrative reconstruction, a person recounts stories they have seen, heard, or read in the media, which then furnishes perspective into the individual's comprehension of media content. In reconstructing the narrative, audience members disclose how they make sense of the programming they watched, heard, or read. One area of investigation is a person's understanding of explicit content. Explicit content refers to the essential events and activities in a story that are displayed through visible action. To illustrate, when retelling stories, young children often have difficulty deciding on the essential points in the narrative. They may omit parts of the story that adults judge to be essential content and may include pieces of the story deemed nonessential.[15] Parents often operate on the assumption that they have all "seen" the same story, when this may not be the case. Consequently, an important first step in media discussion and analysis is to determine the child's comprehension of the story.

Asking an individual to reconstruct the essential elements of a narrative is also an excellent way to learn about his/her interests and preoccupations. For example, young children often embellish a story with their own experiences, sometimes inserting themselves into the narrative. In addition, they may include or emphasize what they regard as important and omit or de-emphasize what they see as unimportant. When describing a James Bond movie, a young child may devote an extraordinary amount of attention describing the Austin Healy driven by the British agent, reflecting his/her interest in cars. In recounting a media narrative, individuals may also add their editorial commentary (e.g., "this was neat"). These remarks can furnish perspective into individuals' assessments of those elements they chose to include in their reconstruction.

Recounting the plot also provides insight into the individual's understanding of *implicit content.* Implicit content refers to those elements of a narrative that remain under the surface, including motivation, the relationship between events, and the consequences of earlier action. Returning to our example, young children have even more difficulty identifying implicit than explicit content.[16] In their narrative reconstruction of plots, they are developmentally incapable of recognizing the implicit elements in a plot.[17] Therefore, as part of narrative reconstruction, it is useful to determine (1) why they think that an event occurred; (2) whether there was a relationship between events in the story; and (3) if there were consequences to the characters' actions.

Affective Response Analysis

This technique asks audience members to focus on their emotional reactions to media programming as a springboard to critical analysis. Visual and aural media are particularly well suited to emotional appeals. Unlike print, which is processed at a cognitive level, photography, film, television, and radio are directed at the heart; we first react emotionally, and then translate these feelings into words. Indeed, one of the primary reasons for attending movies is to provide the audience with an intense emotional experience; a new cliché for movie reviews is the "feel-good movie of the year." Because the response to visual and aural media content is largely emotional, discourse about media content is often reduced to a "Beavis and Butthead" sensibility: a program is either "cool" or it "sucks." But although this type of response initially discourages conversation, affective response analysis offers an excellent launch pad for systematic investigation of media content.

Affective Response and Personal Belief Systems

Affective response to media programs has emerged as a factor in the emotional development of individuals. Media programs give us an opportunity to "try out" emotions in a safe environment. There is little risk involved, since the media experience is private, and our emotional investment is contained within the duration of the program. However, these responses are particularly healthy in contemporary culture, in which many people—particularly men—are alienated from their emotions. Significantly, many genres audience members in touch with a range of primal feelings. The horror genre targets our most basic fears. Melodramas touch off feelings of sadness, pathos, and regret. Comedies make us laugh, action films tap into feelings of rage, and romances evoke feelings of passion, longing, and regret.

Buckingham observes that media programs can be instructive for children, by putting them in touch with their feelings: "[C]hildren are also 'learning how to feel.' They are discovering what counts as an acceptable or appropriate emotional response, and the ways in which such responses serve to define them as individuals, both for themselves and for others."[18] Disney films are distinctive in their ability to introduce to young audiences an array of emotional experiences. During the course of *The Lion King* (1994), children grieve for the loss of Simba's father, are outraged by his subsequent humiliation and exile, and rejoice at Simba's new-found resolve to reclaim his throne.

Buckingham observes that affective responses to media programs can contribute to the formation of self-concept. For instance, fifteen-year-old Jenny describes herself in terms of her responses to media programs—she is the type of person who would "cry at anything."[19] People learn to react to media programs in ways that correspond to culturally acceptable gender roles: women cry, men rage. In addition, individuals' affective responses to media programs often change as they move into new stages of life. Young people who wish to "act like adults" learn to tone down their reactions to media programs.

Affective response analysis therefore furnishes a framework for the systematic exploration of personal belief systems and can serve as the basis for critical self-analysis. Asking individuals to talk about how they felt at particular parts of a program can provide insight into audience members' personal belief systems. Follow-up questions can focus on whether the emotional responses they experienced while watching a program carry over into their everyday interactions, and what these responses indicate about their personal belief systems.

An extension of this line of inquiry is the *pleasure perspective,* which recognizes that media programs do not merely produce negative feelings but are often the source of genuine enjoyment. It is therefore worthwhile to consider (1) what kinds of activities depicted in a media presentation generate a pleasurable response, and (2) what this reveals about a person's interests, attitudes, and values. Programs may also elicit pleasurable secondary emotions; for example, being frightened by a horror film can be followed by a sensation of excitement. Consequently, it can be useful to backtrack, focusing attention on the original emotion and reasons for the secondary response.

Examining affective responses to media presentations also can furnish insight into the source of a person's emotional reactions. Buckingham sees a correlation between how people respond to media presentations and the things that move them in their everyday experience: "The things that make us cry in films also make us cry in real life."[20] In his research with children, Buckingham identified themes found in media programs that resonated in children's everyday interactions: (1) disruption of the family; (2) the impossible romance; (3) pity toward those who are presumed to be vulnerable or innocent (e.g., animals); (4) body violation; and (5) the supernatural.[21]

Coping Strategies

The study of affective response also provides insight into *coping strategies* commonly used to deal with emotional distress. Coping strategies enable individuals to deal with the source of the emotional response and keep their feelings under control. Once established, these coping strategies become a habitual response that helps people contend with emotional stress throughout their lives. The media have emerged as a principal arena in which people learn coping mechanisms. Buckingham identified the following coping strategies that children used in response to disturbing media content:

Denial. Some children disowned their emotions by refusing to acknowledge their feelings, either to themselves or to others. For instance, they may have been scared but would not have admitted it if they were.[22]

Challenge. This mechanism establishes the media experience as a personal challenge: "I should be able to watch." The audience member's ability to endure the discomfort evoked by the media presentation is therefore regarded as a rite of passage that promotes the person to the next stage of development. She is now old enough to persevere through this uncomfortable experience.

Mockery. Some audience members maintain a safe distance from the media experience by installing an emotional filter—mockery or irony—between themselves and their feelings. Audience members therefore may laugh at horror movies, choosing to see them as comic. By making fun of the presentation, they feel superior to the filmmaker and can regain control of the situation. Overreaction is a related coping strategy, as audience members turn the emotion into a safe burlesque by exaggerating their responses. For instance, at a horror movie some audience members scream, scare each other, and run down the aisle of the theater.

Comfort Devices. In response to disturbing content, some individuals seek physical comfort in the form of pillows, toys, or people to hug.

Partial or Total Avoidance. Some people avoid material that they feel incapable of dealing with by hiding their faces at pivotal moments or leaving the screening area.

Reality Checking. Agitated members of the audience may choose to consciously remind themselves that the media presentation is not real. For instance, frightened viewers may force themselves to think of a horror film as "only a movie." Another reality check is to look for flaws in the program, including artistic mistakes, poor acting performances, or logical inconsistencies in the plot.

Distraction. Audience members who are uncomfortable may try to distract themselves by thinking "happy thoughts" or aspects of their everyday lives (e.g., errands they have to run after the film) as a way to regain control and perspective.

Repetition. Some audience members respond to disturbing content by seeing the program repeatedly. By becoming familiar with the material, audience members regain the control they relinquished on the first viewing. Because they are no longer surprised or shocked by the content, they become immune to its effects.

Alibi. Several children in Buckingham's study dealt with the shame associated with their reactions by attributing these reactions to other factors. Some excuses were physical (e.g., "something in my eye"), while others manufactured alternate reasons for their response (e.g., "my sister left town").

Changing the Context. Watching the same presentation at another time, with other people, can help some people put the media experience into perspective.

Understanding the ways in which audience members cope with emotional tensions generated by the media can furnish perspective on the coping mechanisms they use elsewhere in their lives. A useful line of inquiry involves asking individuals to discuss the coping mechanisms they employed during the course of a media presentation. Once these strategies have been identified, it is possible to focus on the source of these defensive mechanisms. Consequently, these coping mechanisms can serve as guides to identify the sources of anxiety in their lives. And, if appropriate, this approach offers an opportunity to change coping behaviors.

Affective Analysis of Media Content

Affective response can also serve as an effective approach to the study of media content. One way to analyze characterization in media productions involves examining the audience's initial emotional response to characters "making an entrance." The first impression an actor makes sets the emotional tone for the entire program and establishes a relationship between the character and the audience. It then can be beneficial to discuss what generated the audience's initial impression. For example, the selection of clothing can elicit a reaction (e.g., admiration or sexual attraction). Or the character may be involved in an activity or engaged in dialogue that moves the audience. Often the character displays an intense emotion that shocks or impresses the audience.

Discussion then may focus on the *intentionality* of this impression: Did the media communicator aim to elicit this response? We have all seen films in which, despite the intentions of the filmmaker, the audience simply does not care about the characters. This lack of engagement affects our interpretation (and enjoyment) of the film. However, if the filmmaker is successful in eliciting an anticipated affective response from the audience, he/she can use these emotions to reinforce the themes and world view of the narrative. In *Titanic* (1997), director James Cameron set up initial scenes designed to establish feelings of sympathy between the audience and the two protagonists, Jack Dawson (Leonardo DiCaprio) and Rose DeWitt Bukater (Kate Winslet). If the audience cares about these characters, Cameron is able to convey themes about the injustice of the class system and the consequences of greed and hubris on the part of the ship's management.

The next area of exploration is whether the audience maintains or changes this initial impression, and what (if anything) causes this change. And finally, based on their subsequent behavior in the story, do the characters deserve that particular initial response from the audience?

The pleasure perspective also provides insight into the media content as a source of enjoyment. Particular elements of a program such as sex, violence, or romantic tension often evoke consistent reactions from an audience member; these same elements may trigger a pleasurable response when they appear in other programs as well. The appearance of particular actors may also serve as the source of continual pleasure. Or, particular programs or genres (e.g., musicals or romantic comedies) may be particularly effective in eliciting positive responses. Consequently, examining pleasurable responses to programs can serve as a starting point for analysis of media content.

However, because the mode of analysis is rooted in personal experience, this line of inquiry is not without risk. Writing about classroom applications, Masterman cautions that a student's response can conflict with others in the class, including the teacher's: "Some people may be disturbed, worried or offended by the very things in a text which others find pleasurable."[23] A pleasurable response can be tied to "dubious or oppressive purposes," such as violence or acts of racism.[24] Teachers are faced with the challenge of maintaining a mutually respectful classroom environment, while encouraging students to be open and honest in their responses.

Affective Analysis: Function

Another critical approach involves examining the *function,* or purpose, of affective response; that is, what objective is served when the media communicator elicits a particular reaction from the audience? This line of inquiry asks audience members to think along with the media communicator. How does he/she want you to be feeling at particular points in the plot? Sad? Happy? Scared? Insecure? Envious? The next step involves investigating why the media communicator is attempting to elicit that intended emotional response from the audience.

Media artists often strive to spark an emotional reaction from the audience for dramatic purposes. *"Show,* don't *tell"* is an adage that can be applied to media presentations. Rather than simply talking about a subject, it is always more effective to evoke the same emotions from the audience that the characters in the presentation are experiencing. The effective media communicator anticipates how the audience should react at each point of the presentation and then strives to elicit that particular response. For instance, Hollywood director George Cukor was not known for his technical expertise. Instead, he surrounded himself with the best available cast and crew and, stationing himself by the camera, acted as his own audience while the action unfolded. If he was moved by the scene, he was satisfied. If not, he would gather his experts around him to discuss strategies that would produce the intended response.

Advertisers manipulate the feelings of the audience to persuade the audience to buy their products. Ads often are directed at one of a number of *intrinsic psychological motivations,* such as guilt, love, need for approval, nostalgia for the past, and fixation with death (including need for control, promises of immortality, fears of failure and of the unknown). For instance, in a 1997 Tide commercial, a woman confesses her shame about her own experience as the youngest of several sisters who had to endure the embarrassment of wearing discolored hand-me-downs. As a mother of several girls, she is determined to spare her youngest daughter from this trauma. Thus, Tide has been transformed into a product that cleanses not only laundry but one's stained emotional past as well. On the other hand, advertisements that display animals or babies are intended to evoke a warm response, which the media communicator hopes the audience will transfer to the product. Advertisers often use humor, snappy music, or celebrities in an attempt to make commercials enjoyable, in order to sell the product.

Affective response can serve an ideological function as well. Douglas Kellner declares that often a positive reaction to content itself is neither natural nor innocent but instead intimately associated with power and knowledge:

> We often are conditioned about what to enjoy and what we should avoid. We learn when to laugh and when to cheer (and laugh tracks on TV sitcoms and entertainment cue us in case we don't get it ourselves). A system of power and privilege thus conditions our pleasures so that we seek certain socially sanctioned pleasures and avoid others. Some people learn to laugh at racist jokes and others learn to feel pleasure at the brutal use of violence. . . . Pleasures are often, therefore, a conditioned response to certain stimuli and should thus be problematized, along with other forms of experience and behavior, and interrogated as to whether they contribute to the production of a better life and society, or help trap us into modes of everyday life that ultimately oppress and degrade us.[25]

Media communicators can maneuver the audience into emotional reactions that reinforce the prevailing ideology of the program. For instance, when violent action is accompanied by a laugh track or silly music, the audience tends to discount the activity as humorous. In addition, Masterman contends that making media messages pleasurable is an effective way to "sell" objectionable ideas: "A narrative seeks to enlist our sympathies for a cause, a character or an idea that we might repudiate given the time for more mature reflection."[26] (For further discussion of ideology, see chapter 1.)

Identification Analysis

Identification fulfills a critical role in the formation of self-concept. Gloria Johnson Powell explains that children discover personality traits in themselves by recognizing them in others:

After the early differentiation of self from the animate and inanimate worlds, the process of self-concept development becomes more social in nature. It begins to involve identification with others, introjection from others, and expansion into interpersonal relationships.[27]

Because people see the world depicted by the media as real, they often measure their own lives in relation to what is happening in a media presentation. Audience members identify with media figures who have been elevated to role models, and with the worlds they inhabit. To illustrate, when Jerry Seinfeld decided to discontinue his hit sitcom in December 1997, fans made a pilgrimage to Tom's Restaurant, the site of the exterior shots used for the coffee shop scenes in the program (although, it should be noted, all of the interior scenes were shot in a studio in Los Angeles). "Where else could we go?" asked Denise Jones, a secretary from Queens who made the sojourn with two friends to have a tuna sandwich (one of the staples of the characters in the show).

For Donna Stephen, a visitor from Houston, the version of New York City portrayed in Seinfeld served as her tour guide during her trip to the city:

> Everything we know about New York City is from "Seinfeld." Like how to bootleg a movie, how to smuggle cafe latte into the movies in your pants, how to fight for a parking space, how to follow the protocol at the Soup Nazi.[28]

Fans were in mourning, seeing the end of the series as a form of death for the characters, who had become very real to them. Fans speculated about the possibility of spin-off series as a reprieve for the other "Seinfeld" characters:

> "I wish I was friends with Elaine," said Teri Goldberg, a 26–year-old. . . . I love her. She's so funny. I feel like I use her expressions all the time. Now if she had her own show, I could almost forget about losing "Seinfeld."
> Lynly Stephen, a speech therapist from Dallas, said she would miss Kramer, also known by his elusive first name Cosmo: "What a bad way to wake up, and me even here in New York. I just worry, what will happen to Cosmo. If Jerry wants to quit, fine. Let Cosmo have his own show."[29]

Identifying with a celebrity like Seinfeld, Madonna, or Michael Jordan becomes a public declaration of self. David Buckingham observes,

> Taste . . . is not a reflection of some inner essence: on the contrary, it is about claiming particular social affiliations, whether consciously or not. In imply-

ing that we "identify" with certain people on television, it would seem, we may also be "identifying" ourselves for the benefit of others.[30]

It is often a matter of concern that identification with media personalities and situations leads directly to imitative behavior. However, identification is a widespread and normal part of the formation of identity, and people have always looked to external sources (e.g., parents, actors, actresses, sports figures) as role models. Although identification is a *precondition* of imitation, it is not a guarantee that people will adopt the modeling behavior.

The identification process can operate in one of the following ways with respect to media presentations:

- Audience members adopt the point of view of one of the protagonists.
- Audience members identify with characters similar to them.
- Audience members identify with those they aspire to be like.
- Audience members feel what is happening to the character as if it were happening to him/her.
- Audience members identify with the situations in which the characters find themselves.
- Audience members identify with behaviors they encounter in media programs.

In addition, individuals may "try on" aspects of personality that they admire in a media figure. To illustrate, children sometimes engage in *fantasy participation,* in which they insert themselves into the program. Fantasy participation can help children prepare for the world offscreen, as they picture what they would do in different circumstances to alter the situation.[31]

Unfortunately, Aimee Door observes that media portrayals of minorities offer limited opportunities for identification.

> If minority children look for models of the same ethnicity as themselves, they find few to choose from on television. Those they do find have a limited range of personality characteristics, occupations, and social circumstances to emulate. If, on the other hand, they look for role models who are powerful and successful, then they would probably emulate white characters.[32]

Indeed, the cumulative media messages about social class suggest that in order to become successful, one must relinquish one's identification with these subcultures:

> If [minority children] look to minority characters as role models, then they might learn to be less knowledgeable, wealthy, assertive, or dominant than would white children, to defer to whites, or to accept largely white versions

of their minority culture. If they look to white characters as role models, then they might learn white values and behaviors vis-à-vis work, money, aggression, competition, cooperation, family life, and so on. All of which may require giving up some distinctive elements of one's own ethnic culture.[33]

Identification Analysis: Media Content

Identification analysis offers a way to analyze media content. This approach asks individuals to examine the elements of a media presentation within the context of their own personal experience.

Character identification is a valuable source of information about what people consider attractive or engaging behaviors, values, or attributes. Audience members' identification with particular characters can furnish perspective on their interests, aspirations, and values. This line of inquiry includes the following steps:

- Identify favorite characters and explain what you liked and disliked about them.
- Clarify the nature of the character identification: *likeness* (finding a resemblance with the character), or *aspiration* (wishing to emulate the character). This strategy can provide insight into your perceived gender, ethnic, racial, and class identification, as well as information about what you consider attractive or engaging behaviors, values, and attributes.
- Name additional attributes of the character that you did *not* include in your original list of attributes. This may lead to discussion about qualities that may not be readily apparent but are, nevertheless, essential to the overall positive portrait of the character.
- Discuss the role that the attributes of the character play in the successful outcome of the story. For example, a violent temperament is often key to resolving problems in media programs. At the same time, other attributes may help the character succeed within the context of the narrative—some of which, perhaps, you do not identify with or immediately think about. The next step is to examine the role that these attributes play in the outcome of your own life "narratives." Does being tough or violent guarantee success?
- Discuss whether there are *missing* attributes in some characters that prevent you from succeeding within the context of the narrative.
- Name characters to whom you *cannot* relate. This can stimulate discussion about expectations: What can be regarded as unrealistic or "too

perfect" characters, or characters with attributes that you may regard as unobtainable in your own life.

- Discuss how you relate to villains. This line of inquiry often reveals that we are sometimes attracted to some of the character traits of the antagonists and, conversely, find the heroes to be *less* appealing. One way to account for this phenomenon is that audience members identify with some of the flaws of the antagonists. Another possibility could be that characterization (and human personality) is more complex than the absolute distinctions presented in the media. There can be evil in good and good in evil. Consequently, villainous characters may display an energy, creativity, and sexuality that in some respects accounts for their success as villains.

Narrative analysis enables you to examine your own value system in response to choices made by characters in media programs. Put yourself in the situation depicted in the media program and respond to the following questions: (1) How would you feel about being in that situation? (2) How would you react?

Then compare the narrative to your own experience: (1) Does the situation remind you of your own life? (2) How would the characters handle your situation? Would it work? Why or why not?

Viewer identification can also provide insight into the *ideology* of a narrative. The media text encourages you to identify with the primary protagonists, who are the sources of power in the presentation and aligned with its prevalent ideology (for further discussion, see chapter 1). By imagining yourselves in the role of the primary figure in the program, we identify with the sources of power and "buy into" assumptions about what constitutes "the good life" within the context of the media presentation. Questions to consider include:

- As the lead character, what could you accomplish?
- What opportunities would be available to you?
- What advantages would you have? What could you "get away with" because of your position?

A related line of inquiry involves *oppositional viewer identification,* which involves identifying with a character other than the protagonist: a villain, a member of a subculture, a member of the opposite sex, or a supporting character. Again: What could you accomplish (as one of these characters)? What opportunities would be available to you? What advantages would you have? What could you "get away with" because of your position?

To illustrate, a team of educators, college students, and staff members used this approach with some success at the Hogan Street Regional Youth Center, a juvenile offender facility in the state of Missouri. Judy McMillan, a teacher at Hogan, described these adolescents, some of whom have committed serious crimes, as a strange anomaly: "None of the teenagers have been off of their block, but all of them have been to Hollywood."[34] Consequently, movies are a primary source of information for these teens about gender roles, as well as definitions and strategies for success. The teaching team presented film clips from *Boyz N the Hood* (1991) as a vehicle for discussion about behavior and personal choice. One clip depicts a confrontation between two groups of African-American teenagers: verbal exchanges between the groups become heated, and challenges are issued. At that point, the team stopped the film and the teenagers talked about what principles were at stake: valor, personal dignity, and concern for reputation. The teenagers agreed that these values were an important part of their own lives as well. At that point, the team played the remainder of the scene, in which several characters are shot. The subsequent discussion focused on the consequences of the code of conduct displayed in the film: Were there other options available that would have enabled the characters to retain their dignity and self-respect?

Identification Analysis: Function

This line of inquiry investigates the underlying reasons *why* a media communicator promotes the audience's identification with characters or situations in programs. One function in entertainment media programming is dramatic effect: Identifying with the characters engages the audience, as they see some version of themselves on screen. Media communicators often exploit the audience's identification with celebrities to promote a product or idea. If the audience identifies with Bill Cosby or Michael Jordan because of their entertainment or sports skills, they also may be receptive to their "suggestions" regarding purchases. In other cases, actors take advantage of the viewers' identification with a part they play by appearing "in character" to sell products. For example, several cast members of "Northern Exposure" have transfered their personas from the show to commercials.[35]

The Limits of Identification

This line of inquiry could also be termed *de-identification*, in that it focuses attention on the limits of identification. As mentioned earlier, although film, television, and the other media may appear to reflect the audience's experience, the media construct a reality that is impossible to emulate in real life. Production elements such as editing make the world depicted in the media appear exciting by presenting selected moments. The addition of a musical score dramatizes even pedestrian acts like shaving or crossing the street. Through special effects and stunt specialists, characters appear capable of astonishing acts of strength and daring. And because the action is scripted, our heroes and heroines never lose their keys, accidentally spill their food, or die in the middle of the story.

Through the use of makeup, editing, lighting, and digital manipulation, actors always look magnificent. After continual exposure to these idealized figures, ordinary people can be disappointing. Ironically, even the stars themselves cannot measure up to this standard of beauty:

> Asked the secret of her unlined looks seen in close-up on the cover of *Vogue* at age 45, [actress and model Isabella Rossellini] denied having tips to share. "Well, you can't go by the photo," she says, "Because obviously, the photo is an enhanced version of me, you know. It generally takes hours of makeup and fantastic lighting, a great photographer. So I don't think I look as good in life as in my photos."[36]

Examining these production and performance elements reveals the ways in which identification with media characters promote unrealistic expectations on the part of the audience.

Media Production Approach

Becoming familiar with production techniques can help develop a critical understanding of media by providing individuals with the opportunity to apply media literacy theory in a practical setting.

Educational Applications

The study of media production adds a distinctive and important component to media literacy education. An understanding of media production can work toward the goal of improving the media industry by preparing practitioners who combine technical skill with an understanding of the responsibilities of the media communicator. Media production fulfills a number of learning objectives, including:

Seeing Media Production as a Construction of Reality. Hands-on media production experience enables individuals to learn for themselves how stylistic considerations reinforce the manifest message of the media communicator, or convey latent messages that the process of constructing a media message alters the reality they are attempting to capture. They discover that the choices they make in production (e.g., what to include and omit, word choice, and selection of images) have an enormous impact on how audience members respond to the media presentation.

For instance, the "shakey-cam" camera technique suggests that the program is spontaneous and that the subject has been selected randomly, so that the audience should believe what they see. The amateur, crude motion of the camera contrasts with the slick professional approach of mainstream media and is therefore considered hip and avant-garde. Advertisements hope that these stylistic messages of authenticity and trendiness will be transferred to the product.

Developing Aesthetic Appreciation. Hands-on production introduces the production team to the considerations of style and structure. This practical experience enables the crew to recognize these formulas in mainstream media presentations. In the process, they become aware of why TV dramas, news, and newspaper stories are presented in a certain way. At the same time, hands-on production provides opportunities to experiment in order to move beyond these conventions.

Understanding the Process of Media Production. In the production of a program, the crew learns to identify the background, interests, and predispositions of the audience. In addition, they must define the goals and objectives of the project—what they want to accomplish, and what messages they wish to convey. A script must be developed that combines clear visuals and narration. Other considerations include pre-production planning, including research, legal issues, budgeting, and casting.

Developing Social Skills. Media production is a collaborative enterprise in which the success of a project is dependent on the ability of the crew to work together. The production team must develop a close working relationship defined by mutual respect, a sense of compromise, and problem-solving skills. Alison Byrne Fields, associate director of the Institute of Public Media Arts, declares, "When students work in a group project, they have to figure out how to negotiate their differences in order to achieve an agreed-upon goal. They no longer have the ability to make autonomous decisions about content and style, which affects the meaning of the piece. The process gives people experience working within a diverse culture."[37]

Examining Media Literacy Issues. Media production presents an opportunity to explore media literacy principles and concerns not generally found in mainstream programming. To illustrate, -ISM (N.), a national project sponsored by the Institute for Public Media Arts, is an educational video documentary project designed to help colleges strengthen teaching and learning about issues of diversity. Schools throughout the United States are selected to participate in the year-long course, which consists of interdisciplinary approaches to issues of diversity, coupled with experiential learning, personal reflection, and video production.

The goals of the project include: (1) teaching about issues of diversity; (2) learning about issues of diversity; (3) establishing a commitment to innovative diversity education; and (4) strengthening the connection between academic affairs and student life. The -ISM (N.) project relies heavily on video production to achieve these goals:

> Video directly engages young people through the same medium from which their generation gets most of its information, including information about difference and power. -ISM (N.) puts videocameras in the hands of students, so they can tell their own stories about diversity issues. Students can use video to document personal experiences with diversity and to witness the experiences documented by their peers. Student videos also provide personal stories, students and instructors can connect to broader theoretical and historical lessons about diversity issues.[38]

In the first semester, video documentation is used as a personal diary to reflect on how issues of diversity influence students' sense of identity. In the second semester, students expand on their personal experience as they work in teams to develop video documentaries that look at diversity issues in institutions and communities. Student video projects produced in twelve colleges and universities throughout the country during the spring of 1996 focused on a range of issues related to diversity:

- Twenty-five percent of the videos dealt with racism. For instance, at Pitzer College, students covered a protest by minority workers at a Los Angeles hotel.
- Over 10 percent of the videos discussed "self-segregation" on college campuses. Students at Tulane University produced a group video that focused on the diversity of the crew—students of different races and religions who worked together to produce the video.
- Six percent of the videos addressed the issue of sexism, from the objectification of women in the media to domestic violence.

- Nearly 25 percent of the videos consisted of students exploring ways in which sexual orientation and racial and religious background have shaped the formation of self-concept and identity.[39]

Media Arts Programs

Media arts programs promote media literacy through a combination of production and critical analysis. This approach promotes self-discovery and growth through artistic expression.

The media arts approach has been used successfully with youth throughout the United States. Since 1986, the VIDKIDCO Youth Media Production Workshop, in Long Beach, California, has provided a summer program, in which young people produce innovative media arts (including video, audio, computer animation, and multi-media). Martha Chono-Helsley, media artist for VIDKIDCO, explains,

> Workshops . . . combine the components of media literacy, artistic exploration and interpretation with hands-on technical production training. . . . Each session begins with introductory studies in media literacy that help participants explore and understand mass media in our society and in the arts. . . . Participants are able to view work by contemporary video artists and independent producers that stimulate in-depth discussion about content and aesthetics. This exposure to "alternative/independent" work helps to break down the barriers of what television can be. The emphasis of the content of the VIDKIDCO projects are that of the participants—their perceptions, views, understanding and communication of knowledge.[40]

Advocates of this approach emphasize that media arts programs are not designed to produce media professionals. Instead, the goal is to increase understanding of the production process and to experience the thrill of creation in a variety of media.

Media arts programs bring perspectives and issues rarely addressed in mainstream media to the attention of the public. To illustrate, the Video Data Bank (VDB) distributes videotapes by independent artists that fall into the following categories: Behind the Scenes (broadcast and print journalism ethics, biases, and coverage); Advertising and the Consumer Society; Stereotyping; Alternative Histories; Culture Jamming; Politics/Media and the Exercise of Democracy; The Global Environment; The Information Superhighway, Censorship and Access; How to Read TV; Media Violence(s); and Peer Group Issues (dropping out, gangs, suicide, drugs, pregnancy, etc.).[41]

An emerging genre of media arts programming is the *video diary,* a form of personal storytelling in which videographers use the conventions of the medium—narrative structure, plot, and character—to tell their stories to a broad-based audience. Although the diaries record the artists' personal experiences, these videos also represent larger individual and cultural issues. Ellen Schneider explains,

> Why, we asked, were [the artists] willing to make private moments public? "To use my reunion with a grown sister I've never known as a kind of emblem for the black family experience in America today," answered Meredith Woods in St. Paul. "A personal search for justice," said Jeffrey Tuchman in Los Angeles, who shot 20 hours of tape when he accompanied his father back to Germany to confront the Nazi officer who killed his grandmother. "We wanted to offer an unscripted glimpse into our lives," replied Herbert Peck in New York, whose diary documents his wife's normal pregnancy through the birth of a son with Down's Syndrome. "Video diarists are taking risks . . . but also showing the power of what TV can be."[42]

Programs featuring video diarists have been presented on public television stations in New York, St. Paul, Los Angeles, and San Francisco.

Public Access Activities

In the United States, public access stations are community-based media education centers that generally are established as part of the local cable franchise's contractual obligation to the community it serves. The production of local access programming facilitates public dialogue, community development, and social change. Access centers are one of the few venues where members of the community can build media literacy skills and put their knowledge directly into use by making and circulating their own local television programming.

Public access television promotes and initiates media literacy efforts by (1) developing programs that explicitly include media criticism; (2) including techniques of analysis in production training; (3) providing special training for K–12 teachers who want to integrate video production activities into their curriculum; (4) providing special emphasis on working with youth; and (5) forming a media education study group.

Public access centers across the United States integrate media literacy concepts into the various stages of their production training procedures, including orientation, pre-production, and editing sessions.[43]

Media Chronicles

In the 1970s, scholars began to record oral histories, in which they documented the personal reminiscences of older citizens as a means of studying cultural history. Mass communication has assumed a very personal role in the lives of its audience; consequently, watching old films, TV shows, or listening to radio programs can spark personal recollections of otherwise forgotten pieces of cultural history.

The mass media have become a pervasive part of American culture. We continually receive information through the channels of mass communication whether we are at home, in the car, or in the supermarket. Technological advances enable media programming to accompany people everywhere. To illustrate, with the invention of the car radio and the transistor, the radio has become a constant escort—to the beach, when we jog, and even while we shower.

Because of the repetitive nature of the commercial media industry, the public is inundated with the same programming over a relatively brief time span. Radio stations play their most popular tunes once per hour. Reruns and spinoffs abound on television. The advertising industry bombards the consumer with the same images and slogans in order to establish audience recognition and patronage. Much of the information we receive is retained involuntarily. Members of the family may have programs blaring in another room that we cannot avoid hearing.

As a result, media programming often assumes a personal significance that transcends its aesthetic or entertainment value. Hearing an old song on the radio may awaken memories of a summer long ago, perhaps, or of old friends, or a first romance. In that sense, it often is not the song that we are reacting to (in fact, we may dislike the particular tune). However, the media program has become internalized as a part of our personal experience, and we may feel nostalgic about a program because it has put us in touch with ourselves and our pasts. Ty Burr declares, "Perhaps consumers are buying the 'Titanic' CD the same way they'd buy a souvenir hat at a fairground, to relive an admittedly wrenching roller coaster ride once they're home."[44]

For instance, playing the tune "Take Me Out to the Ball Game" reminded one old gentleman in St. Louis, Missouri, of his youth, when he would skip school and take the streetcar to Sportsman's Park to watch the Gas House Gang—the St. Louis Cardinals baseball club, featuring Dizzy Dean, Pepper Martin, and Frankie Frisch. He even recalled watching the St. Louis Browns playing the New York Yankees and seeing Babe Ruth hit a home run.

Media chronicles furnish insight into historical events as well. For instance, many songs, films, and radio programs of the depression era commented on this period of American history (e.g., the popular tune that began, "We ain't got a barrel of money . . ."). Presenting snippets of these programs may trigger personal memories about this historical period. Media can also be associated with social movements. For instance, the cult film

Easy Rider (1969) assumes a significance for members of the 1960s counterculture. Seeing this film twenty years later may evoke memories about the social and political experiences of this social group.

Media programs also stimulate personal recollections about a particular stage of life. Adolescents embrace specific films, songs, and television programs that express their concerns. Or, media programs may be associated with seasonal activities. Christmas music and movies stir memories of family and of past holiday seasons.

A media chronicle project involves presenting a series of popular media programs from a particular era to individuals. The facilitator then records individuals' personal recollections which have been stimulated by the program.

To illustrate, Joseph Schuster's freshman seminar at Webster University participated in a media chronicles exercise on November 4, 1997. Students brought CDs to class and played songs that had assumed a personal significance for them. The students then were invited to share any of their personal recollections triggered by the song. The following is an edited transcript of their recollections:

> *Song:* "Fight for Your Right" by the Beastie Boys
>
> *Angie Kilber.* It just completely reminds me of my entire four years in high school. Because it talked about, first of all, I don't want to go to school. Mom, please don't make me go. But I had to go anyway, because she was one of those, really into school parents. And then the second verse is like smoking and you can't do that. And I started smoking when I was sixteen and my parents hated it and now they finally understand now that I'm a. . . . It was just this big ordeal throughout high school that I could not smoke. It was just bad. And my dad was just being a hypocrite and it says that in the song too.
>
> And it also reminds me of the summer after my senior year. Because finally, it was all over. This past summer I was like wow, I love the song. Now I'm not in high school anymore. I don't have to do this anymore. I don't have to put up with it. My parents don't care that I smoke. And I was so happy. And I brought it to a friend of mine's house where we used to go all the time. He was one of my best friends. He had a really big party here. And we played this song. And everyone there screamed through the entire song really really really loud. And I will never forget it. Because we were all sitting in . . . thinking of this song.
>
> *Plesah Mayo.* This reminds me of the beginning of my senior year. Because my dad was living in Colorado Springs. He'd got stationed there. It was just me and my mom alone here together. And she was driving me up the wall. . . . And she'd make me come home at 10 o'clock during the summer and stuff like that. Even on weekends. And I was getting really upset with this because

all my friends stayed out late. I was sixteen but I was going into my senior year. And my friend Tracy used to take her brother's car all the time and it had a CD in there. And what happened is I start getting so sick of my mom, and I'd sneak out at night. And there were times when Tracy would come and pick me up at night and this song would be playing and I'd be like yeah, rebellion. But then it just kind of reminds me of all the stuff I did . . . in the school year. I did irritate my mom. I'd go to parties really late at night. . . . But now I really feel bad . . .

Shay Malone. This song reminds me of my freshman year in high school. . . . We couldn't have our prom because the principal stole our money. So, I remember all the ninth graders trying to figure out what they were going to do. And this guy stood up and he had on a cowboy hat and he just start singing this song. And the whole auditorium started singing this song. Because we wanted our prom.

Lisa Pavia. I was involved in a youth group. Every year we have 300 teenagers crowding in this theater for a skit-night on Thursday night. And it's a very long night because we have a lot of kids . . . and they all do skits. The leaders are all together and they are all the same age. And they have as much time as they want. So, they did a medley of songs. And my very first year there I'm like, who are these weird people? And they're dancing around to this song. It was very very cramped. And a lot of people were sweating. And we just want to get out of here. But that [song] kind of took us away from that. And we were all like singing and having a good time. And we all got to jump onto the stage and do the Rocky Horror Picture Show at the end.

Callie Pitt. This is not one of those happy associations memories. Like a senior's last day or a bunch of people getting together listening to this. This was possibly one of the worst first date songs. My best friend's boyfriend fixed me up with his brother. And I met his brother before. And we got along fine. But apparently, some rumors had reached his school about me that were not true. . . . He went over, called his friend and said come get me there's somebody here I don't want to be around. This song was playing in the background. So every time I hear that I think Bryan was really a jerk . . .

Song: "Crash Into Me," The Dave Matthews Band

Bernard Cummings. This song reminds me of the last show in high school. It was The Boys Next-door. I just remember the entire cast being in the dressing room just listening to. . . . It felt sad. . . . We said how much we love each other, how much we miss each other. . . . We started thinking about how the theater department would survive without us. And we were oh well, we have this guy here, this girl here, she can do it.

Gretchen Olson. It was from this past summer. Right before I left for college I had to make some money. So, I got a job at a video store in my hometown. And there was this guy who worked there who was my age but he'd gone to another high school. . . . And I got just this massive crush on him. . . . We'd close the store at night and he put Dave Matthews in the tape deck. So, while we were cleaning up the store, all the lights off in the store, and this song would be playing. And our boss would be like, hey you guys want a beer? And we all would sit up front, sit on the counter drinking our beer just listening to this song and like wow, these are the best days. And I'd go yeah, these are the best days . . . so much. And I always think about that when I hear that song.

Angie Kilber. Mine isn't sappy, happy memory at all. This song reminds me of the day I got fired. Cause it was playing when I left. . . . And I loved that job. I'd been there for two years. And I knew everything about it. I trained people because I worked there for so long. Then one day the district manager . . . told me that someone had said that I had stolen something. And it was really a big misunderstanding because I would have never stolen from the company or anything like that. And I was trying to tell them that and it just made them more mad because they felt I was lying to them. . . . It made me very angry. And listening to that song makes very angry. Because when I left the store there was that song on a stupid tape they play over and over again. . . . And I had to leave. . . . Just hearing that song makes me very very angry. As if you can't tell. . . . I didn't know I could get this angry just hearing a song. I didn't know that just hearing something could make me that emotional.

The college students' media chronicles illustrate why individuals have such a passionate attachment to popular music. The songs triggered memories about relationships, people, and meaningful episodes in their lives.

Recalling popular media can bring past experiences into the present. Gretchen treasured "Crash Into Me" because it served as a vehicle to freeze a moment in time and space. ("We all would sit up front . . . just listening to this song and like wow, these are the best days.") Indeed, at one point in Lisa Pavian's recollection, she moves between past and present tense: ("It was very very cramped. And a lot of people were sweating. And we just want to get out of here.") For Lisa, hearing the music triggered other senses as well, such as sight and smell, making the memory even more real.

Popular music also put the students in touch with a range of emotions. Gretchen associated "Crash Into Me" with romantic feelings, while in reaction to "Fight for Your Right," Callie began, "This is not one of those happy associations memories." As Angie recalled an unhappy memory associated with the song, she re-experienced the anger that she had felt at the time. She observed in amazement, "I didn't know that just hearing something could make me that emotional."

Some students associated songs with significant moments in their lives. Shay's recollection focused on an incident in which "Fight for Your Rights" emerged as an anthem for her high school class, expressing their indignation and sense of betrayal when the principal absconded with their prom funds. Some students linked popular songs to rites of passage commemorating significant personal changes, such as proms or graduation. A song may also remind the listener of a broad time span ("entire four years of high school") or embody a general attitude toward the world. For Angie, the Beastie Boys song articulated her general distaste for her high school years. Song lyrics may articulate the personal feelings and experiences of the listener. (Angie declares, "And then the second verse is like smoking and you can't do that. And I started smoking when I was sixteen and my parents hated it. . .").

Popular music also makes meaningful connections between people. Whether the students in the class hailed from Madison, Wisconsin, or Crestwood, Missouri, sharing the same musical tastes served as a unifying experience for the members of the class. Taste in music also provided significant information about their classmates, serving as an indication of other interests and personality traits. As Angie commented during the debriefing session, "I think that it's a good thing because [Shay] had kind of the same thing going on about [the Beastie Boys] song. Because that was my whole rebellion. I hated school so it was kind of the same for her. And just the fact that she liked it. I don't know, I get along good with people who like the same music I do, for some reason."

Empowerment Strategies

After having gone through an extensive experience in media literacy, one is left with what may be termed the *quintessential so-what:* that is, what steps can individuals take to act on their knowledge and understanding of the media system and media content? The Aspen Institute National Leadership Conference on Media Literacy raises this critical issue of possible applications of this body of knowledge: "Is media literacy important only to the extent that it enables one to be a better citizen in society? What is the role of ideology in the process? To what extent is an individual 'media literate' if she just appreciates the aesthetics of a message without going further with it?"[45]

The Empowerment Circle

Empowerment strategies encourage audience members to assume an active role in determining media content. Rather than expect that the media industry will protect citizens from irresponsible images and messages, the empowerment view holds that individuals must assume responsibility for understanding the political, social, and economic influence of the media. Thus, empowerment strategies enable audience members to change the way in which they respond to and interact with the media. Both Eddie Dick and

Elizabeth Thoman advocate a four-step approach through which media literacy can effect social change; they refer to it as the empowerment circle, and it consists of the following:

1. *Awareness.* This stage involves using tools of media literacy to examine and understand the impact of media messages, including: (1) becoming well informed in matters of media coverage; (2) discussing media programming with friends, colleagues, and children.
2. *Analysis.* Examining the political, economic, social, and cultural factors that shape media messages. This may involve the following steps: (1) developing a sensitivity to programming trends as a way of learning about the culture; (2) keeping abreast of patterns in ownership and government regulations that affect the media industry.
3. *Reflection.* Considering the role of the media in individual decision making, lifestyle, attitudes, and values.
4. *Action.* Deciding on appropriate strategies on the basis of the first three steps. These strategies can include: (1) discussing media content with friends, colleagues, and children; (2) exercising critical choices in personal use of media; (3) writing letters to the editor or to a TV station; (4) meeting with the staff of the newspaper, TV, or radio station; (5) boycotting the advertisers of a program or newspaper; (6) promoting the instruction of media literacy throughout the school system (K–12) by contacting members of the local board of education, PTA, and principals; (7) joining media literacy organizations.[46]

Emancapatory Media Programming

Another action step consists of the production of *emancipatory media programming*—programs that challenge the institutions and values of the dominant culture. Mainstream programs such as "Saturday Night Live" and "TV Nation" raise questions about the underlying assumptions of the dominant culture.

Public Response Strategies

Yet another empowerment action step involves the development of public response strategies for media policy legislation. The Center for Media Education has proposed a twelve-step action plan that citizens can adopt to help assure that the public interest is made a part of media and telecommunications policy:

Concentration and Control

1. *Media Mergers.* Public interest groups need political support to help make the case against current and future media mergers.
2. *Ownership Limits.* Write letters to FCC commissioners and congressional representatives supporting strong ownership safeguards.
3. *Broadcaster Accountability.* Citizens and community groups can file petitions with the FCC to deny transfer of licenses. They can challenge new owners to live up to their public interest obligations, as well as participate in broadcast license renewals. Also, citizens should fight the proposal at the FCC to extend license renewals from five to eight years.
4. *Cable Accountability.* Urge local officials to demand public interest obligations and safeguards in return for the cable companies' use of public rights-of-way.
5. *Crucial Appointments.* Write President Clinton to support appointments of officials truly independent of the telecommunications industry.

Access and Affordability

6. *Universal Service.* File and organize in support of access for the poor, and for community institutions, at the FCC and state regulatory agencies, making sure that information highway access is meaningful and rates truly affordable.
7. *Consumer Pricing for Broadband Service.* File petitions with your local public utility commission calling for a consumer-oriented, low-cost, flat-rate tariff for ISDN (Integrated Services Digital Network) service.
8. *Competition and Consumer Protection.* Join coalitions of national public interest groups and state public advocates to file at these regulatory agencies, giving them the necessary political support to take on local monopolies by denying them unfair advantages in the marketplace.
9. *Children's Television.* Write to the FCC to urge that it require broadcasters to air a minimum amount of educational programming for children as part of their public service obligation.
10. *Spectrum Auctions.* Tell your representatives and the FCC that the spectrum [wavelength] should be auctioned off, and that the proceeds reinvested for public use.
11. *Open Access for Video Programming.* Support nondiscriminatory access for independent video providers on the new Open Video Systems platforms created for phone companies in the Telecommunications Act. Support advocates who are also fighting at the FCC for a low rate [cost] of programmers on cable companies' leased access channels. Special provisions and rates for educational programming on telephone and cable systems are also needed.

12. *Intellectual Property.* Support the Digital Future Coalition, which is fighting for policies that ensure accessible, affordable, and noncommercial information for the public.[47]

Empowerment Strategies in the Classroom

One of the fundamental objectives of media education is the development of critical autonomy, so that the audience can develop an independence from the messages conveyed through the media. In order to achieve this objective, Len Masterman argues that media education must avoid the hierarchical, authoritative structure characteristic of most classroom environments:

> This approach follows closely that practiced by Brazilian educator Paulo Freire, who argued for a pedagogy which would liberate rather than oppress or domesticate. His approach rests firmly on a belief in our human potential to reflect critically upon our experience, to discover what, within our own and others' experiences, oppresses and limits our thinking and our actions, and finally to act in order to transform those debilitating factors in the interests of all human beings and of the ecological systems of which we are a part.
>
> First and foremost, Freire trusts the potentiality and inclination of human beings to move in these directions. Secondly, he also recognizes that most of what passes for education mitigates against this movement for liberation.[48]

Barry Duncan has identified a few strategies designed to promote empowerment in the classroom:

* Try to encourage students to transfer their insights into other areas: schooling, the family, the world of work; otherwise, much of our endeavor will have limited impact.
* Model a variety of individual response to media texts . . . so that students can be introduced to the notions of consent, negotiation, and resistance to popular culture texts. Explore the connections between knowledge, pleasure and power.
* Media studies should be inquiry-centered and investigative. There should be plenty of room for independent study.[49]

Conclusion

Autobiographical Analysis

Because discussion and analysis begin with personal response to media content, autobiographical analysis is an excellent way to approach media literacy in the classroom, as well as in nonacademic settings such as community groups, retirement centers, church organizations, and facilities for at-risk children. This autobiographical approach broadens the scope of media literacy education. Although people in retirement centers may not have the capability or inclination to apply themselves to the academic rigor of media literacy analysis, the autobiographical approach becomes educational in a new sense, that is, providing opportunities for personal discovery and growth.

Explanatory Note: Audience Interpretation of Media Content

Understanding the role of the audience in the interpretation of media content is critical to autobiographical analysis. Two schools of thought exist with respect to the role of the audience. According to the *hegemonic model,* the audience's interpretation of text generally is aligned with the values and beliefs of the dominant culture. Although a mass media text may be open to several interpretations, the text dictates a "preferred reading" from the perspective of the media communicator. Within this construct, the audience assumes a passive role in the communications process. (For further discussion on the hegemonic model, see chapter 1.) The *reception theory* maintains that the audience assumes an active role in interpreting the information they receive through mass media. The reception theory acknowledges that audience members have distinct, identifiable interests and look for specific objectives or gratifications in media programming, based upon factors such as age, gender, economic status, race, and personal experience.

Which perspective on audience interpretation is correct—the hegemonic model or the reception theory? It is clear that there must be a middle ground between these two positions. Audience interpretation is a process: While audience members are encouraged to assume the point of view of the preferred reading, at the same time they negotiate their own meaning, based on their own personal background and experiences. Cary Bazalgette and David Buckingham observe,

> While the text might "prefer" or "invite" a particular reading, and thus prevent or restrict others, it might also invite multiple readings—although the limitations and the ideological consequences of that diversity cannot be guaranteed or determined in advance. At the same time, readers are not seen simply as free-floating individuals, able to make meanings of their own choosing. . . . Readers do indeed make meanings, but they do so under conditions which are not of their own choosing . . . [The power of the media] is not a possession either of texts or of audiences, but as something which is embedded in the relationship between them.[50]

Keys to Autobiographical Analysis

I.   Narrative Reconstruction

    A. In detail, relate the story of the media program you just saw (read, heard, etc.).

B. Explicit Content
1. What were the significant events in the story?
2. What is the primary plot of the story?
3. What are the subplots, if any?
C. Implicit Content
1. What is the relationship between the significant events in the story?
2. What are the characters' motivations for their actions?
3. Are the consequences to specific behaviors defined?

II. Affective Response Analysis

A. Affective Response and Personal Belief Systems
1. The Origins/Causes of Affective Response
   a. Describe your emotional responses to the media presentation.
   b. How did you feel at various points in the program?
      1) What in particular made you feel that way? Describe or recall specific incidents in detail.
   c. How does your emotional reaction to the media presentation carry over into your everyday lives?
      1) Do you react in the same way to events *outside* of the media?
      2) What do these responses reveal about your personal values system?
2. Pleasure Perspective
   a. What aspects of a media program generate a pleasurable response in you?
      1) What is your favorite program, and why do you enjoy it?
      2) Describe your reaction to the program (e.g., Why is it funny? What is the source of the humor?) Be specific.
   b. What does this exercise reveal about the program?
   c. Do these same elements trigger a pleasurable response when they appear in other programs?
   d. What does this reveal about your interests, attitudes, and values?
3. Coping Mechanisms
   a. Reconstruct the media presentation, focusing on your emotional and physical responses.
   b. What coping mechanisms did you employ? At what points in the presentation?
   c. Do you use any of the coping mechanisms elsewhere in your life?

       1) Are there similarities to the events/themes in the media presentation and to events/themes in your own life?

       2) Do you use these coping mechanisms in response to other events/themes in your own life?

       3) Is the use of the coping mechanisms effective? Explain.

  B. Affective Response Analysis: Media Content

    1. The Entrance of a Character

      a. How did you feel about the character when you first saw him/her?

      b. What accounts for your emotional response?

       1) What was the character doing?

       2) What was he/she wearing?

       3) What did he/she say?

      c. Did the media communicator intend to elicit this response?

       1) If so, how does making this emotional connection between character and audience support the themes and world view of the narrative?

      d. Did you maintain this initial impression?

       1) If not, why? And what (if anything) caused this change?

       2) Based on his/her actions in the remainder of the story, did the character deserve the emotional response that he/she elicited from you?

  C. Affective Analysis: Function

    1. How did you to feel at particular points in the narrative?

    2. Why does the media communicator want you to feel this way?

    3. Do your affective responses provide insight into the media messages? Explain.

    4. Do your affective responses provide insight into your personal belief system? Explain.

III. Identification Analysis

  A. Identification Analysis: Media Content

    1. Character Identification

      a. Identify favorite characters and explain what you liked and disliked about them.

       1) Clarify the nature of the character identification.

         a) Likeness: Do you see a resemblance between yourself and the character?

         b) Aspiration: Would you like to emulate the character?

      b. Which attributes of the characters make you choose the character as a favorite?

        1) Are these attributes generally regarded as positive or negative? Explain.

        2) Is this character a hero or villain in the narrative?

    c. Name additional attributes of the character that you did not include in your original list of attributes.

    d. Discuss the role that the attributes of the character play in the successful outcome of the story.

    e. Were there missing attributes in some characters that prevented them from succeeding within the context of the narrative?

    f. Are there characters in the narrative whom you may like or admire but cannot relate to? Explain.

    g. How do you relate to the villains in the narrative?

2. Narrative Analysis

    a. Discuss the role of the admirable character attributes you have identified in the successful outcome of the story.

        1) What role do these attributes play in the outcome of your own life?

        2) Are there other attributes that you have not identified that play a role in the outcome of the narrative? Explain.

    b. Put yourself in the situation depicted in the media presentation.

        1) How would you feel about being in that situation?

        2) How would you react?

        3) Does the situation remind you of your own experience? How?

    c. Compare the narrative to your own personal experience.

        1) Does the situation remind you of your own life? How?

        2) How would the characters handle your situation?

        3) Would it work? Why or why not?

    d. Imagine yourself in the role of the primary figure in a media presentation. What insights does this provide into the sources of power and assumptions about what constitutes "the good life?"

        1) As the lead character, what could you accomplish?

        2) What opportunities would be available to you?

        3) What advantages would you have? What could you "get away with" because of your position?

    e. Oppositional Viewer Identification: Identify with another character in the media presentation (e.g., villain, a member of a subculture, a person of the opposite gender, or a supporting character).

    1) What could you accomplish as one of these characters?

    2) What opportunities would be available to you?

    3) What advantages would you have?

    4) What could you "get away with" because of your position?

B. Identification Analysis: Function—Why is the media communicator promoting the viewer's identification with specific characters or situations?

C. Examine the limits of identification (De-identification).

    1. In what ways does the media presentation construct a reality that is different from your everyday experience? Be specific.

    2. What production elements are used to construct this reality?

    3. Are the actions of the characters unrealistic? Explain.

IV. Media Chronicles: Questions to ask when conducting a media chronicle

A. What does this program remind you of? (Be specific, detailed).

B. Follow-up Questions

1. How old were you when the program was popular?

2. What were you doing when it was popular?

3. Can you describe the environment in which you watched the program?

    a. With whom did you watch the program?

    b. Where did you watch the program?

    c. What were you doing while you were watching the program?

4. Can you recall the first time you saw/heard the program?

5. Can you recall how you felt (scared, amused) while you watched/listened to the program?

6. Does the program remind you of any people/experiences?

7. Are there any cultural artifacts (e.g., cars, dress) or behaviors appearing on the program that had personal significance in your own life? Explain.

8. Do you remember any of the characters?

    a. Which characters did you like? Dislike? Why?

    b. Did you identify with any of the characters? Why?

CHAPTER 3

NONVERBAL COMMUNICATION ANALYSIS

When body language and words are in conflcit, people believe body language.
—Daryl Perkins
Mark S. Normon & Associates[1]

Overview

In interpersonal communication, the most conspicuous and direct vehicle of expression is a verbal exchange. However, nonverbal communication is a surprisingly sophisticated and efficient system for conveying meaning as well. According to J.S. Philpott, over two-thirds of the total impact of a message is the result of nonverbal factors.[2]

Nonverbal communication behavior generally has been linked to the study of interpersonal communication but is applicable in the critical analysis of mass communications as well.

Nonverbal communication analysis provides insight into the ways in which nonverbal communication behaviors reinforce verbal messages in the media. In visual media (photographs, film, and television), actors employ nonverbal behaviors such as body posture, accents, or subtle facial expressions and eye movements to convey messages and reinforce themes. Even in radio, which relies only on sound, vocal modulation, rhythm, and pitch have an enormous impact on the impressions received by the audience.

Figure 3.1. **Christine Todd Whitman**

Nonverbal communication is a surprisingly sophisticated and efficient system for conveying meaning. This photo captures a moment from a 1997 political debate between Governor Christine Todd Whitman of New Jersey and her Democratic opponent, State Senator James E. McGreevey. Whitman's body language (e.g., gestures and facial expression) suggest that she is in an active role. In contrast, McGreevey's nonverbal behavior reflects a defensive posture. P. Greenburg/NYT Pictures.

For example, on January 27, 1998, President Bill Clinton sternly denied having had a sexual relationship with Monica Lewinsky and urging her to lie about it. Clinton angrily declared,

> I want to say one thing to the American people. I want you to listen to me. I'm going to say this again. I did not have sexual relations with that woman—Miss Lewinsky. I never told anybody to lie, not a single time— never. These allegations are false, and I need to go back to work for the American people.

As Clinton spoke, he wagged his finger at the reporters (and the cameras) for emphasis. This combination of verbal and nonverbal communication was extremely effective. News reports commented that this twenty-second pronouncement was "dramatic," and "buoyed his supporters and riveted attention on Lewinsky."[3]

Nonverbal communication analysis provides insight into the character and disposition of the media communicator. Independent from the content, nonverbal behavior such as posture, body type, or dress sends messages about the speaker's self-image, competence, confidence, and trustworthiness.

To illustrate, in October 1997, Clinton addressed an enthusiastic crowd in Buenos Aires, Argentina. Reporter James Bennet's description of Clinton's nonverbal behavior indicated that the president felt relaxed and confident in this supportive setting: "Forehead furrowed as he grappled with each inquiry, the President gestured broadly with his free hand, palm open and up. He walked toward his questioners to lock eyes, at one point climbing a step down from the stage."[4] In turn, these nonverbal cues also influence the audience's attitude toward the speaker—how likable he/she is—which, in turn, can affect the audience's receptivity to the speaker's message.

Nonverbal communication analysis examines ways in which media communicators use "scripted" nonverbal strategies to create a particular image or impression. Media figures carefully orchestrate their nonverbal behaviors as part of impression formation and management strategies designed to make their verbal messages more convincing. The study of various nonverbal impression management techniques enables individuals to effectively present their message.

For example, in the spring of 1997, Air Force pilot Kelly Flinn enlisted the services of image consultants as she faced possible court-martial for having had an extramarital affair. As Flinn left the legal affairs building at Minot Air Force Base in North Dakota, she was photographed clutching a bouquet of flowers. Public relations adviser Tony Capaccio explained that this nonverbal behavior was carefully crafted to marshall public support for Flinn's case:

> To her public relations advisers, the roses were no accident. Rather, they were props in an aggressive, high-stakes campaign to build public support for the embattled officer. "We wanted to give her a sense of humanity," says Judith Webb, vice president of Atlanta-based Duffey Communications. "The flowers were a softening thing. . . . It was a suggestion we made and something the family did. . . ." The roses illustrate perfectly the way that images often become the reality the public remembers.[5]

This image management strategy had an immediate impact on the public's perception of Flinn and, in addition, influenced the way in which the media covered the story.

Another example of nonverbal impression management occurred in 1997, when sportscaster Marv Albert was accused of sexual misconduct.

Figure 3.2. **Marv Albert**

An example of nonverbal impression management occurred in 1997, when sportscaster Marv Albert was accused of sexual misconduct. This carefully scripted nonverbal behavior was designed to convey a message about his innocence. AP/Wide World Photo.

Albert was photographed entering the courthouse, holding hands with his fiancée, Heather Faulkner. Asked about this carefully scripted nonverbal behavior, a class of college students commented that the gesture sent messages declaring Albert's innocence. Holding hands is "wholesome," a "romantic and platonic gesture which counterbalances the more sordid sexual aspects of the accusation." In addition, holding Albert's hand is "both a physical and emotional expression of support by Albert's fiancée."

Nonverbal communication analysis furnishes individuals with tools to detect "unscripted" behaviors that are at variance with the verbal message. People interviewed in front of the camera are often unwilling to express their true feelings verbally. However, their nonverbal behaviors may display their actual thoughts and feelings.

The media—particularly television—have altered the contemporary American political landscape by blurring the distinction between public and private activities. Joshua Meyrowitz observes that modern political candidates are always on stage and consequently must maintain a steady state of performance. Before the age of television, politicians could retain some semblance of privacy. Today, however, political figures no longer have the luxury of "backstage activities"—areas of privacy hidden from public viewing.[6]

Meyrowitz contends that this backstage visibility has led to a decline in the image and prestige of political leaders. The opening up of traditional backstage behavior means that citizens now know, in intimate detail, about the private behavior of those in authority. For example, the media feeding frenzy that accompanied the Clinton sex scandal allegations represents a radical departure from the past, when the press overlooked sexual misconduct by presidents Franklin Roosevelt, Dwight Eisenhower, and John F. Kennedy. The scrutiny of politicians' private behavior has challenged our public conception of "appropriate behavior."

But more to the point of this chapter, the public are now witnesses to their leaders' nonverbal, "backstage" behavior. Ironically, at the same time that the media have permitted the public to be "close" to politicians, this media scrutiny has inhibited leaders' ability to govern. Politicians must monitor their every action and reaction to protect the desired image they wish to project.

A striking demonstration of the potency of unintended gestures in the media occurred during the third 1992 presidential debate between Bill Clinton and George Bush. The town meeting format was more favorable to Clinton's public performance style. During the debate, Clinton employed a series of carefully crafted gestures designed to add a personal dimension to his performance. At one point reporter Marissa Hall asked a question about the economy. Clinton approached Hall, smiled, and made it a one-to-one conversation. His scripted open-hand gestures were synchronized perfectly with his words to convey an aura of warmth and openness. While Clinton was answering the question, Bush was clearly visible in the background. As Clinton spoke, Bush glanced down and, turning his wrist slightly, peeked at his watch. This gesture spoke volumes about Bush's lack of engagement in this debate. In a broader sense, the gesture served as a metaphor for Bush's lackluster campaign and his diminished chances at re-election; clearly, his "time was up."

Nonverbal communication analysis furnishes perspective into the cultural attitudes, values, behaviors, preoccupations, and myths that define a

Figure 3.3. **George W. Bush**

Nonverbal communications analysis furnishes individuals with tools to detect unscripted behaviors which are at variance with the verbal message. In this 1992 presidential debate, the camera captures George Bush as he is glancing at his watch, signaling
his lack of interest in the proceedings. AP/Wide World Photo.

culture. To illustrate, Erving Goffman identified patterns of nonverbal behavior in advertisements which provide insight into gender relations in American culture. Goffman discovered a preponderance of *function ranking images* in ads: "In our society when a man and a woman collaborate face-to-face in an undertaking, the man . . . is likely to perform the executive role."[7] The principle of function ranking also includes images of instruction; in advertising, men are more likely to be shown depicted instructing women, which "involves some sort of subordination of the instructed and deference for the instructor."[8] When females are depicted as engaged in a "traditionally" male task, such as fixing a car, a male is present to "parenthesize the activity, looking on appraisingly, condescendingly, or with wonder."[9]

Goffman also found that, in advertising, women often are victims of "mock assault games" with men. For example, in Newport Cigarette ads, male models dunk females in water, pour water on their heads, and hold them aloft in precarious positions. The women in these ads are smiling; they are not threatened but, rather, impressed by this display of dominance. But though the mock assault games are set within a comedic context, Goffman declares, "Underneath this show a man may be engaged in a deeper one, the suggestion of what he could do if he got serious about it."[10]

Male models in ads often encircle the female model with their arms. This gesture establishes the male as protector from outside attack. However, at the same time, the encircling arm prevents the female from withdrawing from the male. Goffman notes that "the extended arm, in effect, marks the boundary of his social property."[11]

Nonverbal communication analysis provides insight into the role of nonverbal cues in the depiction of media stereotypes. Media communicators rely on nonverbal communication cues, such as body type in the depition of stereotypes. People with heavy builds (endomorphic body types) often are cast as characters who are lazy, warm-hearted, sympathetic, good-natured, dependent, passive, sloppy, and indolent. Examples include Norm from *Cheers* or any part played by the late John Candy or Chris Farley. Characters with thin, fragile frames (ectomorphic body types) are often stereotyped as tense, fussy, critical, suspicious, nervous, pessimistic, anxious, self-conscious, and reticent characters. *The Odd Couple's* Felix Unger comes to mind. And finally, characters with lean, athletic frames (mesomorphic body types) are cast as protagonists who are highly confident, task-oriented, energetic, talkative, aggressive, and dominant.

Characters also are stereotyped in terms of age. Media consultant Jane Squier Bruns relates a story in which her ex-husband, media consultant Bob Squier, produced a political spot for the Democratic Party designed to raise concerns about the Republicans' policy on Medicare. The commercial contained visuals of a grandmother tending to her infant grandchild, while the voice-over declared that Republican initiatives would jeopardize the health care of young and old alike. Bruns's granddaughter Emma was cast as the infant. The role of the grandmother was played by an elderly, dowdy woman who wore a frumpy housedress. Bruns, a vibrant, attractive woman who is also an actress, was told that she could not be cast for the part because she did not fit the stereotypical image of a grandmother—even though she is Emma's actual grandmother.[12]

Height frequently is associated with particular male character stereotypes. Leading men are generally taller than their female love interests. When women do appear with shorter men, the male characters are generally cast as comedic figures who are timid and powerless. Consequently, when diminutive Alan Ladd was cast with taller actresses, the crew had to dig trenches for the women to stand in to even out the height differential.

A Cautionary Note

Nonverbal cues provide excellent indicators of a communicator's intention and attitudes, which then can serve as a springboard to further analysis of media messages. But several mitigating factors must be taken into consideration when conducting a nonverbal communication analysis. First, the culture to which a person belongs can have an impact on the meaning behind nonverbal communication cues. In addition, we must realize that nonverbal behaviors sometimes have innocent explanations. For instance, a person may assume a particular posture because his/her back hurts. As Groucho Marx commented, "Sometimes a cigar is only a cigar." The study should identify an individual's typical patterns of nonverbal behaviors, in order to systematically interpret (1) where and when these behaviors appear, and (2) divergences from the typical nonverbal behaviors. In conducting nonverbal analysis, it is essential to develop consistency in the identification of nonverbal behaviors through an orientation, training, and pre-testing.

Functions of Nonverbal Communication

Nonverbal behaviors fulfill a number of functions during the course of a conversation. Identifying the function, or purpose, of nonverbal communication behaviors in media presentations can provide considerable insight into messages.

- *Clarification.* Nonverbal behaviors may emphasize points or can dramatize the verbal message in pantomime. For example, hand gestures can punctuate the verbal message, indicating which points are of vital importance.

- *Persuasion.* Nonverbal behaviors can be employed to enlist the agreement or cooperation of the listener. For instance, an earnest look or slap on the back may be an appeal to support the verbal message.
- *Regulation of the Communication Process.* Nonverbal cues can be used to facilitate the communication process. A puzzled expression asks the communicator for clarification, whereas a fixed gaze may reassure the communicator that the listener is interested and paying attention.
- *Expression of Emotion.* Nonverbal cues may express a range of emotions, including anger, nervousness, sadness, happiness, sympathy, satisfaction, fear, love, and jealousy. Nonverbal cues also can furnish information about the communicator's attitude toward the subject matter. Posture or eye contact can disclose how the person *feels* about what is being said. In addition, nonverbal behavior may disclose the speaker's attitude toward the other person(s) involved in the conversation. Finally, nonverbal cues can express the communicator's feelings about the environment, context, or circumstances in which the conversation is taking place.
- *Expression of Intimacy.* Nonverbal behaviors may indicate the level of intimacy that exists between the parties engaged in conversation. Touch, eye contact, or proximity signal attentiveness, interest, and emotional engagement between the participants. Nonverbal cues such as an icy stare can maintain distance between the communicators. Lovers often position themselves in close proximity to one another and may touch (e.g., hold hands, kiss) while conversing.
- *Social Control.* During a conversation, nonverbal communication can establish a powerful subtext concerning interpersonal relations. Nonverbal cues often reflect disparities in status and power. During a conversation, a relationship, however brief, is formed based on a shared interest—the topic of conversation. As in all successful relationships, the two parties must adhere to rules of decorum that govern a communication exchange. These unwritten rules include the length of time that two people look each other in the eye, the distance between two people engaged in conversation, and the proper (or improper) boundaries for touching. A person who is allowed to violate the rules of conduct assumes a dominant role in the relationship, such as standing close to the other person or touching him/her on the shoulder.

However, violations of communication rules can also signal a *loss* of social control. Guests on news or talk programs constantly interrupt each other. This aggressive approach is not only a sign of disrespect but an effort to discredit others. Significantly, the focus of tabloid talk shows like "The Jerry Springer Show" revolves around the violation of these communications rules. Much of the "excitement" of the program involves guests interrupting each another, hurling insults, and pummeling the other guests.

Nonverbal communication cues may fulfill more than one function at a time. For instance, a gesture may express intimacy while, at the same time, serve a persuasive purpose. In addition, nonverbal communication behaviors may fulfill both a *manifest* and *latent* function. Manifest functions are direct and clear to the audience. We generally have little trouble recognizing these messages when we are paying full attention to a media presentation. Latent messages are indirect and beneath the surface, and, consequently, escape our immediate attention. Latent functions refer to instances in which the media communicator's intention may not be immediately obvious to the audience. In fact, it is surprising how frequently the manifest function is irrelevant—or at least, subordinate—to other, latent purposes (like impressing the audience, nurturing relationships, or expressing emotion). As an example, a person may touch another for the manifest purpose of suport or sympathy, when, in fact, this nonverbal behavior may have a latent sexual meaning.

Types of Nonverbal Behaviors

Identifying specific nonverbal behaviors can provide information with regard to the message, the communicator, and the dynamics of a communication exchange. Although many of these behaviors apply universally, the meaning of some nonverbal cues may vary within different cultures. In Britain, tapping one's nose signifies secrecy or confidentiality; in Italy it is a friendly warning. In Thailand, a person moves his/her fingers back and forth with the palm down to signal another person to come near. In the United States, we beckon someone to come by holding the palm up and moving the fingers toward our body. The Tongans sit down in the presence of superiors; in the West, we stand up.[13]

However, some universal nonverbal behaviors do exist among cultures that provide insight into a speaker's motivation, attitude, and character.

Facial Expressions

Facial expressions are a reliable source of a person's emotional disposition. The face can register a range of responses, including evaluative judgments (e.g., pain, pleasure, superiority, determination, surprise, attentiveness, and bewilderment), degree of interest or disinterest in the subject, and level of understanding.

People tend to attribute positive character traits to individuals who smile, including intelligence, a good personality, and being a "pleasant person."[14] Smiling also assumes gender-based meanings. Women tend to smile more frequently than men, perhaps reflecting a subordinate desire to please. However, because smiling can be a social construction for women, their behavior may be scripted (i.e., covering other emotions) and, consequently, more difficult to interpret.

People in the public eye, such as political figures, high-profile corporate executives, and broadcast journalists, are trained to develop their *presentational* facial expressions as part of an overall "impression management" strategy. Media relations consultant Tripp Frohlichstein trains his clients to maintain an "open face" while in front of the camera: "Keep your eyebrows up and smile when appropriate. This helps you better convey your pride, as well as intensity. When the eyebrows are flat, so are your voice and feelings. When your eyebrows are down, so is the interview, and you may be perceived as angry or negative."[15]

However, one way to identify scripted facial expressions is by observing the speaker's immediate facial reactions. For an instant, a speaker often reveals his/her genuine feelings; however, this expression is quickly replaced by a presentational expression. Some facial cues include the following:

- Raised eyebrows indicate surprise.
- A set jaw reveals anger, determination, tension, resolve, or decisiveness.
- A chin retraction is a protective action or a signal that something is scary or frightening.
- Flared nostrils express anger.
- A nose wrinkle signifies dislike, disapproval, or disgust.

Eye Behaviors

The eyes have a mystical quality that defies rational explanation. Look in the mirror, covering your face with your hands and leaving only your eyes exposed. Think of something sad, then something funny, and finally something that makes you angry. It is uncanny how these simple orbs can express powerful emotions: eyes narrow with anger, grin with joy, and fill with tears when sad.

Modern politicians employ media advisers to assist them in the best ways to make eye contact with as many voters as possible when giving campaign speeches. Direct eye contact with the camera, reporter, or audience heightens the credibility of the candidate. To illustrate, during the infamous Kennedy–Nixon debates, the majority of voters listening on the

Figure 3.4. **Richard M.Nixon**

Eye behavior can be regarded as a barometer of a person's character and intentions. During the famous Kennedy-Nixon debates, the majority of radio listeners felt that Nixon "won" the debate. However, most of the television audience believed that Kennedy had won. This disparity can be attributed to Nixon's shifty eye behavior on camera, which made him appear dishonest and untrustworthy. AP/Wide World Photo.

radio felt that Nixon "won" the debate. However, the majority of the television audience believed that Kennedy won. This disparity can be attributed, in part, to Nixon's shifty eye behavior on camera, which made him appear crooked and untrustworthy.

The length and direction of eye contact can also be used to assert dominance and control. In *Death and the Maiden* (1995), Dr. Miranda (Ben Kingsley) is a character who repeatedly tortured and raped Paulina Escobar (Sigourney Weaver) while she was a political prisoner under a now-defunct dictatorship. At one point in the film, Miranda recounts how he relished his power over her. In the final sequence of the film, Miranda is positioned

Figure 3.5. **Eye Behavior**

The direct eye gaze conveys a sense of credibility, honesty, or assertiveness. Photo by Jamie Clark.

Figure 3.6. **Eye Behavior**

Averting one's gaze (left) suggests a lack of interest, disbelief, or disengagement. The downward gaze (right) indicates subordination or deference. Photo by Jamie Clark.

above Paulina while both are seated at a concert listening to Schubert's "Death and the Maiden." The camera circles slowly from the orchestra to a close-up of Paulina seated in the lower orchestra section with her husband. The camera guides us as she slowly turns her head and looks directly up toward the box circle where Miranda is seated with his family. At this point, the camera closes in on Miranda staring down at Paulina. Briefly he turns toward his son, smiles, pats him on the head, and then turns back, resuming his fixed stare down at Paulina. The camera then returns slowly to focus on Paulina again. She avoids Miranda's stare, sitting rigidly with a tense, fixed, forward gaze. This eye interaction reinforces the hierarchical relationship between the two characters. Further, the elliptical path traced by the camera from Paulina to Miranda and back to Paulina informs us the issue is closed. Dr. Miranda will remain in his position of power and will never be punished for his transgressions.

Posture

Posture refers to a stance or positioning of the body or a body part. Postures send a range of messages about a communicator's character. An upright posture communicates confidence and integrity. A slumping posture conveys a sense of cowardice, meekness, sadness, or depression.[16] Having good posture—standing tall—is an indication of empowerment, authority, and rank in society.

Examining posture in media presentations provides insight into the heirarchy of power among the characters. Erving Goffman points out that in many advertisements, females pose in a "cant" position, in which the head or body is bowed. The latent message of this body language is deference, submission, and subordination.[17] To illustrate, a recent Nike ad featured tastefully nude portraits of five male and three female athletes. The male athletes are standing erect, their figures filling most of the page. In contrast, the three women are diminished in both body position and in relation to the size of the page. One woman is stooped on the lower left side of a two-page spread. The second is crouched at the bottom of the page and the third, in a sexually receptive position, spanning over two pages, is semi-reclining on her back with her legs in the air. Through posture, the ad reinforces a hierarchy in which the men are deemed more significant.

Posture can also indicate the speaker's attitude toward the audience. Leaning toward a person expresses a positive position, while slumping communicates a negative attitude. Posture is often used to reinforce verbal messages in media presentations. In a commercial for *Sports Illustrated,* a man standing behind the bar in his "rec room" leans forward (toward the camera) to tell us about a special offer to subscribe to the magazine. This posture conveys a sense of intimacy and informality, which in turn suggests friendship, honesty, and trustworthiness. He is not trying to "sell us anything" (actually, he is); instead, he just wants to let us in on a good thing.

Gestures

Gestures refer to the act of moving the limbs or body as an expression of thought or emphasis. Some gestures with specific meanings include: the chin stroke (pensiveness, concentration); chin rub (dubiousness, questioning); and the chest beat (strength, power). Another common gesture is the palm punch, in which the fist of one hand is punched rhythmically several times against the palm of the other. According to Desmond Morris, this angry gesture has a primal, symbolic significance: "This has a common meaning of a mimed blow against an enemy, redirected onto the palm of the gesturer. In such cases the gesture indicates a state of barely controlled rage."[18]

Openness gestures (e.g., unbuttoning coats, uncrossing legs, moving toward the edge of a chair) convey a sense of confidence, encouraging interaction. On the other hand, defensive and nervous gestures are considered unattractive and undesirable. Slouching suggests passive attitude, sloppiness, and incompetence. Crossed arms and crossed legs suggest that the communicator is inaccessible and defensive. Fidgeting, tugging at clothing, and playing with objects signal that the communicator is nervous.

Hand gestures may enhance a speaker's credibility. Peter Bull likens the hand gestures of political candidates to those of a conductor. Hand gestures are carefully synchronized with rhetorical devices to emphasize points as well as direct audience response—either encouraging or halting applause. Political candidates have learned to emphasize rhetorical contrasts by first holding up one hand to issue a statement, and then holding up the other hand as they deliver a contrasting statement. When candidates wish to demarcate a hierarchical organization or give a three part list, they emphasize each part with ambidextrous hand movements, in which they move their hands simultaneously or one after the other. Punching a headline is also facilitated by the use of single or bilateral hand gestures. Candidates synchronize these gestures with vocal stresses, pauses, or tone peaks.[19]

Another hand gesture is the "steeple," in which the tips of all five fingers of each hand are touching to simulate a church steeple. Because the fingertips are pointed toward heaven, this is a very positive gesture that indicates confidence, integrity, contemplation, and sincerity.

To illustrate, the film *Primary Colors* (1998) presents mixed messages

Figures 3.7–3.12. **Posture**

Posture can express thought, reveal character, or reflect attitudes. Examples include the following (photos by Jamie Clark).

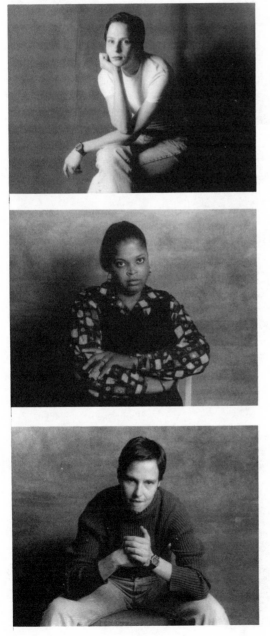

3.7 A pensive attitude

3.8 A defensive posture

3.9 An active, assertive position

3.10 A relaxed, confident demeanor

3.11 An assertive stance

3.12 A thoughtful attitude

about candidate Jack Stanton, who is loosely based on Bill Clinton. Stanton is a womanizer who is dishonest in his personal life. However, he is also an idealist who enters public service to improve the lives of all of America's citizens. Stanton employs the steeple gesture when he is at his best in the film, reflecting about his vision for a better America.

But as stated before, the meanings of gestures may vary enormously between different cultures. For instance, in the United States, the sign in which the thumb and index finger are joined in a circle, means "A-O.K." This gesture has a variety of connotations in other cultures: "In Latin America, this gesture is regarded as obscene and insulting, with associations with excretory functions. In France, this gesture means 'zero' or 'worthless.' In Japan, the thumb and forefinger making a circle is used as a symbol for money."[20]

Proxemic Communication

Proxemic communication refers to the way in which space configurations convey meaning. The use of space falls into three distinct categories:

Personal space consists of the area immediately encircling our bodies. Personal space is protected by the boundary we maintain between ourselves and others, which each of us considers our own territory.[21] The boundaries of personal space may be culturally determined. Members of Arab nations typically stand closer when conversing than do Europeans.[22] The boundaries of personal space may also vary *within* a culture. In the United States, women tend to stand closer together than men.

However, when communicating, all individuals negotiate a comfort zone for interaction. Any violation of this space creates feelings of discomfort and apprehension. As mentioned earlier, close proximity between people is often a sign of intimacy. However, trespassing on an individual's personal space also may signal an imposition of control, reflecting (and reinforcing) status or power differences.

Group formation refers to where people are positioned in relation to one another. The arrangement of people within a group reflects the attitudinal position that a person assumes with regard to the activity. For instance, as a student, you may sit in the same place each day in the classroom, even if the seats are not assigned. To be sure, habit plays a role in your seat selection. However, your choice of seats also reflects whether you are comfortable participating in class discussion or prefer to be less actively involved in the class sessions.

Group formations also indicate status. People in control often assume a place in the center of the group, with more marginal members on the fringe.

This hierarchical principle also applies to seating arrangements. In America, people at the head of the table are in control. The individual seated to the left of the head of the table often has the least status in the group.[23] In Japan, the most important person sits at one end of the rectangular table, with those nearest in rank at the right and left of this senior position. The lowest in class is nearest to the door and to the opposite end of the table from the person with the most authority.[24]

Group formation also indicates whether the assemblage of people forms an open or closed society. People standing in a closed formation are excluding others, while groups in an open formation are more inclusive.

In *Contact* (1997), group interactions throughout the film send messages of inclusion and exclusion. Dr. Ellie Arroway (Jodie Foster), a scientist, finds herself in a subordinate position to males despite her superior knowledge and expertise. In one scene, while Ellie stands at the end of a table in front of the door giving a presentation, her former boss, Drumlin (Tom Skerritt), sits relaxed, in the middle of a group of peers. The group arrangement requires that Ellie confront the entire group, mostly males, while Drumlin receives their nonverbal support. In the final scene, Ellie is finally positioned in the center of a group—teaching science to children. Within the context of the film, she has assumed her "rightful" place in society—not as a scientist but as a caretaker/teacher.

Fixed space refers to the characteristics associated with particular locations. In media programs, particular activities are associated with specific rooms, such as the kitchen, bedroom, or parlor. Rooms may also serve as metaphors for aspects of characters' psyches. For instance, in the film *Gaslight* (1944), the attic represents the subconscious. Mattias Thuresson provides the following plot synopsis:

> Young Paula Alquist (Ingrid Bergman) marries the charming Gregory Anton (Charles Boyer). An elderly aunt of Paula's was murdered a few years ago in her home at Tresvenor Square. Paula inherited the apartment which the newlyweds make their home. Slowly but methodically Gregory convinces Paula that she always forgets things, is nervous, and unwell. He also makes sure that she does not get out much and only has minimal contact with other people.[25]

Gregory's ruse enables him to dig around in the attic for the aunt's hidden jewels without attracting attention. It is in the attic that the audience finally discovers Gregory's innermost thoughts and secrets, which he has kept hidden beneath his charming exterior. Paula remains oblivious to the nefarious intentions of her husband and does not fully remember (or understand) the events leading to her aunt's death—until she finally makes the journey up to the attic and confronts her husband, as well as her own subconscious fears and buried memories.

Arranged space refers to the placement of objects within a fixed space (e.g., home, office). The arrangement of a room often serves as an indicator of the social dynamics among the people who inhabit the space. For example, the primary television viewing area in a home can furnish perspective into family dynamics. Americans often dedicate a special space—the TV room—to much of their social interactions. The furniture in the TV room often revolves around the TV screen, even though this arrangement may make it awkward for people in the room to converse with each other.[26] Where people sit in relation to each other as they watch TV is also an interesting microcosm of family dynamics. Often the person perceived as dominant has the choice of the prime seat, and is in charge of the remote control. On the other hand, people from France, Italy, and Mexico position furniture to encourage interaction among each other. Conversation is important for them and facing chairs toward a television screen stifles conversation.[27]

In media programs, sets provide authenticity, making the world of fiction appear real. In the film version of *Portrait of a Lady* (1997), the filmmaker meticulously included trappings from the period, including clothing, furniture, and curios which transported the viewer to nineteenth-century England and Italy. In addition, the sets are an integral part of many media genres, making the audience feel familiar in these surroundings. For instance, we expect that a saloon in an old western contains swinging doors, a player-piano, long bar, and spittoons on the floor.

Arranged space can also function as a metaphor that reinforces themes and central concerns in the presentation. For example, in the 1970s sitcom "All in the Family," Archie Bunker's easy chair represented authority. But while the chair was exclusively Archie's domain, everyone sat in it during the course of an episode, suggesting that Archie's traditional notion of the family structure had become archaic and dysfunctional, so that Archie's son-in-law sitting in his chair represented a societal shift in power.

Tactile Communication

Tactile communication, or touch, can serve as a demonstration of support, reassurance, intimacy, sexual interest, or as an expression of emotions (e.g., anger, exhilaration). However, as mentioned earlier, touching violations also can be an assertion of power and control by high-status individuals.

Touching behaviors can reinforce verbal content or convey independent latent messages. For instance, politicians have mastered the art of holding a handshake for an instant longer than is normally expected, sending a message of personal regard, intimacy, and trust.

The specific meaning of touch is determined by the following factors:

- *Culture.* High contact cultures include Arabs, Latin Americans, and Southern Europeans. Cultures less inclined to touch include Northern Europeans and Americans.[28]
- *The nature of the relationship.* Lovers touch each other in different ways than mere acquaintances.
- *Region of the body that is touched.* A tap on the shoulder has a different meaning than a pat on the bottom.
- *Age.* Young and older people touch most frequently when communicating.
- *Context.* The place and occasion in which the touching behavior occurs helps determine its meaning. What might be suitable at a drive-in movie might not be acceptable at the office.
- *The type of touching behavior exhibited.* There are subtle yet discernible differences between pats, squeezes, brushes, and strokes.

Primary Colors (1998) provides an interesting comment on the use of tactile communications in the political arena. In one scene, campaign manager Henry Ferguson (Paul Guilfoyle) and campaign aid Henry Burton (Adrian Lester) watch presidential candidate Jack Stanton campaigning. Political consultant Jemmons translates the meaning behind the touching behavior exhibited by Stanton in the scene:

> You know, I've seen him do it a million times now. . . . When [he puts] that left hand on your elbow or up on your biceps like he's doing now, very basic move, he's interested in you, he's honored to meet you. If he gets any higher, gets on your shoulder like that, it's not as intimate. It means he'll share a laugh with you or a secret, a light secret, not a real one, but very flattering. If he doesn't know you that well and wants to share something emotional with you, he'll lock you with a two-hander. Well, you'll see when he shakes hands with you, Henry.

Significantly, Governor Stanton (a thinly disguised Bill Clinton) displays these five gestures with various characters throughout the course of the film. After the election, Stanton greets Henry with "the two-hander," which the audience understands as a sign of affection. However, had Henry not dropped out of the campaign at an earlier stage, he might have merited a hug.

Physical Appearance

It is undeniable that physical appearance has an impact on the ways in which people relate to one another. Attractive people are considered socially desirable, credible, and more persuasive than people seen as less attractive. In addition, good-looking people consistently receive preferential treatment from others.[29] Not only do we admire attractive people, but we identify with them and sympathize with their situations. Thus, even though film stars represent unapproachable ideals of beauty, audience members enjoy projecting themselves into the roles and situations of these attractive people.

Characters in popular media programs often are categorized according to their appearance. Heroes and heroines are physically appealing and wear brighter colored clothing. In contrast, villains often are physically displeasing in some way—unshaven, scarred, or disheveled and in dark clothes. Thus, ugliness is equated with evil. This practice can lead to falsely labeling an attractive person as "good" and an unattractive person as "bad."

Physical beauty also is presented as a measure of superiority; people on-screen are attractive because, on some level, they *deserve* to be. Handsome heroes assume control of their lives and successfully fend off the challenges of the villains. As they battle the villains, these handsome heroes are "in the right"—the inference being that these characters are correct precisely *because* they are attractive. The heroes often are called upon to protect others—most often an attractive female. The implication is that only beautiful women are worth protecting.

In advertising, alluring models are situated as the center of attention, with ordinary, less attractive people staring enviously at the them (ostensibly because of their appearance, but by extension, because of the product they are displaying). These ads promote their merchandise as a modern form of alchemy, which transforms base metals into gold; that is, ordinary folks will look like the glamorous models in the ads simply by using their products. For instance, in a Pantene shampoo ad, a woman moves her head in slow motion, her lustrous hair swaying gracefully and the light accentuating its texture and color. The ad suggests that the shampoo is responsible for her lovely hair. However, a careful consideration of the ad can unmask this illogical premise. After looking at the commercial, Leah Silverblatt, age nine, was asked whether the shampoo made the model's hair that pretty, or if the advertisers selected a model who had beautiful hair in the first place. She immediately replied that the model probably had great hair to begin with.

The world of popular media programming operates according to a hierarchical system based on appearance. One way in which we know that supporting characters are not as important as the stars is because they are not as attractive. In romantic comedies, beautiful people are searching for equally gorgeous partners. Conversely, unattractive people are suited only for each other. Comedy (or, worse, tragedy) occurs when people try to seek matches outside of their particular station. The cumulative media message is "know your place" when it comes to appearance.

When Harry Met Sally (1989) is a romantic comedy that traces the relationship between Harry Burns (Billy Crystal) and Sally Albright (Meg Ryan). Harry and Sally maintain a platonic friendship; however, the audience knows that the two are "right" for each other (in part because they are both attractive), and the dynamic of the film involves the two principal characters discovering what the audience already knows.

Since they are only friends, Harry and Sally agree to fix one another up with dates: Harry with Marie (Carrie Fisher), and Sally with Jess (Bruno Kirby). They go on a double date, but it is clear that the two couples are mismatched physically. Jess has an obvious beer belly, which hangs over his belt. And although actress Fisher is normally very pretty, her hairstyle, dress, and makeup are designed to make the character of Marie look plain.

While Harry and Sally struggle to find their romantic—and physical— counterparts, Jess and Marie get married. Unlike their attractive friends, Jess and Marie are content; their aims are not too lofty, and they happily settle for a partner whose appearance situates them within the same class in the hierarchy of appearance.

Eventually, Sally and Harry discover that they have been meant for each other all along. Order is restored to this universe, with the attractive and not-so-attractive couples finding their appropriate matches.

Significantly, this hierarchy system does not apply when other virtues are deemed more compelling than physical attractiveness. This occurs chiefly with men, when the compensating virtues are wealth and power.

The emphasis on appearance is not limited to entertainment programming and advertising. Appearance has become an essential factor in American politics. During the 1996 presidential campaign, Bob Dole deemed it necessary to dye his eyebrows in order to present a more youthful appearance. Newscasters also must be attractive. For instance, news anchor Christine Craft was demoted from her position at a Kansas City television station at age thirty-six. Her boss, she said, explained that she came across on the tube as "too old, too ugly and not sufficiently deferential to men."[30] Now a Sacramento lawyer and Bay Area talk-show host, Craft sued the station.

Accessories

Accessories are adornments that enhance personal appearance, including clothing, makeup, hairstyle, eyeglasses or contact lenses, jewelry and handbags. Accessories send powerful nonverbal messages about an individual's credibility, interpersonal attractiveness, power (e.g., suits, uniforms), likability, and competence. Through selection of attire, automobiles, and hairstyles, we are able to assemble an identity. Style has become a way to advertise ourselves within mass culture; our choices of accessories tell others who we are, what we stand for, and what others can expect from us.

In media programs, costumes serve as an external expression of character. Wearing a trenchcoat in many of his films reinforced Humphrey Bogart's tough, ruthless image. Costume may also symbolize an *attitude*. In the 1950s, James Dean, Marlon Brando, and Elvis Presley adopted a very distinctive look, complete with motorcycles, leather jackets, tee shirts, and sideburns. More than mere fashion, these accessories became an emblem of teenage rebellion and angst. The costumes worn in media presentations often become fashion trends, reflecting the audience's identification with characters and their worldviews.

Costumes can serve as a dramatic device that represents thematic concerns in media programs. In the gangster genre, the mob's flamboyant wardrobe is associated with violence, wealth, and power. Eugene Rosow comments, "The most reliably consistent trait of movie gangsters was their sartorial progression from dark and wrinkled nondescript clothing to flashy, double-breasted, custom tailored striped suits with silk ties and suitable jewelry."[31] The wardrobe of gangsters epitomizes their paradoxical position in society: They appropriate the styles of high fashion to blend in and gain acceptance, but their clothing style is too extreme, and they are further ostracized by society. Thus, they cultivate an "identified school of stylishness that, far from operating as camouflage, ultimately functioned like warrior dress."[32] In *Casino* (1995), director Martin Scorsese used costumes to accentuate the excesses in the lifestyle of the gangster. During the film, Ace (Robert De Niro) changes costumes fifty-two times; his wife Ginger (Sharon Stone) goes through forty costume changes.

Clothing often reflects the gangster's rise from small-time crook to successful mobster, and his subsequent fall. Ace's demise is dramatized through the use of wardrobe. Toward the end of the film, Ace rises from his desk wearing a meticulously coordinated outfit (shirt, tie, socks, and shoes)—minus his trousers. This signals a radical departure for a man who throughout the film has had a fixation with appearance. Clothes define a gangster's identity—both to himself and the audience. Therefore, slipping into sartorial neglect signals the beginning of his fall.

The popularity of a particular fashion trend may assume cultural significance. According to Professor Harriet Woroby, Joan Crawford's trademark (dresses with shoulder pads) caught the public's fancy because her attire was an expression of emerging cultural attitudes and preoccupations:

> In the 1940s, Crawford was in her shopgirl/independent woman stage, starring in films such as *Mildred Pierce*. The shoulder pads indicated that she had power and helped her compete with her male co-stars. Women began to wear them because they wanted to emulate her. The clothes coincided with cultural events in the 1940s, when women had to join the workforce because of the war and were reluctant to give up this independence.[33]

At times accessories *become* the message. Cheri Bank, medical reporter for WCAU-TV in Philadelphia, recalls presenting a moving story on a medical breakthrough involving the early detection of birth defects. "I anticipated calls from expectant mothers who wanted more information about the procedure. However, the first call I got was from a woman who wanted to know where I bought my earrings."[34]

Vocalic Communication

Vocalic communication refers to the quality of the voice, which conveys meaning, independent of the words themselves. Vocalic elements include the following:

- *Volume* refers to relative loudness or softness of our voices. Loudness can signify dominance or conviction, while a low volume may convey insecurity, submissiveness, or evasiveness.
- *Tone* involves the characteristic quality or timbre of the voice. A deep tone suggests authority, power, and confidence. Nasal voices are regarded as unattractive, lethargic, and foolish. Breathy voices are judged to be youthful and artistic for males, but artificial, high-strung, or sexual for females.
- *Pitch* refers to the relative position of a tone in the musical scale; that is, whether the voice is high or low. Flat voices are construed as sluggish, cold, and withdrawn. On the other hand, variety in pitch often is regarded as dynamic and extroverted. A high-pitched voice may signal lying.[35] Ending a sentence with an elevated pitch signals that the speaker is asking a question. However, this rise in pitch may also indicate that the speaker is uncertain about what he/she is saying. Conversely, lowering the pitch at the end of a sentence is a sign of certainty and authority.
- *Rate* refers to the pace or rhythm of delivery—how rapidly or slowly we speak. A person is generally regarded as speaking with greater intensity

and earnestness as his or her speaking rate increases.[36] But media consultant Tripp Frohlichstein warns, "Too fast and listeners can't follow you. Too slow and you become ponderous and boring."[37]

- *Duration* involves the length of time a communicator takes to emit a given sound or sounds. Taking too much time during a conversation is a dominance device, as the speaker seeks to control the conversation, including the topics of conversation.

- *Diction* refers to the clarity of pronunciation and articulation. Garbled diction can signify confusion, ignorance, or deceit.

- *Silence* is the absence of sound. Silence can be a dominance device, used for control and intimidation. The power of actors like James Dean or Clint Eastwood often comes not from what they say but what they do not (or are unable to) express. However, in other contexts silence can be soothing and encouraging.

- *Laughter* is an involuntary, physical release of emotion that expresses a variety of emotions, including joy, approval, surprise, discomfort, anxiety, sympathy, or ridicule. Various categories of laughter convey different meanings (e.g., chuckles, giggles, snickers, and guffaws). Television programs are punctuated by laughtracks, indicating to the audience not only *what* is funny, but *how* funny the situation is. The context of laughter can also determine meaning. For instance, people who are nervous or feel that they are in a subservient position often may laugh at inappropriate times.

Vocal cues such as dialect, tonal quality, inflection, speed of delivery, or accent transmit a wide range of information. Psychologist Richard Wiseman declares that vocality can be a more accurate barometer of the communicator's intention than eye contact or gestures: "If you want to find out if a politician's lying ... you're better turning away or shutting your eyes and just concentrating on the sound track."[38]

An accent can signify a geographic location, like the post vocalic "R," which identifies a Bostonian or the Southern drawl. Accents often charm the audience. However, an accent also can interfere with the communication or undermine the seriousness of the message. For example, a running gag in the television series "I Love Lucy" consisted of Lucy Ricardo poking fun at her husband's Cuban accent (Lucy asks, "What do you mean, 'I've got a lot of 'splainin' to do?' ").

Dialect, tonal quality, inflection, speed of delivery, pitch, and pause inform the audience about the speaker's educational level, class, cultural orientation, and nationality. In films like *Do the Right Thing* (1989) and *Soul*

Food (1997), black dialect serves as an expression of African-American identity. Film and cultural historian Clyde Taylor observes, "When . . . personality of the speaker, the manner of speech, the cultural resonance of the words and images, the social and cultural connotations, the art of the message spoken . . . takes on the character of performance, we may likely think of the speaker as an oral historian."[39]

In contrast with exploitive films, which minstralize, vaudevillize, and mimic black speech, authentic black speech in indigenous films like *Slam* (1998) reveal not only black values, but the many "distinctive and richly expressive characteristics," such as semantic ambiguity, bold extravagant metaphor, and a prophetic mode of utterance.[40]

African-American cultural expression is also found in black music, which often moves black speech patterns into melody. Interestingly, re-searchers have compared the melodic pattern of some African-American music to the cooing of mothers to their infants. According to jazz musician Phil Wilson, the pattern of jazz is like call and response. He comments that jazz was a means of dialogue among black musicians. While playing in all-white night clubs, black musicians used jazz improvisation as dialogue to alert each other of ensuing trouble.[41]

Vocal cues also furnish insight into the emotional context of the speaker's remarks, including the *type* of emotion (e.g., anger, disappoint-ment) and *degree* of emotional intensity. Vocal qualities also affect the impression that a speaker makes with the audience. A pleasing voice con-veys credibility and personal attractiveness of the speaker. In broadcast journalism, reporters' voices are trained to be low in pitch, appropriately loud, and resonant to give them an air of authority.

Behavior Analysis: Nonverbal Cues

Nonverbal cues can provide considerable insight into human conduct. Terry Corpal, professor of criminal justice and a retired secret service agent, observes that nonverbal indicators provide a rich source of information about an individual's frame of mind and attitude: "By themselves, these behaviors may signify nothing. Collectively, they provide a tremendous amount of information about the person."[42]

These nonverbal behaviors can be found in media presentations as well. Actors adopt these mannerisms to express their characters' internal motiva-tions and emotions. In addition, individuals covered by the media often lapse into nonverbal behavior patterns unconsciously: consequently, exam-ining these unscripted nonverbal signals can provide perspective into spe-cific types of behaviors.

Deception

Deception is a category of human behavior that includes doubt, lying, uncertainty, or exaggeration. One way to detect deception, according to Deputy Tom O'Connor, is by looking for "evasive nonverbal behaviors." When questioning a suspect, O'Connor typically begins by asking a series of routine questions, in order to gauge the subject's normal nonverbal behavior pattern. O'Connor then asks more direct, probing questions and notes any involuntary nonverbal changes in behavior:

> The key from my perspective as a policeman is that we must put a person in a stressful situation (one in which they know that their responses have consequences, such as a loss of reputation or confinement). White lies often are undetectable because there are no huge consequences related to being caught. Nonverbal behavior cues are based specifically on what they do after they have heard and fully understand a critical question addressed to them.[43]

In this stressful situation, a person who is caught in a lie must concentrate on formulating a credible response. At this moment, the suspect is prone to let down his/her guard, displaying involuntary, unconscious nonverbal behaviors. O'Connor looks for downcast eyes (particularly before responding to a question), low level of eye contact, shifty eye behaviors, biting of the lip, or noticeable changes in the pattern of breathing or frequency of swallowing. Other nonverbal signals of inner turmoil include rubbing the hands or dry mouth.[44]

Suspects may also engage in a series of evasive nonverbal behaviors, such as dropping their head or clearing their throats, which O'Connor describes as "a delay tactic—buying time to formulate an acceptable response."[45]

Another signal of deceit consists of hand-to-face gestures to cover up a lie. Allan Pease observes that young children often cover their mouths with their hands "in an attempt to stop the deceitful words from coming out."[46] A variation of this hand-to-face gesture is the nose touch. Desmond Morris explains,

> Touching the nose unknowingly . . . during a verbal encounter often signals deceit. The person performing the action is unaware of it, which makes it a valuable clue as to their true feelings. Why unconscious nose-touching should be closely linked with telling lies is not clear, but it may be that, at the moment of deceit, the hand makes an involuntary move to cover the mouth—to hide the lie, as it were—and then moves on to the nose. The final shift from mouth to nose may be due to an unconscious sensation that mouth-covering is too obvious—something that every child does when telling untruths.

Touching the nose, as if it is itching, may therefore be a disguised mouth-cover—a cover-up of the cover-up. However, some individuals report that they have felt a genuine sensation of nose ringing or itching at the very moment they have been forced to tell a lie, so that the action may be caused by some kind of small psychological change in the nasal tissue, as a result of the fleeting stress of the deceit.[47]

Another signal of deceit is when suspects fidget in their chairs. O'Connor observes that some suspects physically change their position when they are caught in a lie: "Their subconscious desire to leave the room is strong, so they move their bodies closer to the door."[48] Sometimes a suspect actually will cross his/her legs, with one foot pointed toward the door—the place where he/she would like to be headed.

Sexual Attitudes

Sexual attitudes are often communicated through nonverbal indicators. Men are permitted to be more sexually aggressive and therefore are more overt in their nonverbal cues, including winking and the dominant gaze. Preening behavior (e.g., a man's smoothing his collar, or smoothing his hair) is another sign of sexual interest. Another nonverbal sexual overture occurs when a man turns his body toward the object of his attention and points his foot at her. According to Pease, the gesture in which thumbs are tucked into the belt or the tops of the pockets also indicate sexual readiness: "The arms take the readiness position and the hands . . . highlight the genital region."[49]

Because women are more culturally constrained, they have had to be less direct in their expression of sexual interest. Consequently, women utilize a larger catalog of nonverbal sexual interest indicators. The sideways glance, in which the eyes look sideways at the companion from a lowered head, signals secret approval. The head toss, in which the woman's hair sways over her shoulder or away from the face, is also considered a signal of preening. Licking the lips, slightly pouting the mouth, or applying cosmetics to moisten or redden the lips are all indicators of a courtship invitation.[50]

Another nonverbal sexual cue is the body stroke, in which a female absentmindedly caresses her own leg. According to Morris, the latent meaning of the gesture is, "I find you attractive."[51]

When people find their companions attractive, they may unconsciously do to their own bodies what they would like their companions to do to them. . . . A casual stroking of the body while listening to a companion, or while talking to them, indicates a desire to be caressed by them, regardless of what

Nonverbal Indicators

Positive and Negative Responses

Positive responses include the following nonverbal signals:

- For-leaning during encounters
- Body and head orientations that directly face the other individual
- Open-body positions
- Affirmative head nods
- Moderate amounts of gesturing and animation
- Close interpersonal distance moderate body relaxation
- Touching
- Initiating and maintaining eye contact
- Smiling
- Postural mirroring (exhibiting similar or postures (Leathers, 81)
- Palms turned toward other person
- Open hands

Negative responses include the following nonverbal cues:

- Indirect bodily orientations
- Eye contact of short duration
- Averted eyes
- Unpleasant facial expressions (e.g., frown, wrinkled brow, downturned mouth)
- A relative absence of gestures
- Bodily rigidity
- Visual inattentiveness
- Closed bodily posture
- Incongruent postures
- Bodily tension (Leather 81–2)

Social Control

Numerous nonverbal indicators reflect the dynamics of social control among people engaged in conversation. Indicators of *dominance* include:

- Continuous gaze (staring)
- Controlled talk time
- Frequently interrupting other party
- Long pause before answering
- Dynamic and purposeful gestures
- Relative expansiveness in postures
- The option to touch
- The option to stare
- The option to approach another person closely
- Silence (as intimidation or controlling device)
- Straddling chair
- Sitting on desk
- Feet on desk
- Elevation (sitting higher than the other party)
- hands on hips
- Standing while other is seated

Indicators of *submission* include:

- Gaze avoidance
- Hesitant speech pattern
- Constricted and closed postures
- Limited range of movement
- Hunched body
- Downward-turned head
- Body tension
- Soft voice with little volume
- Excessive smiling

Likability

People who give off a *warm, positive image* often display one or more of the following nonverbal indicators:

- Close interactive distances
- Socially appropriate touching
- In-context and sincere smiling
- Body relaxation
- Open body positions
- Direct eye contact
- Attractive facial and/or body appearance
- Appropriate dress
- Vocality—A speaking voice which is pleasant, relaxed, emotionally expressive, friendly, which sounds confident, dynamic, animated, and interested
- Animation (facial animations, appropriate vocal volume, vocal warmth, smiling and laughing, gestural and body animation)

The following nonverbal indicators project a *negative* impression about a person:

- Unpleasant facial expressions
- Relative absence of nonverbal behaviors (e.g., gestures)
- Visual inattentiveness
- Closed bodily posture
- Unspontaneous nonverbal behaviors
- Inappropriate nonverbal behaviors
- Vocality—Monotone, narrow range of volume

statements are being made at the time. Leg stroking is the most common form of this reaction.[52]

Jan Hargrave observes that when a woman sits with one leg tucked under the other and points the folded leg toward the person she wants to attract, the message communicated is, "I feel very comfortable with you. I'd like to get to know you better."[53] Another female sexual posture is the leg twine, in which one leg is twined tightly around the other. Morris explains, "Because of the tight way in which the legs wrap around one another, it gives the impression of self-hugging, and this adds a mild sexual quality to the gesture."[54] Open legs while sitting or standing and rolling hips while walking are also considered indications of sexual interest.

However, these nonverbal cues are not always reliable measures of sexual interest. At times, it is simply comfortable to position yourself in a particular way. Consequently, it is reasonable to regard these nonverbal cues as indicative, but certainly not a guarantee of sexual interest.

The body language of women in the media reflects the cultural polarization between "good" and "bad" women in America. Traditional images of the virtuous woman display a modest, submissive demeanor, which include soft smiles and a slightly tilted head. She refrains from looking directly at the object of her attention, instead looking with lowered eyes or with a sidling glance. Her body language also expressess her vulnerability; she often places an object (e.g., her hair, hands, or a male) between herself and the camera as a shield. "Virtuous" women refrain from behavior or postures that might excite men. The model may sit sideways. If seated in frontal view her legs are usually closed, or knees folded to the side. These women also typically keep their arms close to their bodies.

The "bad," or immoral woman assumes a more direct pose. Her head is straight, and her eyes look directly into the camera. These women adopt open postures, such as moving their arms away from their bodies and opening their legs, signifying sexual receptivity or aggressiveness. In entertainment programming, women who assume these nonverbal behaviors are generally villainesses or temptresses, who are beyond redemption. For example, in a scene from the film *Basic Instinct* (1992), Catherine Tramell (Sharon Stone) positions herself in a sexually provocative posture in front of a group of male interrogators to distract her questioners and control the interview.

In many media programs, these "bad" women are often killed off (as unfit to live) or exiled. To illustrate, in *High Noon* (1952), Helen Ramirez (Katy Jurado) is the former lover of town marshal Will Kane (Gary Cooper). As the "bad girl," Helen's dark hair and complexion and direct, defiant gaze and posture are juxtaposed with the pure blonde appearance and demur demeanor of Amy (Grace Kelly), who Kane has decided to marry. Ironically, when an outlaw Kane had put in prison returns with his gang to take revenge, it is the spurned Ramirez who defends Kane, while Amy leaves him. But despite Helen's good heart, she must be punished for her moral transgressions, and she is forced to leave town.

More recently, however, these conventional "bad" nonverbal behaviors have become more prevalent in mainstream media presentations. Samantha L. King found that the October 1997 issue of *Vogue* featured six ads in which the models were posed with their legs apart—and in several of the ads, the model's pelvis is thrust forward, so that it is the closest body part to the camera. This development can be seen as a positive statement about the artificiality of the cultural duality of women. The models appear comfortable with their sexuality as a vital part of their total identity; this nonverbal behavior, then, reflects a growing acceptance of the total integration of a woman. On the other hand, King observes that this trend also can be regarded as a further exploitation of this "bad girl" image: "In these ads, the company logos are placed prominently near the models' spread legs, in an effort to attract the attention of the readers. The ads definitely associate their products with sex."[55]

Smoking Behaviors

Smoking is a powerful form of nonverbal communication conveying a range of information. Smoking behaviors can indicate an individual's level of self-esteem. For example, blowing smoke through the nostrils is a sign of a superior, confident individual. Pease observes that the direction in which smoke is exhaled is another indicator of self-concept:

> A person who is feeling positive, superior or confident will blow the smoke in an upward direction most of the time. Conversely, a person in a negative, secretive, or suspicious frame of mind will blow the smoke down most of the time. . . . Blowing down and from the corner of the mouth indicates an even more negative or secretive attitude.[56]

Pease also sees a relationship between how positive or negative a person feels and the speed at which he or she exhales the smoke: "The faster the smoke is blown upwards, the more superior or confident the person feels; the faster it is blown down, the more negative he feels."[57]

Smoking behaviors may also express a negative feeling or attitude toward others. Blowing smoke straight ahead (in the direction of the other person) can be a statement of aggression, dislike, contempt, dominance, or indifference. Pease declares that extinguishing the cigarette also can be an expression of attitude toward others: "If the smoker lights a cigarette and suddenly extinguishes it earlier than he normally would, he has signaled his decision to terminate the conversation."[58]

Smoking behaviors also can reveal a person's emotional condition. Some people smoke to release tension. Cigarette gestures such as tapping the cigarette end on the ashtrays are indicative of inner conflict. Twisting, flicking, or waving the cigarette is another signal of emotional turmoil.

Figure 3.13. **Smoking Behavior**

Because of its strong visual properties, smoking often is associated with romance in media programs. In *Now Voyager* (Warner Brothers, 1942), Jerry Durrance (Paul Henreid) suavely opens his cigarette case and extracts two cigarettes. Lighting both, he then gallantly hands one to Charlotte.

Smoking has always played a significant role in media presentations, for numerous reasons. Smoking behavior is particularly well suited for visual media. As the characters inhale and exhale cigarette smoke, the audience can see their breath, which brings the action to life. Smoking behavior also is an effective way to project character and attitude in film and television, where internal processes are difficult to express. Pease notes,

> In motion pictures, the leader of a motorcycle gang or criminal syndicate is usually portrayed as a tough, aggressive person who, as he smokes, tilts his head back sharply and with controlled precision blows the smoke towards the ceiling to demonstrate his superiority to the rest of the gang. In contrast, Humphrey Bogart was often cast as a gangster or criminal who always held his cigarette inverted in his hand and blew the smoke down from the corner of his mouth as he planned a jail break or other devious activity.[59]

Because of its strong visual properties, smoking often is associated with romance in media programs. The smoke establishes a mysterious ambience, creating a texture in the air as it catches the lights. An actor who exhales a cigarette in the direction of his love interest sends a visual line, or *vector* from himself to his companion; this vector connects the couple physically and, metaphorically, in an emotional sense as well. In addition, smoking gestures (e.g., lighting someone's cigarette, removing a cigarette from a cigarette case) can be handled with savoir-faire. A classic example from film is found in *Now, Voyager* (1942), in which Charlotte Vale (Bette Davis) falls in love with a handsome and suave European, Jerry Durrance (Paul Henreid) on a South American cruise. In one scene, as the couple come to an understanding about their feelings for each other, Durrance proposes, "Shall we have a cigarette on it?" He suavely opens his cigarette case and extracts two cigarettes. Lighting both, he then gallantly hands one to Charlotte.

Smoking on screen also has strong sexual implications. As Richard Klein observes, the phallic properties of cigarettes play a suggestive role in sexually volatile scenes: "In those aroused by the spectacle of masterly women giving themselves leisure (all nostril, mouth and fingers), smoking languorously and slow, the moment of lighting up seems to spark the most energetic erotic excitement."[60] Often when two characters meet and establish a sexual chemistry, one or both pulls out a cigarette. Enjoying a cigarette after making love is a familiar cliché in film and television.

Smoking can serve as a theatrical prop, providing opportunities for dramatic pause and emphasis. George Burns and Groucho Marx incorporated cigars into their acts to define their comedic personas, as well as to punctuate their style of delivery. By lighting the cigars, they controlled the timing of their lines. They also waved cigars around for emphasis and (in Groucho's case) wagged the cigar in a suggestive way after a sexually suggestive quip.

Cigarettes also are used as a dramatic device to advance a plot. Lighting a cigarette establishes a pause in the action for new disclosures and fresh insight into character and relationships. Cigarette smoking often functions as a bonding ritual between characters in the narrative; the communal aspects of smoking (e.g., offering someone a cigarette, lighting up together) offer opportunities for characters to pause in the action and honestly share their thoughts and feelings. In *Rebel Without a Cause* (1955), Jim Stark (James Dean) and gang leader Buzz (Corey Allen) pause for a smoke before dueling in a dangerous "Chickie Run." During this brief interlude, the two rivals reflect on the quest for meaning in a changing and impersonal world. Jim asks Buzz, "Why are we doing [the Chickie Run]?" Buzz replies, "You've got to do something." But as soon as they have finished their cigarettes, they again retreat behind the facade of appearance and resume their competition. The implication is that the cigarette is somehow critical to this intimate and significant moment.

Smoking is a part of the world view of many films and television programs, reinforcing the notion that cigarettes are integral to the culture. Cigarettes accompany certain activities, such as socializing at bars. Cigarettes also are one of the trappings associated with glamorous professions such as detectives, gangsters, or journalists. Often it is the coolest, hippest characters who smoke.

Smoking also is a narrative technique used to express and reinforce thematic concerns in media programs. For instance, smoking is often presented as a rite of passage to adulthood. *Stand by Me* (1986) is an initiation film about a group of young boys and significant experiences that move them toward adulthood. The film includes a scene in which the young boys, smoke cigarettes as they sit around a table, playing poker. In some cases, smoking is presented as evidence that a young person already has achieved adulthood. In *Huckleberry Finn* (1995), young Huck is left on his own. Having already assumed adult responsibilities, he enjoys the privileges as well—in this case, smoking.

Cigarettes also serve as a symbol of rebellion against adult authority. In *Rebel Without a Cause,* Jim Stark lights up as a sign of his dissatisfaction with the hypocritical rules of adult society general and his parents in particular. More recent films like *Trainspotting* (1996) offer a more nihilistic world view. The characters are on their own, with nothing (not even parents) to rebel against. Locked in the present, smoking cigarettes (and shooting heroine) represents a rebellion against the self, against their futures.

Given all of the cumulative messages about smoking, entertainment programming remains a very powerful indirect advertisement for the tobacco industry, in addition to direct advertising campaigns. Despite an intense anti-smoking campaign, cigarette smoking by high school students increased by 36 percent between 1991 and 1997. Smoking increased by 28 percent among white students, 34 percent among Hispanic students, and 80 percent among black students.[61]

Essay: Nonverbal Communication Analysis of Alcohol Moderation Ads

In the 1980s, citizens' organizations pressed for strict regulation or a complete ban on beer and alcohol advertising. Fearing that television beer advertising would suffer the same fate as tobacco, three major brewers (Anheuser-Busch, Coors, and Miller) launched campaigns to promote "responsible" drinking. Although these campaigns were designed to caution against the overindulgence with alcohol, a close examination of these public service announcements (PSAs) reveals that the nonverbal messages actually reinforce the brewers' regular commercials and marketing strategies. Despite the verbal appeals for moderation in these ads, the nonverbal communication elements continue to promote the consumption of alcohol.

An ad for Anheuser-Busch promoting designated drivers presents images indistinguishable from their customary commercials that promote beer consumption. In fact, this spot includes several visuals taken from their pro-drinking" ad campaigns. One of these segments takes place in a crowded bar, where a group of young adults gathers in a ritual of comradeship and group solidarity. Another segment shows two women playing a basketball arcade game at the bar, while the rest of the group cheers them on. College students who observed the "responsible-drinking" ad commented that the depictions of friends having a good time, the focus on entertainment, and the appealing visuals of the product were similar to typical beer spots.[62]

Juxtaposed with these pro-drinking images, the voice-over in the Bud ad issues the moderation message: "Friends know when to say when." However, the loud music and ambient bar noises make the voice barely audible. And regardless of the voice-over, the images reinforce the message that "good times with friends" is synonymous with drinking Budweiser.

The Coors "Now, Not Now" ads present a sequence of shots, demonstrating when it is acceptable to drink. The voice-over narration in each scene tells the viewer when "It's the Right Beer Now" or when not to drink ("But Not Now"). Significantly, the most compelling visuals accompany the scenes in which the characters *are* drinking. The scenes depicting the right times to drink Coors include three young, handsome men boating and water skiing; a playful interlude between a young man and woman on a beach; a crowded bar scene with a close-up of three friends, who have their arms around each other laughing; a beach party with a crowd of young adults; and males bonding around a camp fire. The actors in all of these social scenes are attractive, happy, and are holding a can or bottle of Coors. The images suggest that beer is the essential elixir of youth, virility, glamour, healthy living, and the key to a good time.

In contrast, the "Not Now" scenes show people in isolation rather than in group settings. If more than one person is in the scene, (e.g., two men hunting), they are not communicating with each other. Some of these scenes depict older males—a group conspicuously absent from the pro-drinking segments. Thus, the group encouraged not to drink is not the primary group that Coors wants to target anyhow. The images of young adult males not drinking are also scenes of darkness and isolation.

Immediately before two of the socially active scenes, close-ups of Coors light are placed up front and center. One is a slow motion close-up of a frosty cold can of Coors light that rotates into full view. The second shot shows two bottles of Coors light emerging out of icy water into a tight close-up of the Coors Light labels on the bottles. With the accompanying up-beat music, the male voice says "Coooors light, it's the right beer now." These two shots undermine the manifest message of moderation by suggesting that whatever the viewer is doing, it is the right time to drink Coors light.

DeJong, et al., declare that these "moderation" advertisements violate the industry's own code of ethics and encourage overindulgence.[63] A nonverbal analysis of these ads would support this view.

Conclusion: Nonverbal Analysis of Media Content

I.   Nonverbal communication analysis can help the audience member to decipher media messages by following the lines of inquiry:

   A. Do the nonverbal communication behaviors reinforce verbal messages? Explain.
   B. Do the nonverbal communication cues provide subtextual information about the speaker? Explain.
   C. Are there "unscripted" nonverbal behaviors that are at variance with the verbal message? Explain.
   D. Do the media communicators manipulate nonverbal behaviors to create a particular image or impression?
   E. How does the study of nonverbal communication furnish perspective into cultural attitudes, values, behaviors, preoccupations, and myths that define a culture?
   F. What role do nonverbal cues provide in the depiction of media stereotypes?

II. Nonverbal Communication Behaviors

Nonverbal Communication Behavior Chart				
Facial Expressions	Eye Behaviors	Posture	Gestures	
Proxemic Communications	Tactile Communication	Vocalic Communication	Physical Appearance	Accessories

Analyze the nonverbal behaviors in a media presentation. Apply the following set of questions to the appropriate nonverbal behaviors cited in the above chart:

   A. What types of nonverbal communication behaviors does the subject display?
   B. What functions are fulfilled by these nonverbal communication behaviors?
      1. Do these nonverbal communication behaviors classify information? Explain.

2. Are these nonverbal communication behaviors intended to persuade? Are they successful?

3. Are these nonverbal communication behaviors used to regulate the communication process? Explain.

4. Are these nonverbal communication behaviors intended to establish/maintain the communication relationship? Are they successful?

5. How do you interpret the nonverbal communication behaviors?

6. What emotions are conveyed through nonverbal communication behaviors?

7. Do the nonverbal communication behaviors support or conflict with the verbal communication?

C. What do these nonverbal communication behaviors reveal about the subject's character, state of mind, or attitude?

D. What do these nonverbal communication behaviors suggest about the subject's status or credibility?

E. What messages are conveyed by the communicator's nonverbal communication behaviors?

1. Do the nonverbal communication behaviors reinforce verbal messages?

2. Do the nonverbal communication behaviors reveal "unscripted" nonverbal behaviors that are at variance with the verbal message?

3. Do the nonverbal communication behaviors reveal "scripted" nonverbal impression management behaviors? What are the intended messages?

III. Additional questions used to analyze specific nonverbal communication behaviors:

A. Posture
1. What are the characters' postural styles (rigid, relaxed, nervous, calm, friendly, contentious, attentive)?
2. What messages do these postures convey?

B. Proxemic Communication
1. What kinds of proxemic communications are taking place?
2. Personal space.
   a. What is the physical distance between the characters?
3. Group formation
4. Fixed space

    a. What does the architecture tell you about the characters' lifestyles?

    b. Describe the environment on an emotional level (warm, formal, private, familiar, distant, confining).

C. Tactile Communication
1. Which characters touch each other? Who initiates the touching?
2. What does the touching signify?

D. Vocalic Communication
1. What tone of voice is used?
2. Is there an accent or dialect?
3. How fast do different characters speak?
4. Are there long silences or pauses, and what does this mean?

E. Physical Appearance
1. What is the shape of the body (obese, thin, muscular)?
2. What does the body type tell you about the character?
3. What are the comparative heights of the characters?
4. Does this signify anything as to dominant or subordinate relationship?

F. Accessories
1. How are the characters dressed and what does this tell you about them (social class, education, ethnic origin)?
2. What artifacts do the characters wear?
3. What types of clothing are the main characters wearing?
4. What other material accessories (e.g., home, technology) do the characters have?

CHAPTER 4

MYTHIC ANALYSIS

Introduction

In contemporary culture, with its emphasis on rational, scientific explanation, there is a tendency to discount or deny the value of myth. However, writing in 1873, Max Mueller argued that mythology exists in the modern age, whether or not we are willing to acknowledge it: "Depend upon it. There is mythology now as there was in the time of Homer, only we do not perceive it, because we ourselves live in the very shadow of it, and because we all shrink from the full meridian light of truth."[1]

Today, the oral tradition—the primary source for passing myths from generation to generation—has nearly disappeared. In this vacuum, the media have emerged as primary channels for the transmission of myth. Mircea Eliade contends that although times have changed, people continue to seek solutions to life crises, albeit unconsciously, through the channels of mass communication: "A whole volume could be written on the myths of modern man, on mythologies camouflaged in the plays that he enjoys, in the books that he reads. The cinema, that 'dream factory,' takes over and employs countless mythical motifs—the fight between hero and monster, initiatory combats and ordeals, paradigmatic figures and images."[2]

A mythic approach can help make media content accessible in the following ways:

- identifying the *mythic functions* of media programming;
- providing perspective on media content as a *retelling* of traditional myths;
- identifying *mythic elements* in media programs (and the meanings behind

these elements) as a way to approach critical analysis of the narrative;
* recognizing *cultural myths* in media programs that furnish perspective into that culture.

Overview of Myth

A myth is any real or fictitious story, recurring theme, or character type that gives expression to deep, commonly felt emotions. Myths may be grouped into three general areas: *nature myths, historical myths,* and *metaphysical myths.* Myths can be multilayered, so that they may operate on several of these levels simultaneously.

In the prescientific age, nature myths provided explanations for natural events, including meteorological, astronomical, terrestrial, chemical, and biological phenomena. Nature myths describe the origin of things, like the formation of rivers, or some momentous occurrence experienced in the past, such as the great deluge, or flood.

Historical myths chronicle significant events and rulers of previous civilizations. These tales serve as prehistories of ancient civilizations, which often kept no written records. Historical myths may also provide information on the genealogy of gods, kings, and peoples, as well as the naming of particular places and people.

Metaphysical myths furnish insight into creation, birth, death, divine presence, good and evil, and afterlife. According to Gilbert Highet, mythology is an elemental part of the human experience, an effort to understand the mysteries of being human and an inhabitant of this world:

> The central answer is that myths are permanent. They deal with the greatest of all problems, the problems which do not change because men and women do not change. They deal with love; with war; with sin; with tyranny; with courage; with fate; and all in some way or other deal with the relation of man to those divine powers which are sometimes to be cruel, and sometimes, alas, to be just.[3]

Thus, many myths deal with the *deep truth* of human experience. Regardless of whether myths are factually accurate accounts of historical events, myths speak to an inner truth in a way that science cannot. Rollo May declares, "It does not matter in the slightest whether a man named Adam and a woman named Eve ever actually existed or not; the truth about them in Genesis still presents a picture of the birth and development of human consciousness which is applicable to all people of all ages and religions."[4]

In myths, gods are often portrayed as having human shape, feelings, and motives, though on a grander scale than their mortal counterparts. This personification makes the mysteries of the universe more intelligible to human beings. At the same time, the stories of the gods can be regarded as allegorical tales about human beings, which enable us to put the experiences of men and women into meaningful perspective.

Mythic Analysis

Function

Myths serve a variety of functions, or purposes, many of which now are fulfilled by media programming. Roland Barthes observes that one of the disarming features of myth is that its functions appear to be so natural; that is, though the functions may be obvious and assumed, they are not consciously thought about by the audience:

> [Myth] transforms history into nature. We now understand why, in the eyes of the myth-consumer, the intention . . . of the concept can remain manifest without however appearing to have an interest in the matter: what causes mythical speech to be uttered is perfectly explicit, but it is immediately frozen into something natural; it is not read as a motive, but as a reason.[5]

This principle also applies to myths conveyed through the channels of mass communication. Although media programs often serve a variety of mythic functions, the audience tends to accept these programs as natural, without question. Consequently, a useful approach in mythic analysis is to consider media programming in terms of the following traditional functions of myth.

To Inspire Awe

Myth has the ability to move people out of everyday experience, into the realm of the extraordinary. Because preternatural events and heroic exploits are not part of everyday existence, we seek myth to affirm that the extraordinary is possible, that witches, ghosts, and supermen exist, and that people are capable of grand and transcendent acts.

In like fashion, media programming has the ability to transport its audience to a different realm of experience. Film, television, and recorded music operate on an affective (or emotional) level, so that audience members do not merely understand the story on a cognitive basis but are moved beyond their own immediate experience. Indeed, one of the primary functions of special-effects films like *Star Wars, Twister,* and *Titanic* is to immerse people in an alternative experience.

Myth and media share another awe-inspiring capability as well. Both myths and media presentations contain elements of horror, destruction, and tragedy that evoke feelings of fear and dread among members of the audience. Both the story of Oedipus and news reports of the Oklahoma City bombing remind people of the horrific possibilities of life.

To Facilitate Self-Actualization

Rollo May observes that by putting human beings in touch with their own submerged feelings, myths can have a cathartic, or healing, effect: "In reading the mythic tale, we feel cleansed as if by a great religious experience. . . . The world and life have a deeper quality that reaches down into a person's soul. . . . Love and joy and death confront one another in these depths of emotion."[6]

Part of the attraction of media programming—even popular, formulaic programs—stems from this self-actualization function. Dramatic programs feature conflicts between good and evil, life and death, and questions of living honorably in an unjust world. Sitcoms are morality plays, in which characters contend with the consequences of their transgressions—often deceit or betrayal of their community. Disney cartoons such as *Hercules* or *The Little Mermaid* focus on issues of identity. Thus, even if programs appear repetitive, simplistic, and unchallenging on the surface, they satisfy our hunger to see innate conflicts acted out by characters on-screen.

In addition, human beings seek myth as a way to break through their personal isolation, enabling them to move into a full sense of membership in the community of human beings. Jerome Bruner declares,

> In his life-form the individual is necessarily only a fraction and distortion of the total image of man. He is limited either as male or as female; at any given period of his life he is again limited as child, youth, mature adult, or ancient; furthermore, in his life role he is necessarily specialized as craftsman, tradesman, servant, or thief, priest, leader, wife, nun, or harlot; he cannot be all. Hence the totality—the fullness of man—is not in the separate member, but in the body of the society as a whole; the individual can only be an organ.[7]

Media programming offers individuals an opportunity to share these experiences with others, whether they are rooting for their favorite team on "Monday Night Football" or reveling in a "feel-good" movie.

To Provide Order

Myths furnish explanations in the face of what appears to be an overwhelming and chaotic world. In that sense, myths provide reassurance, as well as a sense of direction: they communicate where we have been, where we are, and where we are going. In the same way, a media presentation presents an ordered world view that offers the comfort of structure to people's lives. This might explain why much media consumption is habit-driven. People tend to read the newspaper in the same order and in the same location, or routinely tune into the news before retiring for the night.

To Provide Meaning

Myths also establish and reinforce beliefs. People choose to believe in myths, even though many of the stories involve extraordinary beings and events that challenge logical explanation. Could the infant Hercules strangle snakes that were placed in his crib? Did God create the world in six days? Belief in these myths involves an act of faith that transcends logic. But even if people are dubious about the literal truth of a myth, they often believe in its metaphorical aspects. For instance, the biblical time frame for creation can be interpreted as relative—God's conception of a day may translate into eons. And even if a myth is untrue, over time it may assume a *mythic reality;* that is, a myth is repeated with such frequency that people believe it to be true.

To Exalt

Myths provide a means for people to honor significant events and people. In like fashion, the media elevate people and events to mythic status. Media attention can transform *ordinary* events into *extraordinary* occasions. For example, the occasion of the Super Bowl has been transformed into Super Sunday. Conversely, the media magnify achievements merely by focusing on them; if it appears on television, it must be important.

In contemporary society, the media have assumed a *mythologizing* function in contemporary society. The pervasiveness of media coverage gives the media figure an air of omniscience. Michael Jordan is everywhere—on television, in print, and in films. The close-up shots of Jordan make him appear omnipotent. While certainly Jordan's skills on the basketball court are superb, media coverage endows him with an air of invincibility. "ESPN Sportscenter" highlights Jordan's spectacular plays while editing out his missed shots or errant passes. Slow motion replays accentuate his graceful moves and keep him suspended in midair for an indefinite period of time.

The media have truly merged reality and myth. Advertisements frequently present its spokespersons performing mythic deeds to boost their appeal. One TV ad features Larry Bird and Michael Jordan matching baskets, beginning with moderately difficult shots, and concluding by bouncing a ball off of a series of buildings into the hoop. Entertainment programming also has begun to merge reality and myth. In *Space Jam* (1997), Michael Jordan operates in a magical world, in which he talks with animals and, thanks to special effects, defies gravity and other mortal constraints.

At the same time, however, the media *demythologizes* mythic figures and events. The intense scrutiny of the media magnifies the human flaws of those people who are in the public eye. Editor Tony Frost of the tabloid paper the *Globe* asserts that his paper is responding to a basic desire to tear down our mythic heroes: "We have inherent morality. We believe in the lowest common denominator. Very few stars behave the way they should in private. That's what makes them interesting. We put them up on the pedestal, and they fall down and it's their own doing. . . . Bam, we've got a story."[8]

To illustrate, pro golf sensation Tiger Woods was the object of adulation after his victory at the 1997 Master's Tournament. However, after this initial torrent of positive attention, the media began to pick at the image they had constructed. The twenty-one-year-old Woods was criticized for turning down an invitation to appear with President Clinton on the fiftieth anniversary of Jackie Robinson's debut in major league baseball, which took place two days after he won the Master's. Woods was immediately put on the defensive: "For one thing, I had planned my vacation already; it was already set. And, two, why didn't Mr. Clinton invite me before the Master's? That didn't happen, and as soon as I won, he invited me. I think it would have been best if he'd have asked me before, with all the other athletes that were involved."[9]

Woods's reputation was further tarnished in an article in *Gentleman's Quarterly,* in which he was alleged to have used foul language and made offensive jokes about blacks and lesbians. However tasteless his comments may have been, Woods made the point that his remarks were intended to be private. "I was just unknowingly talking to a limo driver who was miked."[10]

In this climate of intense media scrutiny, it is increasingly difficult for human beings to maintain an exalted status. As in the case of public figures like Bill Clinton and Bill Cosby, the foibles of individuals are uncovered and brought to public attention. While intriguing to audiences, this phenomenon contributes to a sense of public cynicism, as people are stripped of their belief in mythic heroes.

To Instruct

When they are accepted as truth, myths represent the accumulated knowledge and wisdom of a society and, therefore, serve as a primary source of information dealing with history, natural phenomena, and religious and ethical principles.

In the same vein, people model their conduct and define their expectations based upon the activities of media figures. Some programs instruct through positive examples. However, other media presentations instruct by glorifying negative, self-destructive, self-indulgent, or violent behavior.

As Ritual

A ritual is a ceremonial act that is an extension of the belief system of an organization, religion, or myth. Rollo May explains the relationship between ritual and myth: "[Rituals are] physical expressions of the myths. . . . The myth is the narration, and the ritual—such as giving presents or being baptized—expresses the myth in bodily action."[11]

Rituals reaffirm faith in the essential validity or authenticity of the myth. Henry A. Murray observes that the ritualistic retelling of myths, such as the story of the birth of Christ at Christmas time, serves "to propagate and periodically revive and reestablish veneration for the entities and processes it represents."[12] Thus, watching a rerun or a formulaic program may have value as ritual, reaffirming mythic themes and values that are critical to our belief system.

Media presentations often function as rituals that act out and resolve myths. Looking at the media as ritual can help explain the popularity of some programs we watch—either as reruns or simply as variations of the same formula—again and again. To illustrate, Joseph Schuster was astonished to discover how many times students in his script analysis class at Webster University (Fall 1996) had seen *Star Wars:* "I had eleven students in my class. Each student had seen *Star Wars* at least twice. One student reported that he had seen the film seventy-eight times. On average, the students in the class had seen the film approximately 18.3 times."[13]

These students return to *Star Wars* not to find out how the story *ends;* after seventy-eight viewings, this should be rather obvious. Rather, their gratification comes from watching the narrative *unfold,* to reencounter the elemental conflict between good and evil and to experience the satisfying resolution of the narrative.

To Promote Social Solidarity

Myths often present a world view that supports and validates the prevailing social order. Murray regards myths as essentially reactionary, in that they promote conformity to the belief system of those in control of society: "The forces that are aligned with the group's welfare, with its hopes for the future, being beneficent in direction, are exalted as the good powers. The opposing and hence maleficent forces are portrayed as evil."[14]

In particular, cultural myths play a fundamental role in an individual's socialization by telling stories that promote the prevailing standards of success and failure within the culture. In many cultural myths, the triumph of good over evil is dependent on the characters' compliance with its adherence to the values and goals of dominant culture. (For further discussion, see Ideological Analysis, chapter 1.)

Media and the Transmission of Myth

Many contemporary media programs are modifications, variations, or extensions of traditional myths. A popular media hero like Rambo captures the public's attention and adulation because, in many respects, he is a modern version of Hercules. It can be argued that one of the reasons we watch the same formulaic media programs over and over is because these stories are transmitting myths that tell us about ourselves and about the human experience.

Psychoanalysts Sigmund Freud and Carl Jung maintain that myths originate in the subconscious, the repository for all universal human experience. Individuals come into contact with this shared experience through their dreams. Myths, then, represent an *externalization* of the elemental experiences and aspects of Self that each person encounters as part of being human. By projecting these universal impulses, experiences, and conflicts, human beings are able to put their personal experiences into perspective. Murray explains,

> Though the imagery is necessarily derived from the external world, the reference is internal. In no other way, as Plato insisted, can certain profound truths be genuinely conveyed to others. Mythic stories and symbols that depict the "night journey" of the introverted soul, the encounter with the monster in every person's "depths," liberation from imprisoning modes of feeling and of thought, reconciliation, spiritual rebirth, the beatific state of grace and redemption—experiences of this nature—are expressed in language that must be taken figuratively, symbolically, and imaginatively.[15]

Consequently, human beings do not *invent* myths; they *discover* them as part of our universal unconscious. To illustrate, Rayshawn Campbell, a fifth-grade student at Flynn Park School, University City, Missouri, composed an original story which, unbeknown to him, is a variation of the Greek myth of Cronus and Zeus. The ancient version of the myth is as follows:

Cronus was now the lord of the universe. He sat on the highest mountain and ruled over heavens and earth with a firm hand. The other gods obeyed his will and early man worshiped him. This was man's Golden Age. Men lived happily and in peace with the gods and each other. They did not kill and they had no locks on their doors, for theft had not yet been invented.

But . . . Mother Earth was angry with him and plotted his downfall. She had to wait, for no god yet born was strong enough to oppose him. But she knew that one of his sons would be stronger than he, just as Cronus had been stronger than his father. Cronus knew it too, so every time his Titaness-wife Rhea gave birth, he took the newborn god and swallowed it. With all of his offspring securely inside him, he had nothing to fear.

But Rhea mourned. Her five sisters, who had married the five other Titans, were surrounded by their Titan children, while she was all alone. When Rhea expected her sixth, she asked Mother Earth to help her save the child from his father. That was just what Mother Earth had been waiting for. She gave her daughter whispered advice, and Rhea went away smiling.

As soon as Rhea had borne her child, the god Zeus, she hid him. Then she wrapped a stone in baby clothes and gave it to her husband to swallow instead of her son. Cronus was fooled and swallowed the stone, and the little god Zeus was spirited away to a secret cave on the island of Crete. Old Cronus never heard the cries of his young son, for Mother Earth let noisy earth sprites outside the cave. They made such a clatter, beating their shields with their swords, that other sounds were drowned out.[16]

Later, Zeus successfully deposed Cronus and, releasing his brothers and sisters, established the reign of the gods on Mount Olympus.

Rayshawn's story contains some remarkable similarities to this Greek tale:

Once there was a mean giant named Jim. He couldn't stand kids. He always would try to eat them. One day the kids were playing outside past their curfew. So Jim followed them home. When they got in, he waited for a while. Jim knocked and knocked again. They didn't open the door.

Jim shouted,"Let me in." The kids said,"We know it's you, Jim. So back off. Leave us alone." So he slipped behind their house and waited until their mom got home. She said,"Let me in," sweetly. They let her in.

Then Jim went to the bakery and bought some sugar. When their mom left again, Jim ate the sugar to make his voice sweeter. He went back to their house and knocked on the door. He said sweetly, "Let me in." Then they opened the door.

Jim chopped their heads off and ate their bodies. He put their heads on the post. When their mom got home she saw their heads on the post. She said, "Ooooo Jim got my babies." She heard a "Zzzz" sound and saw Jim. Immediately, she cut open his stomach took her kids' bodies out and sewed their heads back on. Then she put two big stones in Jim's stomach. When Jim woke up, he was thirsty. He went to the lake. And when he bent down, he fell into the lake, sank to the bottom, and turned into stone.[17]

Both versions focus on male authority figures who are threatened by members of the younger generation. The children are protected by the mother, so that they can fulfill their destinies. Interestingly, both tales used the same motifs—swallowing the children and the mother substituting stones for her children.

The media serve as a primary vehicle for the transmission of classic mythic tales in contemporary culture. To illustrate, the story of Hercules has been recounted countless times in the media, including the movies of the late 1950s and early 1960s (starring Steve Reeves), the 1997 Disney animated feature film, and the current popular Australian syndicated television series. A worthwhile question to consider is: *Why is the myth being presented at this time?*

A related line of inquiry explores ways in which modern adaptations depart from the original. In the contemporary Australian television version of Hercules, the hero is slimmed down, clean-shaven, and displays a sensitive side as well as his physical prowess. His speech is a curious mixture of ancient-sounding vernacular, 1960s slang ("Bummer," he comments when things go awry), and 1990s expressions. In one episode, Hercules comes up against a sorcerer who uses technology (e.g., laser weapons and airplanes) as magic to achieve his nefarious ends.

The 1997 Disney animated version of the Hercules moves the myth even further into a modern context. According to film critic Deborah Peterson, in this contemporary adaptation, Hercules is simply a boy seeking acceptance and a sense of identity:

> As a teen, Herc is a buster of a boy, taunted by bullies who call him "Jerkules" because of his unbridled strength. Herc is despondent because he doesn't fit in and his dad tells him that his real father is Zeus, the thunderbolt god. With that knowledge, Herc is soon bound for Thebes (aka "The Big Olive") where he plans to turn himself into a hero fit for immortal life with the gods.[18]

Disney animator Gerald Scarfe modeled the mythological characters after modern cultural icons, so that the classic myth was filtered through popular culture: "I kind of thought when I was doing Hercules, we thought the young Paul Newman, or even the young Elvis . . . [the female protagonist Meg is] sort of a sexy Barbara Stanwyck type."[19]

Frequently, contemporary characters have been reconfigured in the media, in the role of mythic characters. For instance, a 1996 TV commercial for Gatorade, featuring Michael Jordan, is a modern adaptation of the mythic Labors of Hercules. The spot begins with the camera moving swiftly over a flat plane, stopping at a tall, mountainous tower. This journey is accompanied by ominous, dramatic drum beats. A boy (young Michael Jordan) looks at the mountain, which suddenly is transformed into a supernatural being, with its face embedded in the rock. The mountain spirit admonishes the young man, "Don't expect too much from yourself, Michael." His ascent up the mountain is a metaphor for life's journey, as well as Michael's climb to the top of his profession. Michael swigs a bottle of Gatorade—a potion which prepares him for his adventure. As young Michael begins his journey, the mountain spirit presents the boy with a series of challenges—labors that he cannot possibly achieve: "Start on varsity . . . Ha!" "You can't play on the level at North Carolina. Be realistic." "Why go back to basketball? You'll embarrass yourself."

By including these references to Jordan's life and achievements, the storyteller/advertiser is working off of the audience's familiarity with Michael Jordan as a cultural mythic hero. The mountain spirit then tempts young Michael, trying to divert him from the selfless play that has marked him as a basketball immortal: "Forget the team! Think of yourself."

At this point the character—now the mature Michael Jordan—stops to wipe his brow as he scales these "impossible" heights. (This gesture also reminds us that achievements of this magnitude can make a person develop a terrific thirst.)

Jordan finally completes his ascent and stands on the ledge, against the sky. The camera looks up at him, triumphant. Suddenly, he is holding a bottle of Gatorade; the sunlight hits the bottle, so that the Gatorade glows with a magic power. The mountain spirit asks, "Had enough?" The next shot is a close-up of Jordan, who turns toward the camera. He looks powerful and in control. He retorts, "Just getting started." Once again, Jordan has withstood the forces that defeat normal mortals.

Embedded in this contemporary version of the ancient Hercules myth are various levels of messages. First, the commercial charts the internal journey that people must undertake, regardless of their station in life. Life is a series of labors, and it is in meeting these challenges that we grow and discover what is best in us. The audience also celebrates the indomitable human spirit, as Hercules/Jordan triumphs over natural and supernatural obstacles. Finally, of course, we have a commercial message suggesting that the triumph of Michael Jordan (and by extension, ourselves), is due to the regenerative powers of Gatorade. This advertising appeal capitalizes on (and contributes to) the mythic persona of basketball star Jordan, as a way to sell a product.

Amistad (1997) is a reconfiguration of the biblical myth of David and Goliath, in which an individual conquers the formidable forces that threaten freedom. In the biblical tale, the Philistines gathered their troops to defy the Israelites. Goliath, a warrior of great physical stature, challenged the Israelites to choose a man from among them to fight a duel. The young shepherd boy David volunteered to accept this challenge.

Earlier, David had demonstrated his valor while tending his father's sheep. Suddenly, several lions appeared and snared a ram from the flock. Undaunted, David pursued the lions, struck them with a stone, moved the ram to safety, and then killed the intruders. At the time of battle, Goliath drew his sword and approached the shepherd. Calmly, David took a stone from his scrip and casts it with his sling. The stone struck Goliath in the forehead, whereupon he fell to the ground and died. Seeing their champion defeated, the Philistines fled.

The beginning of *Amistad* establishes an association between David and the film's protagonist, Cinque (Djimon Hounsou). In a literal correlation, Cinque kills a lion to protect his Mende tribe. In an early scene, Cinque awakened to find that a lion entered his small village. Recognizing the lion as the one who previously killed two villagers, he picked up a stone and hurled it at the lion, hitting him between the eyes. The lion fell instantly to his death.

After being captured and taken prisoner on a slave ship, Cinque frees himself and his people from their chains and slays their overseers. After the Africans are arrested, Cinque's story metaphorically becomes the rock that John Quincy Adams threw at the Supreme Court to free the Mende from a return to slavery or a possible death sentence.

After two separate trials, it appears that the weapons of the law were prevailing over the Mende's battle for freedom. Cinque readies his people for their last and final battle against the Supreme Court, informing their lawyer John Quincy Adams (Anthony Hopkins), "We won't be going in there alone. . . . I will call into the past, far back to the beginning of time to beg them [my ancestors] to come and help me at the judgment. . . . They must come, for at this moment, I am the whole reason they existed at all." As the biblical David believed that this was really God's battle, Cinque looked to his ancestors to provide help and protection.

In Adams's argument before the Supreme Court judges, the lawyer explains the Mende tradition of calling on the spirits of their ancestors for wisdom and strength. He then walks over to the wall lined with portraits of America's founding fathers. After calling out their names, he informs the Supreme Court judges that perhaps it is time to call on their American ancestors for guidance. Adams declares that Americans owe their individuality, their freedom, to their ancestors. "We have been made to understand and to embrace the understanding that who we are is who we were." Thus, the wisdom and strength of Cinque's story defeats the monstrous forces of oppression and win the Mende's freedom.

Mythic Elements

Mythic elements frequently appear in media presentations. Murray maintains that mythic elements such as themes, characters, motifs, and images serve as a code for the reader, which furnishes a wealth of meaning to the text: "[The inclusion of mythic elements is] very commonly sufficient to bring the complete mythic event to the consciousness of those who are familiar with it."[20] Identifying mythic elements in media presentations can therefore enrich our understanding and appreciation of the content.

Mythic Themes

A theme refers to the central idea expressed in a narrative, whether implied or explicitly stated. Mythic themes raise issues pertaining to the human condition, as well as human beings' unique relationship to the universe. These mythic themes correspond to what Rollo May has identified as a series of *existential crises* that accompany the stages of human development. Media programs often contain mythic themes that articulate these existential crises.

Birth. Some myths focus on the miracle and mystery of birth. Myths often feature a hero whose birth has extraordinary significance (e.g., Jesus, Moses). These myths reflect human beings' efforts to assign meaning to this seemingly random act of nature. A cosmic variation of this consists of myths that attempt to explain or account for creation: both *how* and *why* the world was created. Myths also provide accounts of the origin and nature of gods.

Contact (1997) is a film in which a young woman (Jodie Foster) detects the presence of life on another planet. Much of the plot focuses on her efforts to validate her findings and then convince her male supervisor to take her (and her work) seriously. However, underlying the story is the reason that the protagonist is attracted to her work and why she is so excited by her discovery. She (and the audience) are taken back to essential questions about creation and the order of the universe.

Awakening. This stage originates in young children between the ages of five and six, when they first become aware that human beings are born of the union between man and woman. One theme related to the stage of awakening is the Oedipal longing, named after the famous Greek myth. Sigmund Freud interpreted this myth from a sexual perspective—the son's desire to eliminate his rival (father) and possess his mother. However, Carl

Jung applies a spiritual interpretation to the Oedipus myth, focusing on the image of the mother as the source of life. Within this context, the Oedipus myth responds to humans' growing awareness about their inevitable separation from the protected womb of the mother. Although separation is a part of life, this step is, at the same time, a form of death, as the individual can never again recapture the same sense of safety and connectedness to the source of life.

This existential crisis is reflected in stories in which characters must let go of loved ones as they pass away. For instance, in Disney's *Bambi* (1942), the young deer and his mother are trapped by hunters and are forced to flee. In her efforts to save her son, Bambi's mother is killed. Once he has reached safety, Bambi (and the audience) become aware of the tragedy and mourn the loss.

A derivative story involves characters who separate forever, which is a form of death-in-life. In *E.T.* (1982), the extraterrestrial's return home means that he must bid farewell to Elliott, his new earth buddy. The emotional moment of E.T.'s departure signals a form of death—as defined by a final separation. A third variation of this theme involves tales of abandonment, in which a character must cope with feelings of rejection and isolation. A comedic example of this theme is the *Home Alone* films.

Additional thematic concerns associated with this stage of awakening include:

- A statement of need and helplessness in a perilous, unnourishing, or hostile environment and the wish for an omnipotent, omniscient, and benevolent protector, provider, and director.
- Narcissism and the wish to be omnipotent and superior to others (psychic source of countless self-glorification and heroical myths).
- Curiosity and the wish to obtain an appealing graphic explanation of how babies are created.
- Dread of temptation and punishment (psychic source of numerous images of demonic [satanic] tempters, threatening indignant deities, and myths of crime and punishment [e.g. Sodom, Gomorrah, and the Deluge]).
- Collective motivations, such as fear of starvation and a consequent decline of social and regal vigor in a barren, dry environment leading to ardent wishes for the revival of fertility and of vigor (psychic source of the important death and resurrection myth).[21]

Adolescence. These mythic themes revolve around adolescents' need to assert their independence as they seek to establish their own sense of identity. Fundamental to the stage of adolescence is the drive to test taboos, or limits that have been imposed on human beings, either by nature or society. The desire to break away from one's earthly existence is expressed in the tragic myth of Icarus. Young Icarus and his father Daedalus learn to fly, by constructing wings made of feathers glued with wax. But despite his father's warning, Icarus becomes intoxicated with his new powers of flight and soars too close to the sun; in the process, the heat melts the wax, and Icarus plunges into the sea and drowns.

This existential crisis is also reflected in stories of revolt or rebellion against the established order (parents, society, or gods). Popular films of the 1950s such as *Rebel Without a Cause* with James Dean and *The Wild One,* starring Marlon Brando, focused on this existential crisis. These actors became cultural mythic icons, epitomizing teenage angst and rebellion. Although Dean and Brando were defying their parents or social institutions (police or school) in their films, the act of rebellion itself was ultimately the source of meaning in the films. At one point in *The Wild One,* an adult asks Brando, "What are you rebelling against?" Brando replies coolly, "What have you got?"

One common adolescent thematic issue appearing in both myth and media is the role of *fate verses free choice.* Classical myths like Odysseus raise questions about whether human beings are independent entities who control their own destinies, or if they are merely players who act out a script that has been written for them. In many media programs, the protagonists must carve out their own destiny in the face of a society that has already prescribed their futures. This empowerment theme underlies many advertisements that suggest that their products are key to overcoming our human limitations. . . . Nike tells us "Just do it," while the ads declare, "Gravity, you are no friend of mine."

Another theme connected to the crisis of adolescence is love and romance. Many classical myths, including Aphrodite, Cupid, and Psyche deal with the beauty and transcendent power of love, as well as its many complications—jealousy, loss of trust, and rejection. Film and television programs place a heavy emphasis on the travails of love and romance—responding to the strong adolescent market, as well as the adolescent sensibilities in adults.

Adulthood. The crisis of adulthood focuses on the ultimate acceptance of human limitations (or taboos). The Greek myth of Prometheus offers a classic example of this theme. As the gods distributed the gifts of life to the creatures of earth, humans were overlooked. Consequently, human beings had neither the strength, swiftness, or protective covering (fur or feathers) of other animals. Prometheus, took pity and stole fire from the gods to give to humans. In doing so, Prometheus brought civilization to humans. Once this was discovered, Zeus punishes Prometheus, by chaining him to a rock:

> An eagle red with blood
> Shall come, a guest unbidden to your banquet.
> All day long he will tear to rags your body,
> Feasting in fury on the blackened liver.[22]

Prometheus was doomed to suffer like the humans he befriended; for though he could see beyond his chains, he .vas confined forever.

A contemporary example of people confronting their "adult" responsibilities is the hit television series "Friends." The world of this program is populated by Generation Xers—young adults in their mid-twenties who have followed the rules for success as dictated by their parents. The introductory sequence establishes the characters and the premise of the program. The visuals are bright, fast-paced, and positive—images of New York City, mixed with shots of the characters dancing. The theme song is up-tempo as well. However, the lyrics undermine the optimistic tempo of the music, revealing a troubled subtext within the program:

> No one told you it was gonna be this way . . .
> Your job's a joke,
> You're broke,
> Your love life's DOA.
> You're always stuck in second gear.
> This isn't going to be your week, month, or even your year

In "Friends," the characters find it difficult to make the transition to adulthood. In this world of diminished expectations, these college graduates cannot find work commensurate with their educations. In one episode, Chandler (the only character who holds an executive position), is looking for a temporary secretary. Phoebe, who has been working as a masseuse, asks her friend for the position. "I can do [the job]," she pleads. It is certainly ironic that Phoebe (an educated, if ditzy Generation Xer) must convince everyone—her friends, herself, the audience—that she is qualified for the temp job.

After working for Chandler, Phoebe informs him that his employees don't like him, and that he has become an object of ridicule in the office. Chandler is devastated: "I don't get it. A month ago, these people were my friends. Just because I'm in charge doesn't mean I'm a different person. . . . I just want to . . . [be friends with them]." Chandler is uncomfortable with his new position of responsibility and longs to return to the camaraderie of adolescence.

The characters are terrified about emotional commitment as well; no one in the cast has a lasting romantic relationship. Significantly, one ongoing subtheme in the early episodes involved Ross's "secret" crush on Rachel, which operated at a junior high school level of sophistication and maturity.

The chorus of the theme song brings apparent resolution to this crisis of adulthood: "I'll be there for you . . ." This musical *denouement* is accompanied by group shots of everyone hugging. However, the latent message is that the most this world can offer is the comfort and support of friends—not as a solution to their problems, but as temporary solace and respite from their condition. Ironically, this is precisely what the program is also offering its Generation X audience—a cheap laugh and commiseration with television friends who appear to understand their plight.

Death. In this stage, human beings come to terms with their own mortality. According to Freud, human beings are both terrified and fascinated by death:

> Freud postulates that the organism has an innate tendency to revert to its initial state. This instinct, which would lead to self-destruction, has to be diverted outward by the developing organism. . . . The death instinct represents one of the two major classes or drives and motives, which—for psychoanalysts—comprise all motivational processes.[23]

A common advertising strategy involves positioning the product as a form of security. For example, sales for car phones jumped dramatically when ads began promoting the product as a security device.

Another theme rooted in this stage of life occurs as human beings finally embrace their mortality. According to Rollo May, accepting one's finitude is vital to love and compassion: "We are able to love passionately because we die."[24] Mr. Spock of "Star Trek" epitomizes this theme. Half Vulcan and half human, Spock is strongly attracted to his mortal side, which connects him to a wellspring of feelings that originate in the impermanence of human beings.

Mythic Figures

Mythic figures appear throughout media presentations. The more we understand the mythic antecedents and mythic aspect of these figures, the more we can appreciate the context and impact of their appearance in media presentations.

Sometimes media characters are taken directly from classical mythology. For example, a 1997 television ad for Mercedes-Benz depicts a winged figure racing an automobile. Although the ad makes no effort to identify the character, the wings on his hat are a clear reference to the Roman god Mercury, who was Jupiter's messenger. Added to the mythic context of the ad, the race takes place in an ancient, Roman-looking coliseum. This allusion reinforces the ad's message about the swiftness and agility of the Mercedes, which easily wins the race against Mercury. But beyond this obvious allusion to speed, the selection of Mercury in the commercial has additional implications. Mercury also was the god of commerce and the market, protector of traders such as Mercedes.

For the uninitiated in the audience, the inclusion of these mythic figures in media programming is an introduction to mythology. The audience learns to associate the winged figure with swiftness without formal instruction about Greek mythology.

Mythic Archetypes. Characters in media presentations frequently reflect mythic archetypes. According to psychologist Carl Jung, an archetype is a projection of humans' collective or universal unconscious. In its simplest terms, an archetype corresponds to the various sides of Self in human beings, representing various aspects of the psyche. All archetypes, taken together, make up the Self. The balance, or relationship between the archetypes determines the personality of an individual. The goal of Jungian psychology is to work toward the proper "constellation" of all of the archetypes to achieve a balanced personality.[25]

Archetypes appear throughout human history, serving as a projection of humans' universal experience. Over the ages, these archetypes, or aspects of Self, have been externalized in the form of mythic characters. In like fashion, archetypes are found in media presentations as projections of Jung's universal Self. These archetypes may assume many forms, or archetypal images, which are decided by the culture and the individual storyteller. Thus, Odysseus and Rocky are both archetypal images of the hero archetype.

Mythic archetypes often appear in media presentations in the form of stereotypes. One reason that media stereotypes are so readily recognizable is because they resonate within us; that is, the stereotypes reflect basic sides of the Self. This mechanism enables people to scapegoat others and, in the process, distance themselves from their own impulses.

The *hero archetype* epitomizes the best in human character and achievement. It offers an opportunity for the members of the audience to get in touch with their own heroic attributes.

Joseph Campbell has identified several categories of archetypal hero:

- *Hero as Warrior.* Myths often extol the hero's strength, athleticism, and power. However, in many myths (e.g., David and Goliath), the hero is clearly overmatched physically; however, the hero ultimately prevails, due to heroic intangibles: courage, quick-wittedness, or faith. The adventures of the warrior symbolize the inner challenges confronting all humans. To illustrate, Campbell regards myths in which medieval knights slay dragons as "Slaying the dragon in me: slaying monsters is slaying the dark things."[26]
- *Hero as Lover.* The hero and heroine also may distinguish themselves in love. Examples of young tragic love move from the Greek myth of Pyramis and Thisbe, to Shakespeare's Romeo and Juliet.
- *Hero as World Redeemer.* This mythic hero is a crusader who fights injustice and oppression. Such heroes inspire others through their idealism, selfless commitment, and willingness to risk their own lives for their cause. An example of World Redeemer found in media programming includes the character of William Wallace (Mel Gibson) in the film *Braveheart* (1995).

The Villain. The villain represents the corruption and sterility of society, and of life itself. Northrup Frye observes that villains are "associated with winter, darkness, confusion, sterility, moribund life, and old age."[27] The villain archetype appears in the form of monsters, demons, devils, evil aliens, and vampires. Villains fall into the following general categories:

> *Usurpers* seize the power, position, or rights of another, by force and without legal right or authority.
>
> *Criminals* intentionally break the law or regulations for personal gain.
>
> *Violators* disregard the wishes or preferences of another individual to violate that individual. This can involve either physical violence (e.g., assault or rape) or emotional violence.
>
> *Betrayers* breach a confidence, are disloyal, or deceive another.
>
> *Corrupters* are guilty of spiritual villainy. They are immoral, dishonest, and depraved and can contaminate others by seducing them to betray their own principles.

In myth (and media presentations), evil is consigned to objects, animals, people, and metaphysical beings, such as devils and witches. In this regard, the villain serves as a projection of an individual's own evil, impure, or weak impulses. To illustrate, some myths vilify snakes as the embodiment of evil, an example being the Adam and Eve story. This externalization of evil enables people to distance themselves from these very disturbing impulses within themselves.

The Shadow Figure represents the defects of man's conscious personality. Jung declares, "[The shadow] represents counter-tendencies in the unconscious, and in certain cases by a sort of second personality, of a puerile and inferior character."[28] Like all archetypes, however, the shadow is not an absolute figure, but embodies characteristics that are attractive, though threatening. Jung explains,

> He is both subhuman and superhuman, a bestial and divine being, whose chief and most alarming characteristic is his unconsciousness. . . . The trickster is a primitive cosmic being of divine-animal nature, on the one hand superior to man because of his superhuman qualities, and on the other hand inferior to him because of his unreason and unconsciousness.[29]

The counterpart of the Shadow archetype in the media is the stereotype of the black male. The white man represses, or rather oppresses the black man, who embodies the inferior, puerile side of his own personality. Once the characteristics of the shadow have been displaced onto blacks, the white man safely can assume the role of the superior member of society. Thus, the black's "inferior" nature provides an important antithesis for white society.

The Mentor represents that aspect of Self that is in supreme authority. This superior master and teacher is an ideal figure, the prototype of order and rationality. Christopher Vogler points out that in many myths and media programs, the mentor provides support, motivation, inspiration, and guidance in the course of the hero's journey:

> The relationship between hero and Mentor is one of the most common themes in mythology, and one of the richest in its symbolic value. It stands for the bond between parent and child, teacher and student, doctor and patient, god and man. The Mentor may appear as a wise old wizard [*Star Wars*], a tough drill sergeant [*Officer and a Gentleman*], or a grizzled old boxing coach [*Rocky*].[30]

The mentor often voices the central theme or insight of the narrative. Vogler points out that archetypes often fulfill specific functions within a narrative.[31] At a pivotal moment in the narrative, the mentor expresses a revelation, prophecy, or counsel that the hero (and audience as well) should heed. The hero's success is determined by his/her ability to absorb and apply the counsel of the mentor. The hero may be a *reluctant agent* who requires the assistance of a mentor to act. In *Star Wars* (1977) Luke Skywalker is initially afraid to commit himself to the spiritual leap of faith necessary, to realize his potential as a warrior until he eventually heeds the advice of Obi-Wan Kenobi. However, at some point in the narrative the hero must leave the mentor and venture out on his/her own.

The Anima represents the feminine side of the Self. This archetype corresponds to humans' emotional nature. She is personified in dreams by images of women ranging in nature from harlot and seductress to divine wisdom and spiritual guide. She is the Eros principle in men. Projection of the anima accounts for an individual's falling in love. A man's anima development is reflected in how he relates to others.[32]

Jung describes the anima as the "feminine and *chthonic* part of the soul."[33] Significantly, chthonic is defined as "designating to, or relating to, gods or spirits of the underworld." This suggests that the anima is connected to death and dissolution. Jung elaborates:

> The anima is a factor of the utmost importance in the psychology of a man wherever emotions and affects are at work. She intensifies, exaggerates, falsifies, mythologizes all emotional relations with his work and with other people of both sexes. The resultant fantasies and entanglements are all her doing. When the anima is strongly constellated, she softens man's character and makes him touchy, irritable, moody, jealous, vain, and unadjusted.[34]

Thus, while the anima is in many respects attractive, she is not to be trusted. The charm of this figure obscures a fundamental weakness of character and lack of stability.

However, according to Jung, a permanent loss of the anima within an individual is equally threatening, resulting in: "a diminution of vitality, or flexibility, and of human kindness. The result, as a rule, is premature rigidity, crustiness, fanaticism, one-sidedness, obstinacy, pedantry, or else resignation, weariness, sloppiness, irresponsibility, and finally a childishness, with a tendency to alcohol."[35] Thus, Jung observes that although the anima is essential to the integration of the individual, this "feminine" side of Self is perceived as dangerous.

The archetype of the anima can be found in the media stereotype of women. Members of male-dominated society deal with these conflicting emotions within themselves by assigning prescribed external sex roles to this side of Self. Numerous female figures in media presentations are depicted as temptresses who distract men from the purity of their moral construct, dilute their strength, and divert them from missions. Women are therefore kept at a distance by men, who harbor fears concerning the anima within themselves.

Threshold Guardians are characters who attempt to block the path of the hero and test his/her powers. Threshold guardians often assume the form of henchmen, bodyguards, gunslingers, mercenaries, guards, doormen, or lieutenants of the chief antagonist.

Threshold guardians also may be well-intentioned supporters who, nevertheless, oppose the hero taking a radically different course of action. In this case, the threshold guardian represents our own uncertainties as we contend with change. Vogler explains,

> These Guardians may represent the ordinary obstacles we all face in the world around us: bad weather, bad luck, prejudice, oppression, or hostile people. But on a deeper psychological level they stand for our internal demons: the neuroses, emotional scars, vices, dependencies, and self-limitations that hold back our growth and progress.[36]

The Threshold Guardian appears when the main characters are faced with critical choices. For example, in the classic film *Marty* (1955), the main character (Ernest Borgnine) is a lonely guy who is locked in a perpetual adolescence, living at home and hanging out with his friends. When he finally meets a young woman, Clara Snyder (Betsy Blair), both his mother and best friend are threatened by Marty's "desertion" and discourage Marty from seeing her again. Marty must face these Threshold Guardians (who also voice Marty's own self-doubts) before he is prepared to follow his heart and make a date to see Clara again.

The Herald brings a challenge to the hero and announces the coming of significant changes. In Greek mythology, Hermes was the messenger god, dispatching messages from Zeus. Vogler explains,

> Typically, in the opening phase of a story, heroes have "gotten by" somehow. They have handled an imbalanced life through a series of defenses or coping mechanisms. Then all at once some new energy enters the story that makes it impossible for the hero to simply get by any longer. A new person, condition, or information shifts the hero's balance, and nothing will ever be the same. A decision must be made, action taken, the conflict faced.[37]

Heralds may be manifested as dreams, visions, oracles, or foreshadowing devices. The Herald also may signal the *need* for change. Vogler notes, "Something deep inside us knows when we are ready to change and sends us a messenger."[38]

The Victim refers to weak or vulnerable characters who succumb to the forces of the world, the will of others, and their own self-destructive tendencies. This figure is a projection of the weaknesses within human beings.

This figure is deficient, either morally, physically, or emotionally, and frequently is in need of protection by an outside agent—either a hero or divine intervention. A variation of this figure is the character who has been victimized by forces outside of his/her control, such as fate or injustice. Frequently, female characters are assigned the role of victim in media programs, reflecting cultural attitudes with respect to the female gender.

The Divine Child (*Puer Aeternus*) corresponds to the infantile side of self. Numerous myths feature a child as hero, including Hercules, Moses, and Chandragupta (fourth century B.C.), the founder of the Hindu Maurya dynasty. This character type is marked as special at birth, epitomizing the nobility and divinity within all human beings. Steven Walker observes that this archetype reflects both immaturity and spiritual purity:

> For Jung, what is "infantile, childish, too youthful in ourselves" is also what carries the promise of future development: "the Puer Aeternus means really your most devoted attempt to get at your own truth, your most devoted enterprise in the creation of your future; your greatest moral effort."[39]

The Divine Child appears prominently in contemporary media presentations, reinforcing the American cultural myth of youth culture (see discussion of American cultural myths later in this chapter). Contemporary media programming suggests that the contemporary culture has stifled this side of Self. Programs such as the film *Big* (1988) reflect a universal longing for the Divine Child, along with a skepticism that the adult aspects of Self are capable of finding answers to questions of meaning and happiness in modern society.

Occasionally the function of a character will change during the course of a narrative. Vogler refers to these characters as *Shapeshifters:* "Shapeshifters change in appearance or mood, and are difficult for the hero and audience to pin down. They may mislead the hero or keep him/her guessing, and their loyalty or sincerity is often in question."[40]

In mythology, wizards, witches, and ogres are often shapeshifters. Shapeshifters often alter their appearance through disguises or physical transformation. For example, in *The Wizard of Oz* (1939) Dorothy's friends are able to infiltrate the castle of the Wicked Witch by donning the uniforms of her guards. Characters may also assume emotional masks by hiding their true natures or motives.

During the course of a narrative these characters may shift from one archetype to another reflecting different sides of Self. For example, in *Rocky* (1976), Mickey the trainer is a Wise Old Man archetype. However, he temporarily assumes the role of the Threshold Guardian by taking the fighter's locker away and, in the process, challenging Rocky to realize his own potential. At times, villains serve as Heralds, who either issue a direct challenge to the hero or dupe the hero into becoming involved in a particular situation.

Shapeshifters may also fluctuate within the dual nature of the archetype. For instance, it may be difficult for the hero (and the audience) to determine whether a female character represents the positive aspects of the anima (emotion, warmth, nurturing), or the negative attributes of the archetype (temptress or destroyer). This ambiguity has a dramatic function, introducing doubt and suspense into the story. Vogler declares, "In some stories, it's the task of the hero to figure out which side, positive or negative, he is dealing with."[41]

Narrative Elements

Because myths and media presentations share many narrative elements, the media are particularly well suited to deliver myths to modern audiences. Recognizing mythic narrative elements in media presentations can be a useful way to uncover meaning in a media presentation.

Mythic Plots

A plot is a planned series of events in a narrative, progressing through a struggle of opposing forces to a climax and a conclusion. There is a close relationship between plot and theme. A theme is an abstract idea that is given expression or representation through a character or plot. Thus, the plot (the structured sequence of action) in Odysseus consists of the hero's quest to return home. The theme of the myth, however, involves the hero's search for identity; it is only when he fully discovers who he is that he is ready to return home.[42]

According to Ronald B. Tobias, a finite number of mythic plots have been retold countless times, from days of antiquity to modern media presentations: "We use the same plots today that were used in the world's oldest literature. . . . If you found a plot that had never been used before, you're into an area that is outside the realm of shared human behavior. Originality doesn't apply to the plots themselves but to how we present those plots."[43] Thus, many of the narratives in media programming are incarnations of fundamental mythic plots, which helps to explain their essential appeal.

One common mythic plot is the *quest,* in which characters embark on a journey at the beginning of the story. Examples include Sir Galahad's Quest for the Holy Grail and *Indiana Jones and the Temple of Doom* (1984). Joseph Campbell explains,

These deeply significant motifs of the perils, obstacles and good fortunes of the way, we shall find inflected through the following pages in a hundred forms. The crossing first of the open sewer, then of the perfectly clear river flowing over grass, the appearance of the willing helper at the critical moment, and the high, firm ground beyond the final stream (the Earthly Paradise, the Land over Jordan): these are the everlastingly recurrent themes of the wonderful song of the soul's high adventure.[44]

Throughout the ages, the quest has been a vehicle for mythic themes dealing with the search for identity and truth (see discussion on mythic themes). Linda Seger explains that the quest is an essential growth experience for the main character: "As a rule, the hero is transformed in the course of his journey. As we watch the story unfold, we may think of our own heroic journeys. . . . The journey of the story may also remind us of our own inner journeys, as we seek value and meaning in our lives."[45]

The audience also participates in this quest, making discoveries with the characters during the course of the journey. Often, what emerges as consequential is the quest *itself*; that is, that the relationships, growth, and commitment to the goal is ultimately more meaningful than the actual attainment of the goal itself.

The quest plot frequently appears in stories that focus on the adolescent search for identity (see section on mythic themes). An example from classic mythology is Odysseus's quest to return home after the Trojan War. According to the myth, an impulsive lack of respect for the gods (surely an adolescent act), provoked the gods into orchestrating events, so that it took nearly ten years before Odysseus saw his home. Thematically, Odysseus was not yet ready to assume the mantle of adulthood. In the course of his journey, Odysseus faced a series of trials which tested his resolve and fortitude. Odysseus was forced to contend with the issue of identity, assuming a series of disguises in order to make his way from place to place. Ten years later, he arrived home as an adult, ready to assume his role as King of Ithaca and husband to Penelope. He finally cast off his disguises and vanquished his enemy, who had usurped his throne and threatened his wife.

The *death and resurrection* plot occurs when the hero suffers apparent death, only to return later in the story (e.g., the story of Christ). This plot reflects the cycle of nature: life, death, and resurrection. In media presentations, regeneration may take the form of a wedding, birth, or triumph over villains. Many media presentations feature a "comeback" by a character who has been initially defeated, a la Rocky. Comebacks signify an internal, spiritual renewal, linked to the character's discovery of moral truth or recommitment to the values that enable the hero to succeed. A variation of this plot occurs when the hero's reputation is tarnished. He is either branded as a coward (e.g., *High Noon*) or a fraud (e.g., *The Natural*). In either case, the hero suffers a death-in-life, only to reemerge triumphant at the denouement of the film.

A related plot can be termed the *harrowing of hell,* in which the hero willingly confronts death for the public good. This plot reveals the courage and strength of character of the hero as he/she voluntarily encounters death. At the same time, this plot puts the audience in touch with their own deepest sense of dread and terror as they watch the hero's descent into hell.

In an interview with Bill Moyers, Joseph Campbell discusses the harrowing of hell in *Star Wars* (1977):

> *M:* My favorite scene was when [the heroes] were in the garbage compactor, and the walls were closing in, and I thought, That's like the belly of the whale that swallowed Jonah. . . . Why must the hero do that?
>
> *C:* It's a descent into the dark. Psychologically, the whale represents the power of life locked in the unconscious. Metaphorically, water is the unconscious, and the creature in the water is the life or energy of the unconscious, which has overwhelmed the conscious personality and must be disempowered, overcome and controlled.
>
> In the first stage of this kind of adventure, the hero leaves the realm of the familiar, over which he has some measure of control, and comes to a threshold, let us say the edge of a lake or sea, where a monster of the abyss comes to meet him. . . . In a story of the Jonah type, the hero is swallowed and taken into the abyss to be later resurrected—a variant of the death-and-resurrection theme. The conscious personality here has come in touch with a charge of unconscious energy which it is unable to handle and now must suffer all the trials and revelations of a terrifying night-sea journey, while learning how to come to terms with this power of the dark and emerge, at last, to a new way of life. . . .
>
> You see, consciousness thinks it's running the shop. But it's a secondary organ of a total human being, and it must not put itself in control. It must submit and serve the humanity of the body. When it does put itself in control, you get a man like Darth Vader in *Star Wars*, the man who goes over to the consciously intentional side.[46]

Circe plots deal with the implications of change. One version of this mythic plot involves a person's physical transformation, as in Odysseus, when the sorceress Circe turned Odysseus's crew into pigs. Another variation involves a person undergoing significant change in social, culture, or material status.

In the *imminent annihilation* plot, the characters (and audience) become aware of an impending catastrophe. The emphasis immediately shifts to individuals' personal responses to the upcoming crisis. The crisis brings people closer together, enabling them to admit things that they would otherwise choose to remain unspoken. The approaching crisis also brings out the best and worst qualities in human beings. Often the realizations that occur as people prepare to meet the approaching crisis enables them to successfully meet this challenge. In *Independence Day* (1996), the beginning of the film establishes the impending invasion by the aliens. The remainder of the film examines the personal impact of this catastrophe on the individual characters, the United States, and world at large.

Adam and Eve plots feature stories of temptation and corruption. These stories examine how the average person can be tempted by sex, power, or money to commit immoral or antisocial acts. Tobias explains,

> The story of temptation is the story of the frailty of human nature. If to sin is human, it is human to give in to temptation. But our codes of behavior have established a price for yielding to temptation. The penalties range from one's own personal guilt to a lifetime without parole in the state penitentiary. . . . The battle rages: yes and no, pro and con, why and why not. This is conflict, and the tension between opposites creates the tension. Knowing what to do and actually doing it are sometimes oceans apart.[47]

Paradise plots are an extension of the Adam and Eve plot. In paradise plots, the characters have been in harmony with nature (as well as with their own natures). However, something has upset this harmonious condition, and the characters are cast out of paradise. Paradise plots focus on the characters' efforts to return to an earthly paradise. Paradise myths also symbolize the characters' efforts to regain the original states of innocence and harmony that they have lost.

Mythic Figures: Other mythic plots that appear in media presentations include the following:

- *King Midas*. In myth, Midas was a king who worshiped wealth above all things and got his wish that everything he touched would turn to gold. But the "Golden Touch" proved fatal when his food, his clothes, even his loved ones, became dead gold under his hand. King Midas, like many legends, points to the moral that spiritual, not materialistic, goals are, in the end, the most satisfying.
- *Faust*. This is the story of a man's pact with the devil, exchanging his ultimate salvation for the earthly pleasures of youth, wealth, and love. There are at least two conventional endings to the Faust plot: one in which Satan cashes in on his contract with the damned; and the other in which the central character is saved by the love or self-sacrifice of a virtuous woman, whose purity defeats the powers of darkness.

- *Frankenstein.* The tale about the coming of the machine gave us this plot–theme of "the creator destroyed by his creation." That man should not play God is a powerful dramatic premise.
- *The Fatal Flaw.* "In each man are the possible seeds of his own destruction," which is another way of saying that mankind, being human and mortal, is capable of evil as well as good. This plot was perhaps first told describing a physical flaw, as the myth of Achilles's heel. The Greek hero's mother, attempting to make her son invulnerable, dips him as a child in a magic stream holding him by his heel. But she neglects to bathe that part of his body and so provides his enemies with a way of destroying him. Told in a more sophisticated version, it can unfold as the story of how alcoholism, drug addiction, or any overpowering obsession can bring about a person's downfall.
- *The Fatal Choice.* This plot applies to almost any story in which a wrong or right turn or decision can affect a long chain of events and circumstances.
- *Rivalry.* The original murder plot was Cain and Abel in the Bible. Murder can be told as a suspense or detective story, or it can be the basis of absorbing human drama in which the question of man's responsibility for the welfare of his fellow man is questioned: "Am I my brother's keeper?"
- *The Pact with God.* This plot generally unfolds in one of two ways: A person faced with impending disaster or death vows that if he is saved he will "turn over a new leaf" and be a good man or woman for the rest of his life. The conflict arises when his prayer is answered but he is confronted with a number of temptations that try his character severely. The other usual variation tells of the dedicated man or woman of God confronted with a strong motivation or desire to get out of holy vows and return to the "world."
- *Beauty and the Beast.* In a "Beauty and the Beast" story, a beautiful girl is able, by taking pity on a frightful beast, to transform him into a handsome prince. The moral here is that the eyes of love can make all things beautiful.
- *Damon and Pythias Classic "Friendship" Story.* "Damon and Pythias" illustrates this plot, in which a friend may, or at least offers to, give up his life and fortune for his beloved companion, and the complications arising therefrom. It may be a war story of two service-men or it may be the story of another kind of severe testing of a close relationship between two men or even two women.
- *David and Goliath.* The story of how the "little guy" who, small in stature (or position) but great of heart, wit, and courage, defeats brute

strength in a giant bully points to a heartening moral. The power of "brains versus brawn" in the overcoming of brutality or unreasoning strength by ingenuity and valor is part of man's history as well as his folk literature. The overthrow of a tyrant by a seemingly helpless people would be another application of this tale.

- *The Triangle.* This is perhaps the oldest and most reliable of all plots dating back to the story of Adam and Eve and the Serpent (who in some versions is a woman named "Lilith").
- *The "Savior"(or "Mysterious Stranger").* The story of Jesus is unique, yet it has been retold in other terms and other circumstances. "Mr. X" in soap operas, or the "mysterious stranger" who comes out of nowhere, solves problems, and disappears into nowhere, is an absorbing concept.[48]
- *Revenge* plots focus on "retaliation by the protagonist against the antagonist, for real or imagined injury."[49] These plots deal with issues of civil verses "higher" justice, individual culpability, and the self-destructive aspects of revenge.

Mythic Motifs

A motif is a recurrent thematic element, such as an idea, symbol, or incident, employed in narratives. Motifs appear in both myths and media presentations. Understanding the significance and context of these motifs can enrich one's understanding and appreciation of media text.

In the *personification* motif, objects, plants, animals, and gods are endowed with human features, emotions, personalities, and speech. Thus, figures like Mickey Mouse or Barney assume human characteristics. Even in cases in which they cannot speak, animals like Flipper and Lassie seemingly possess human intelligence and emotions. By making nonhumans act in human ways, audiences are better able to understand the motives and sensibilities of the world at large. This device also establishes a comfortable distance from which myths can comment on human issues and concerns. Science fiction films have extended the personification motif to include aliens; for instance, creatures in "Star Trek," despite their cosmetic differences, operate on a human level. In some science fiction programs, technology has been personified as well. In the *Star Wars* films, the droid, R2–D2, and C-3P0 maintain an all-too-human relationship, bickering and worrying about each other.

The mythic motif of *magic* assumes an extraordinary world of possibilities that transcend natural laws, logic, and human limitation. As Sir James George Frazer notes, magic is a form of wish fulfillment: "A dramatic representation of the natural processes which [human beings] wish to facilitate; for it is a familiar tenet of magic that you can produce any desired effect by merely imitating it."[50]

Magicians such as Merlin are shamans or mystics who use magical powers to see into the future and influence events to promote the welfare of the human community. However, magic also has a darker, more dangerous side. Villains sometimes employ magic to achieve their own self-serving ends or to wreak havoc on the heroes. For instance, Odysseus's adventures led him to the Island of Dawn, which was inhabited by the sorceress Circe. She turned his crew into swine, and it required all of Odysseus's cunning to convince her to restore them to human form.

Occasionally, humans attempt to use magic and, in the process, threaten the natural order; being human, they are ill-equipped to control this power. Examples include Pandora or the Russian fairy tale "The Sorcerer and His Apprentice," which later appeared in the Disney film *Fantasia* (1940).

Magic is a common motif in media programming. One reason that magic is prevalent in media presentations is simply because film and television can produce the illusion of magic. Futuristic technology now has assumed the function of the magic wand. For example, in "Star Trek" people "magically" disappear as they are beamed from one locale to another.

The entertainment sensibility of media admits to the possibility of magic through the willing suspension of disbelief. In the world of media, horses talk, dandruff shampoos make you popular, and the cavalry always arrives on time. Even the technology of the media is "magical"; at the end of a scene, the people and surroundings disappear, replaced by new images.

Significantly, in films such as *Hocus Pocus* (1993), it is the young people who recognize the existence of magic, since they have not yet closed their minds to the paranormal possibilities of life.

Prophecy is a motif in which predictions foreshadow the events of the story. In many classic myths, prophecies are expressed through an oracle— which can refer to either the transmitter of the prophecy or the shrine at which prophecies are made known. Oracles are divine in origin and therefore are regarded as reliable sources of information. However, the prophecies are often presented as enigmatic statements or allegories; the exact meaning behind the prophecy only becomes clear as the story unfolds. In media presentations, an oracle frequently assume more pedestrian forms, such as a letter or a mysterious stranger who provides a clue about upcoming events in the story.

In entertainment media programs, an omen or foreshadowing of events often occurs in the introduction of the presentation. As in the case of *Jaws*

(1975), the music provides an ongoing reminder of the original omen. In a more literal sense, the introduction of media programs such as print or broadcast news provides a "foreshadowing" of what will be covered, as well as the order in which the information is presented. In newspapers, the lead paragraph provides a summary of what the article will substantiate, in more detail. The introduction often also serves as a microcosm of the story, establishing the premise as well as specifying the setting, characters, and situation. The body of the narrative, then, is the fulfillment of the prophecy presented at the beginning.

Mythic Symbols

Mythic symbols operate as a language that, besides being universally understandable, provides a way for individuals to understand and share their experience. According to psychoanalytic theory, mythic symbols originate within the human imagination as a manifestation of the collective unconscious, and thus have a shared meaning for the audience.

The *circle* has a mystical quality, representing the endless, cyclical conception of time (represented, for example, by the zodiac and clock faces). This shape has direction and is complete; as a result, it is associated with endlessness and wholeness. In many cultures, the circle is a symbol of the sun and, as a result, stands for warmth and life.

However, while the circle joins people and things together, it also separates, setting objects apart (e.g., a "social circle"). In that respect, the circle represented protection in ancient civilizations. Stonehenge and Avebury are examples of ancient use of the circle to mark the boundary of a sacred area. Similarly, a Babylonian rite involved laying a circle of flour around a person's sickbed to keep demons away.

The circle was also used by magicians in medieval Europe as a way to delineate sacred space:

> [T]he circle is not only intended to keep something out but also to keep something in—the magical energy which the magicians will summon up from within themselves in the course of the ceremony. . . . If it were not for the circle the energy would flow off in all directions and be dissipated. The circle keeps it inside a small area and so concentrates it. The same motive lies behind the circle of people who link their hands at a seance.[51]

According to Eva C. Hangen, the circle has a universal significance that can be traced through a variety of cultural artifacts:

- *Circle of fire.* Monastic chastity, magic, inviolability.
- *Wedding ring.* Continuing devotion and love.

- *Four circles linked to a fifth, larger one.* The words of wisdom.
- *Two serpents entwined into a ring* (Mexico). Time without end.
- *A circle separating two serpents* (China). The two Principles claiming the universe.[52]

(For more discussion on the significance of shape, see Chapter 5.)

A *reflected surface* such as a mirror is often employed to reveal an individual's unexplored self or inner secrets, furnishing knowledge not yet revealed. An example of this image is the evil Queen's looking glass in *Snow White*, which expresses the truth that the Queen cannot admit to herself. In some myths, a reflected surface serves as a source of prophecy, foreshadowing later events in the story.

In myth (and media), the *primal elements of nature*—fire, water, and air—may hold a fundamental significance. Fire can have a positive or negative connotation, depending on context. Fire can represent evil, as in the fires of hell. However, fire also can symbolize knowledge, power, and enlightenment. In the Greek myth of Prometheus, fire was the element which distinguished humans from other animals. Fire also can be used as a defense against forces of evil (witches) or predators (animals).

As a primal element, water is associated with birth (the water in the womb), and the origin of species (the primordial swamp). In addition, water is a sacred element representing purification. Examples include Catholic Holy Water and the biblical story of Noah and the flood. Water also symbolizes death and rebirth. Baptism is a ritual in which a person undergoes spiritual regeneration by being immersed in water.

Ancient myths divide the universe into three *cosmic spheres:* hell, earth, and heaven. In like fashion, locations on earth often are endowed with a symbolic significance that derives from their proximity to these cosmic zones. Places located at great heights situate human beings close to heaven. Consequently, scenes in which the characters experience a revelation or epiphany often occur on rooftops, balconies, ladders, staircases, towers, or mountain-tops. These elevated areas often provide the setting in which the climax and denouement of the plot take place.

Conversely, lower recesses of the earth are closest to hell; as a result, it is often in these settings that the most sordid manifestations of the human mind and spirit take place. In Quentin Tarantino's film *Pulp Fiction* (1995), Butch (Bruce Willis) is a professional boxer who has been ordered to throw a boxing match; instead, he double-crosses his boss, Marcellus pockets the money he has bet on himself, and prepares to skip town. But as luck would have it, Butch literally runs into Marseilles as the underworld leader is crossing the street.

Marseilles chases Butch into a pawn shop, where the clerk stops the altercation. But then, in a shocking turn of events, the clerk takes them prisoner, forcing them downstairs to the recesses of the cellar. There they are bound and gagged, and Marcellus is sodomized. This scene is disturbing to the characters (and to the audience as well); just as we think that Tarantino's characters could not be more evil, we are introduced to new depths of depravity.

Cultural Myths

Cultural myths are a series of beliefs tied to self-concept; how a people or group sees itself. Examining cultural myths can provide insight into the attitudes and preoccupations that define a society.

Each culture has its own version of mythic tales that address universal mythic themes. Comparing the versions of these universal mythic themes can be a useful way to identify differences between cultures. To illustrate, creation myths are common in nearly all cultures. However, in the Judeo-Christian version, God was preeminent and supreme, existing before the universe. The Book of Genesis declares that He created the heaven and earth in six days, and then He rested. In contrast, Babylonian myth reflects a different conception of divinity, in that the universe preceded the existence of the gods. According to the Babylonian myth, the merging of sweet water (Apsu) with salt water (Tiamat) gave birth to the gods.... Considering Babylon's arid climate, it is not surprising that water was equated with life.

Norse mythology takes yet another perspective on creation. The Norse creation myth focuses on a human-driven world, very dark in orientation, in which the end of the world has already been foretold. According to Norse myth, the fusion of two contrasting elements, fire and ice, created Ymir, the Frost Giant, who had a human form. The giants then produced a new race of gods. The gods conspired to murder their progenitor and used his body to make the earth and the seas. Significantly, in this myth, the gods are not immortal; the gods are created by mortal beings (giants), rather than the other way around. And unlike the two other versions of the creation myth, the Norse gods were not immortal; for the prophecy declared that the gods would die when the giants and demons rose against them.

At times, classical myths are adapted by a culture to provide explanation and meaning within a cultural context. To illustrate, Foster R. McCurley observes that the myth of Adam has been reconfigured into an American cultural myth:

> [The Americanization of the myth of Adam] . . . portrays the American as the innocent primal human, possessing virtually unlimited potential and set at the

beginning of history. This view of Adam, of course, is based on the biblical story of Genesis 2, and does not include the story of rebellion and limitation which follows on its heels in Genesis 3.[53]

Finally, each culture develops its own set of myths, which expresses its predominant concerns and preoccupations. Today, the media has assumed a vital role in the transmission of cultural myths. Through countless hours of watching westerns on film and television, American audiences have become acquainted with the California gold rush, the stand at the Alamo, the battle of Little Big Horn, and the gunfight at the OK Corral. Even if these stories are not factually accurate, they contribute to the myth about the settling of the American West.

Cultural myths also can reveal shifts in societal attitudes, behaviors, values, and preoccupations. For example, situation comedies of the 1950s such as "Leave it to Beaver" and "Ozzie and Harriet" presented an ideal world, in which the nuclear family was the center—both in terms of activity and as the locus of identity.

Following the disruption of World War II, the 1950s were characterized by a longing for stability—a return to normalcy. The 1950s culture valued convention and conformity.

In contemporary sitcoms like "Married with Children" and "The Simpsons," the families are dysfunctional, and the parents' shortcomings impede the children's efforts to grow into well-adjusted human beings. The humor of these programs is based on the audience's familiarity with the cultural myth of the ideal family, acknowledging that the world has changed since the 1950s.

American Cultural Myths

American culture has a rich tradition of cultural myths, which have been reinforced and perpetuated through the media. The *New World Myth* stems from the "discovery" of America by Europeans in the fifteenth century. The New World became a symbol of innocence and hope, in contrast to the tired civilization of Western Europe. The downside of this cultural myth is that Americans display a shocking ignorance and contempt for history. For many Americans, life began with the discovery of the New World.

Manifest Destiny is an extension of the cultural myth of the New World. As the new "chosen people," Americans regard themselves as the standard-bearers of a new civilization. The cultural myth of manifest destiny was the philosophical foundation of the Monroe Doctrine, a political policy originating in the nineteenth century, which held that the United States was the guardian of the Western hemisphere and had both the right and the duty to expand throughout the North American continent. Today, the American news media reinforces this myth of manifest destiny. The amount of international coverage in newspapers and television is minuscule, and the majority of international coverage focuses on allies of the United States or on international news items that directly affect America.

The Mythic Frontier is also an extension of the New World myth. Once again, America offered the prospect of a fresh beginning as the settlers spread west in the nineteenth century. According to Frederick Jackson Turner, the mythic frontier is characterized by "restless energy, individualism, self-reliance, the bounteousness and exuberance which comes with freedom."[54] Having shed the vestiges of civilization, man was free of corruption. This myth was essentially democratic; instead of status being determined by social class, success was based on innate qualities—courage, imagination, determination, honesty, and integrity. The myth of the frontier was also associated with abundance and opportunity. America was blessed with seemingly boundless resources. Farmers would use up a patch of land, burn it, and then move on.

Over time, the mythic frontier evolved into the Myth of the Old West. As depicted in countless novels, films, radio, and television programs, the mythic west generally was set between 1865 (the end of the American Civil War) and 1890. In the face of changes in American culture during the twentieth century, the myth of the frontier has remained strong. The western myth has been incorporated into other genres, such as science fiction (the starship Enterprise exploring "the final frontier"), and the detective program. Western heroes now ride motorcycles, trucks, or convertibles rather than horses.

The Myth of Progress is predicated on a faith that life can get better. In the New World, change (as opposed to tradition) was accepted as a way of life. Immigrants worked diligently so that their children could go to college and find material success. For years, technological innovations improved the comfort level of Americans. Scientific discoveries extended the lifespan of the average citizen. Advertising has responded to this myth by promoting products as "new and improved." These ads link the product to the cultural myth; the message is that new will be improved and that we should purchase a new product because it will be better.

However, Rollo May sees some dangers in what he refers to as "the seduction of the new."[55]

> [T]his addiction to change can lead to superficiality and psychological emptiness. . . . This compulsion toward change can be an effort to escape responsibility, Self, "the anxiety of the human paradox and the anxiety of death." . . . The price for this evasion is a deep loneliness and a sense of isolation.[56]

The Horatio Alger Myth has become emblematic of the American Dream. Horatio Alger was an author of juvenile fiction whose books celebrated the accomplishments of young boys who achieved success through hard work and perseverance. The Reverend Andrew Greeley explains,

> [The Horatio Alger myth] is essentially a breaking with the finite conditions of earthly [really, working-class] life so that one can transcend oneself and scale the heights. . . . [It] symbolizes the desire of all men to be able to rise out of their finite existence. Is the "rags to riches" myth so very different from the magic flight of the god king or the seven steps of Buddha?[57]

The Horatio Alger myth contains a very optimistic message about individuals achieving success by following the American Dream. However, this myth can have negative implications as well. The Horatio Alger myth celebrates the fundamental democratic principle of America—not that everyone will *be* successful, but that everyone has a *chance* to make it in America (no matter how great the odds). The Alger myth provides a rationale for the preservation of the status quo by minimizing the effort required for minorities to overcome the various cultural hurdles. Individual members of subcultures who manage to succeed are offered as proof that the system works for all. (For further discussion, see chapter 1.)

The *All-Sufficiency of Love* holds that romantic love is a mystical force that is essential to a person's self-esteem, identity, and existence. Conversely, loss of love is equated with loss of Self, so that maintaining a relationship—any relationship—is critical to a person's very survival.

Popular song titles provide insight into the American myth of the All-Sufficiency of Love, including the following:

- "There's No Living Without Your Loving"
- "You Are My Everything"
- "You Are My Sunshine"
- "All You Need Is Love"
- "One Hand One Heart"
- "Can't Help Falling in Love"
- "Everything I Do I Do It for You"
- "The Only One"
- "You Got It All"
- "Can't Smile Without You"

The Creation of New Cultural Myths

As societies evolve, new cultural myths emerge, which are then reflected, reinforced, and promoted through the media. For instance, over the last fifty years, the UFO tale has emerged as an American cultural myth. Numerous stories have circulated about the existence of unidentified flying objects, most notably the alleged crash of an alien spacecraft in Roswell, New Mexico, in 1947. A Gallup Poll conducted in May 1997, found that 42 percent of American college graduates believe that flying saucers have visited Earth in some form—up from 30 percent twenty years earlier. This preoccupation with UFOs continues today with the popularity of television's "The X-Files" and feature films such as *Independence Day* (1997) and *Contact* (1997).

Despite the distinctive embellishments of individual UFO stories, the essential structure of the UFO myth is uniform, reflecting a constant set of questions, issues, and concerns. Vladimir Propp's morphology is useful in identifying a unifying structure in the UFO myth. Propp dissected the fairy tale as a genre, divesting it of its individual embellishments in order to identify its skeletal formula. He then traced the sequence of elements in a story to discover the basic structure common to this genre of tales. Propp found that the number of structural elements, or "functions" known to the fairy tale is limited and complete. Each function may contain a number of alternatives, which provides variety within the stories. For example, Function IV is entitled, "The Villain Attempts to Deceive His Victim in Order to Take Possession of Him or of His Belongings." However, three general plot alternatives are available under this general heading: (1) The Villain Proceeds to Act by the Direct Application of Magical Means; (2) The Villain Uses Persuasion; and (3) The Villain Employs Other Means of Deception or Coercion. The basic structure of the narrative is also subject to some degree of variation. Some functions may be omitted from a tale, while the order of the other functions remains the same. At times, the sequence of a tale is rearranged, and interpolated episodes occasionally are inserted in the middle of a tale, complicating the plot.[58]

Seen in this framework, the essential structure of the UFO myth is as follows:

I.   Introduction
    A. Background
    B. Establishing Truthfulness/Veracity of the Account
II. Circumstances Leading to the Sighting
    A. Temporal-Spatial Determination (Time, Day, Location)

    B. Weather Conditions
    C. Status of Protagonist
      1. Personal Background
      2. Accompaniment (Alone/In a Group)
      3. Activity Preceding Sighting
III. Initial Sighting
    A. Reaction(s) of Protagonist
      1. Astonishment
      2. Disbelief
      3. Disregard
      4. Puzzlement
      5. Fear
      6. Curiosity
      7. Helplessness
    B. Rational/Physical Explanation Immediately Offered
    C. Affirmation of Sighting
    D. Alerts Members of "Immediate Circle"
    E. Hero in Physical Contact with UFO
    G. General Impression of Phenomenon
IV. Description
    A. UFO
    B. Aliens
V. Protagonist Seeks Personal Verification
    A. Explanation
    B. Exploration
VI. Confrontation with UFO
    A. More Detailed, Closer Description of UFO
    B. More Detailed, Closer Description of Aliens
    C. Indirect Contact with UFO—Aliens Alter Environment
VII. Protagonist Seeks Outside Verification
    A. Family/Friends/Lovers/Other Objective Witnesses' Response(s)
      1. Disbelief
      2. Belief
      3. Investigation
    B. Authorities (Police/Military/Government)
      1. Response(s)
        a. Disbelief
        b. Belief
        c. Investigation
        d. Cover-up
    C. Decides Not to Seek Verification

VIII. Direct Contact with UFO
   A. Communication with UFO
   B. Physical Contact with UFO
      1. Aliens Are Friendly
      2. Aliens Are Hostile
         a. Protagonist Taken Prisoner
         b. Aliens Hostile to People/Environment
      3. Protagonist Interaction with Aliens
IX. Departure of UFO
   A. Leaves Alone
   B. Takes Someone/Something from Earth
   C. Aliens Are Vanquished
   C. UFO Leaves Undiscovered by Authorities
   D. Leaves Discovered by Authorities

This structure furnishes a complete frame for the UFO tale, while providing for considerable variation within each story. Each general function contains a number of alternatives; the wide possibility of responses to the initial sighting, for example, ranges from a denial of the phenomenon to being in physical contact with extraterrestrials. The basic structure also permits individual embellishments, so that the aliens assume a variety of shapes and dispositions in different stories.

Beyond the differences in specific detail (appearance of the aliens, location, etc.), a slight manipulation of the formula drastically alters the narrative. As in Propp's tales, reversing the order in which functions appear creates wide plot variations. For instance, if the protagonist confronts the UFO (Function VIII) *before* he/she seeks personal verification (Function V), the emphasis of the story shifts from the hero as an active participant in the adventure to the hero as a victim of the phenomenon.

When seen as a whole, this new cultural myth provides insight into concerns, preoccupations, and circumstances that are characteristic of this culture. These myths are distinctly local in setting, as the stories focus on the intrusion of the foreign into very familiar territory. According to Amy Harmon, the origin of the UFO myth is rooted in the political and technological climate of post–World War II society: "The nation's interest in UFO's began at the dawn of the atomic age, when fears over the Cold War and anxieties about new doomsday technologies coincided with thousands of reported sightings in the years that followed the Roswell incident."[59]

Chris Carter, creator of the popular TV series "The X-Files," observes that the emergence of this myth is a response to the narrow and literal confines of our materialistic culture: "We need mysteries, we need stories, we need something beyond the temporal."[60]

In addition, the UFO myth furnishes a new type of mythic character—the extraterrestrial. If not superhuman-like mythic gods and heroes, these extraterrestrials are technologically superior to humans. The aliens serve as a foil for their human counterparts, and thus provide insight into human foibles, aspirations, and concerns.

At the same time, this new cultural myth operates on many of the levels of traditional myths discussed earlier. The UFO myth provides insight into phenomena of the past, ranging from unusual formations in the terrain to unexplainable influences on ancient civilizations that would enable people to interpret, for instance, the Sphinx, or Stonehenge. The UFO myth also answers other phenomenal questions concerning the universe, including the form and substance of other planets.

Finally, the UFO myth also addresses metaphysical questions concerning the distant stars and planets that people have long observed with wonder. Benson Saler and Charles Ziegler note, "The UFO myth serves as an expression of anti-Government sentiment and the age-old yearning to believe we are not alone in the universe . . . the popular belief in superior technological beings. . . . For some, aliens replace or augment conventional religious beliefs."[61]

Human beings no longer are the center of the universe but are part of a larger community. The revelation of a populated universe also raises questions about creation—how, when, and why earthlings were created as part of this larger universe.

The Commercial Invention of Cultural Myths

At times, American cultural myths are invented for commercial purposes. For example, one of the most innovative attractions at Disney's MGM Theme Park in Orlando, Florida, is the Tower of Terror. As passengers ride up an elevator in an old "haunted" hotel, they are told about a group of passengers who never made it to the top floor; but as their elevator plunged to the basement, these people disappeared, never to be found. At this moment, the elevator drops, leaving the passengers breathless and exhilarated. One way to enhance the success of the ride is for the audience to became fully acquainted with the legend before entering the attraction. Consequently, in October 1997, Disney produced a television program, "Tower of Terror," in which the protagonists investigate the legend and "meet" the ghosts. The program appeared on "The Wonderful World of Disney," on ABC, which is also owned by Disney. Thus, the myth is disseminated in the public consciouness as a marketing device to promote the attraction.

Cultural Mythic Heroes

Cultural mythic heroes embody the highest aims and ideals of a society. Taken collectively, mythic figures reflect not only individual sides of Self but a cultural persona as well. For example, the male Hollywood movie stars of the 1930s and 1940s were cultural archetypes who embodied aspects of the American Self. Collectively, these film stars form a composite of the ideal American male during this period. Examples include:

* The Rugged Individualist: John Wayne
* Sophistication, Charm: Cary Grant
* Boyish Innocence, Purity: Jimmy Stewart
* Urban Toughness: Humphrey Bogart
* Dangerous Insolence: Robert Mitchum

The popularity of these actors was based on a constant, identifiable, mythic persona that they brought to each film. John Wayne remained the rugged individualist in each film, whether he was starring in a western or military drama.

When cultural myths remain constant, so do its cultural heroes. Consequently, while the individuals change, the essential type remains the same. For example, John Wayne, Clint Eastwood, and Sylvester Stallone are generational representatives of the Rugged Individualist archetype. The Rugged Individualist epitomizes the virility, ruggedness, self-sufficiency, and independence of the American male.

Cultural heroes are the physical embodiments of cultural myths. For instance, the Rugged Individualist is affiliated with the cultural myth of the frontier. (The Rugged Individualist affirms the cultural myth that people can determine their own fate through the exercise of individual choice.) As Rollo May notes, this cultural hero is distinctly American and would not have appeared in the myths of other cultures: "[Individualism] was unknown in the Middle Ages . . . and would have been considered psychotic in classical Greece."[62] (See earlier discussion on American cultural myth.)

Garry Wills contends that John Wayne's popularity stems from his association with this cultural myth—an association that only grew more fervent as the cultural myth of the frontier became more fragile in the face of cultural change:

> Wayne's innate qualities are not enough to explain so large a social impact. He had to fill some need in his audience. . . . When he was called the Ameri-

can, it was a statement of what his fans wanted America to be . . . he stood for an America people felt was disappearing or had disappeared, for a time "when men were men."[63]

Advertisers have exploited the deep-rooted appeal of this mythic hero by linking products to an archetypal image of the Rugged Individualist. Michael Gill of J. Walter Thompson discusses the success of the Marlboro Man:

> In advertising, as in most fiction, you need to tap into the subconscious of your audience. The Marlboro Man seemed to have done that. . . . With the Marlboro Man, of course, this man is the symbol of the West—the cowboy. There's a feeling of confidence—that he's in charge. He's always either alone or, sometimes, with other men. But he's never with women—that's not part of the myth. . . . When people smoke or drink they're not doing it casually, they're doing it to be associated with something that improves their feeling about themselves.[64]

However positive cultural heroes may appear, these figures also embody some of the shortcomings within a culture. The Rugged Individualist is a narcissistic figure whose self-absorption undermines the spirit of community within a society. Heroes like Dirty Harry are mavericks who regard the system as an obstacle to their heroic mission.

Rollo May observes that the Rugged Individualist is a lonely individual who "has few if any deep relationships and lacks the capacity for satisfaction or pleasure in the contacts he does have."[65] The Rugged Individualist accepts his isolation, giving him a melancholy, if not tragic air. According to May, this alienation is a manifestation of America's cultural rootlessness.[66] America is a country without any common, indigenous myths; immigrants came to America bringing a variety of mythic traditions from their own countries, and mainstream America has not accepted Native American myths as part of its cultural tradition. May contends that this state of isolation produces an anxiety that is expressed in our being a violent people.[67]

At times, a particular archetype may dominate the myths of a culture, signaling imbalances within the culture. As mentioned earlier, contemporary American media programs promote youth culture, featuring versions of the Divine Child (Puer Aeternus). Adult actors are now taking second billing to child stars. Films such as *Ferris Bueller's Day Off* or *Getting Even with Dad* depict children who can adapt to the complexities of modern society, in contrast with their inept, inflexible parents. In these media presentations, adults no longer exercise the authority that traditionally comes with age. Indeed, adults often are absent altogether, as in the *Home Alone* films. Other movies feature adults who act like children (e.g., *Ace Ventura* or *Dumb and Dumber*). However, Jung warns that in order for an individual (or a culture) to achieve psychic balance, the Divine Child archetype needs the salutary wisdom of the Mentor. An improper constellation can result in "dangerous flights of fancy."[68] Further, individuals or cultures with this psychic imbalance may disintegrate when confronted with reality.

As the culture changes, different mythic figures may assume positions of prominence within the society. Reverend Andrew Greeley contends that cultural heroes emerge to fit the times. To illustrate, he cites the elections of Dwight D. Eisenhower in 1952 and 1956, and John F. Kennedy in 1960: "In the early 1950s the American people needed a father god to reassure them. They were provided with one. In the early 1960s . . . the people needed a young warrior god who would lead them to victories in the face of new challenges."[69]

Cultural Symbols

Cultural symbols are representations of an otherwise intangible aspect of the cultural life of a society. These symbols are subtly incorporated into media presentations, without particular fanfare. Recognizing these symbols can enrich the audience's understanding of media messages embedded in the text.

One cultural symbol is *small-town America,* which is defined by basic values such as honesty, loyalty, and volunteerism. This mythical landscape is equated with the simple life, defined by order and permanence rather than the complexity and chaos characteristic of urban life. The nuclear family is the source of strength and identity in the citizens of the town. A classic example of this cultural symbol is the small town in Frank Capra's *It's a Wonderful Life* (1946).

In some respects, the suburb is an extension of the small-town America cultural symbol. According to Hal Himmelstein, suburbia represents a harmony between humans and nature: "[The suburb] was a place where sanity prevailed, a place of full employment; conventional white, white-collar corporate families; clean streets, well-kept weedless lawns, neatly trimmed hedges, and, in the older suburbs, an occasional freshly painted white picket fence."[70] Even the names of many of the suburban developments have a mythic flavor—Olympia Gardens, Arcadia Estates, and Clarendon Hills. Subdivision names like Plantation Estates recalls the American cultural myth of the antebellum South.

The suburb emerged as a cultural symbol in post–World War II America. People who were disturbed by social changes in urban culture retreated to the suburbs as a place of physical refuge. On another level, suburbia was also a psychic retreat, reflecting individuals' unwillingness to confront social problems.

As presented in the media, suburbia symbolizes success and control. Nothing ever changes in Beaver Cleaver's Mayfield. Indeed, the landscape is made up of brick homes, which seem impervious to the forces of nature. In this paradise, the range of problems are reduced to funny, trivial irritants, which are easily resolved within a thirty-minute time frame: Wally discovers girls, Beaver loses his library book.

The *gun* symbolizes power, masculinity, and control. Consequently, the person who wields this weapon is dangerous, violent, and attractive. On the surface, the National Rifle Association's campaign for gun rights is founded on constitutional issues. However, at heart, the primal concern of the NRA is over the gun as cultural, mythic symbol of the American character.

The *automobile* has emerged as a mythic symbol of mobility, control, prestige, and sexual prowess in twentieth-century America. Greeley observes,

> . . . the automobile has taken on a highly important symbolistic role in American culture. . . . It is . . . a manifestation of the inclination he has to worship an object that is particularly dear to him or on which he is especially dependent, and to elevate it from the order of the profane to the order of the sacred.[71]

Kimberly V. Althedge, a student at Webster University, conducted an analysis of *Twister* (1996), pointing out the sacred role of the automobile in the film. *Twister* is the story of two characters, Jo Harding (Helen Hunt) and Bill Harding (Bill Paxton), who are on a scientific quest to locate and study a series of intense tornadoes sweeping across Oklahoma. The selection of the Dodge Ram as a sacred image was hardly accidental; the appearance of the vehicle in the film was part of a product placement arrangement in which the car manufacturer paid the studio to strategically position its truck in the film. Consequently, the film drew from the sacred image of the automobile in the development of the narrative, creating an effective, elaborate commercial for the Dodge Ram.

The Ram assumes a central role in the narrative, sending a message about the value of the truck to prospective owners. For the main characters, the Ram represents sanctuary. When the Hardings are separated from the Ram, their primary goal is to return to the safety of the truck. The Ram also represents mobility, freedom, and independence, enabling the characters to flee the destruction of the twisters.

The filmmakers employ the mythic motif of personification, endowing the truck with human sensibilities. The vehicle serves as a trusted friend and protector; it is dependable, starting and stopping when it is most needed. The Dodge Ram also possesses astonishing recuperative powers. At one point, an object strikes the windshield, leaving a large crack on the surface. By the next scene, it has been magically repaired. In another scene, the tailgate is ripped off of the truck; later in the film, the truck "grows" a new tailgate. In addition, the truck is amazingly durable. In the film, the characters watch in awe as cows and buildings are uprooted by the tornadoes. However, the Ram hugs the road, impervious to the forces of nature.

Even the style of the film is reminiscent of a commercial. The introduction to the characters is an aerial shot of the truck barreling down a road—a formulaic shot used in car ads. The bright red Ram is very distinctive, given that the other vehicles in the film are black. Much of the action in the film is a performance demonstration for the vehicle, with the Ram moving deftly around obstacles and stopping suddenly to avert disasters.[72]

Essay: A Mythic Analysis of "ER" and "Chicago Hope"

In September 1994, after a few faint breaths of hope, President Clinton's national health care legislation died on the congressional floor. The same month, the networks delivered two new medical series, "ER" (NBC) and "Chicago Hope" (CBS). Television reviewer John O'Connor attributes the success of "ER" to . . . "the American public's escalating anxieties over health care in the wake and confusion and helplessness in Washington." "ER" executive producer John Wells sees the series as reassuring an anxious public about their medical care. "People are frightened about going to emergency rooms, about being cared for by people who are compassionate," he says. "*ER* . . . is a place where you go and you sort of know who the people are, and you feel they care about you."[73]

The powerful images organized around "ER" and "Chicago Hope" have been administering a steady dose of anti-anxiety to medicine for over two years. Each week, "ER" reaches 24 million homes and is viewed by an estimated 34.9 million people. It is number one among key demographic groups of adults aged 18–49 who are wealthy and well educated.

Prime-time medicine is providing viewers with the anesthetic they need—a vehicle of passage from the real world of the health care crisis into a "reel" world of "power" where doctors and medical science have the hotline to nature's secret formula. These weekly medical series offer hope of deliverance. They give viewers an essential component to their personal and family security—access to health care. In contrast to the present state of the American health care system, "Chicago Hope" and "ER" (coupled with sex, violence, and youth) offer immediate, compassionate care by heroic, sympathetic, and committed professionals. "ER" and "Chicago Hope" are weekly rituals that reinforce the medical institution's power to define, prevent, and treat illness in American society.

Since ancient times physicians have been viewed as "heroic warriors" and medicine as a noble art. They trod, with religion, in the same mystery of hope and despair. These priest/physicians were mostly specialists who practiced medicine in Houses of Life that were attached to the temples. The myth of medicine and doctors has been heightened since World War II. The progress of medical knowledge has proven to be one of the greatest advances in human history. Vaccines and sanitary measures have had a profound influence on the health of the American people. Killer diseases like smallpox, diphtheria, and tetanus seem to have been eliminated. Antibiotics have conquered life-threatening bacteria. Within a seventy-five-year span, improved surgical techniques, the discovery of antiseptic and aseptic surgical procedures, anesthesia, and blood transfusions catapulted surgery into one of the greatest scientific marvels of all times.

For the first time in history, medicine burst out of its narrow limits. Diseases that wiped out families were now either eliminated or under control, due in great part to discoveries in medical science bringing the wisdom of Ecclesiastes to light. "The Most High hath created medicines out of the earth . . ." and ". . . hath given knowledge to men [physicians], that He may be honored in His wonders." (38: 4,6). These advances changed the American psyche so completely that in 1952, Evelyn Barkin observed that "most patients are completely under the supposedly scientific yoke of modern medicine as any primitive savage is under the superstitious serfdom of the tribal witch doctor."[74]

Within this context, creators of the TV medical drama series built their formulas, setting the pattern of the sacerdotal physicians dedicated to their patients. The image of the doctor in medical drama has ranged from paragons of unfailing, unblemished, all-caring, all-knowing healers "Dr. Kildare" and "Marcus Welby, M.D." to the ensemble of TV doctors on "Chicago Hope" and "ER," who possess emotional and physical problems in abundance.

TV medical drama provides a repetitive ritual in a designated "sacred space" much like religious rituals. According to Mircea Eliade, a sacred space is a designated space, a place set aside. It is the center where the symbolic repetition of mythic rituals is recreated. It affords a break from the profane outside world, to another world, a "sacred" interior where the ritual takes place.[75] "ER" and "Chicago Hope" transcend the present personal time and provide an escape where the viewer submerges himself in what Eliade calls a "strange" time, which is imaginary.

Like a church, "ER" is a sacred gathering place where individuals from all walks of life gather together "united by" what Steven Poole asserts is, "a fear of death and hope of salvation." "ER" creator and writer Michael Crichton, an anthropologist and Harvard medical school graduate, believes that "society needs the insights of the mystic as much as those of the empirical scientist."[76] As the television doctors cure their patients at an amazing (and unrealistic) rate, they offer hope that humans can transcend their mortality. The overhead lighting offers biblical light and dark symbolism. In the most intense dramatic scenes, like the surgical and emergency procedures, the contrasts with either harsh or soft shafts of light falling on the medical personnel suggest knowledge, security, and truth. Fear and ignorance dwell in the background that dwindles into darkness and the unknown. The soft ethereal nimbus that frames doctors during procedures continues the image of hope and heavenly assistance depicted in Werner Van Den Valckert's seventeenth-century painting of *Christ the Physician* and the seventeenth-century Swabian wood-panel painting of the *Limb Transplantation Miracle by Saints Cosmos and Damien.* The head light worn during surgical procedures connotes a luminous ray of God's wisdom while the rest of the room is shrouded in ignorance. The exaggerated lighting in the operating scenes produces a significant emotional effect while, simultaneously, directing our eyes to focus on the heroic performance of the surgeon.

The rhythmic blend of music, camera angles, dialogue, and icons of healing provides a weekly sacerdotal ritual of healing. The slow melodic liturgical music with underlying rhythmic (heart) beats cues us while the camera engages us to join characters such as "ER's" Dr. Greene (Anthony Edwards). Assuming a position akin to the eleventh-century manuscript illustration of *Christ Healing the Lepers and Other Healing Miracles,* Greene, along with his disciples, begins his healing rounds amidst the congregation.

Weekly, millions of viewers enter the sanctuaries of "Chicago Hope" and "ER" and entrust their fears of disease and trauma to televisions priests/physicians. By removing disease from the context of real life, these "magico-medical rituals" treat diseases as events that never extend beyond each episode. In most episodes, by the hour's end, television doctors make the correct diagnosis, stabilize chaos, and cure the majority of patients who flock to the sanctuaries of "Chicago Hope" and "ER." Even in those cases in which death occurs, the hospital serves as a sanctuary in a broader, spiritual sense, in that the patients (and, vicariously, the audience) accept the inevitability of the illness and death. Steven Poole believes it is a useful catharsis for viewers to see the patient either happily cured or die an illusory death.[77] This, of course, carries all the trappings of expected miracle cures.

TV drama rarely reflects the real-life definition of illness and dying. "Nobody's dying tomorrow—not in that room," Dr. Jeffrey Geiger (Mandy Patinkin) reassures pediatric surgeon Dr. Karen Antonovich (Margaret Colin) prior to surgery on Siamese twins. The close-up and warm ray of soft lighting on the right side of Geiger's face provides a convincing portrait of a Geiger enlightened by God. The following scenes support this image. Cued by accelerated, rhythmic, percussive sounds vitalizing our visceral chords, we join Geiger and his surgical team on their march to victory, during which time Geiger subtly turns his head toward the heavens. The sense of drama heightens, as the underlying rapid percussive sounds increase and the patients (the Siamese twins) are wheeled into the operating room. While preparing for the surgical ceremony (masks and blood pressure cuffs applied, IVs inserted), silence emerges and Geiger gathers and implores his team, "for those of you with God in your life, please make contact now." The camera then guides us slowly over the faces of the medical personnel in their moment of heavenly contact. Given this spiritual invocation, it is a certainty that both twins survive. With slow lyric chords plucking our heart strings, chief of surgery Phillip Watters glances over to head operating room nurse Camille (Roxanne Hart) and nods his approval. The message is that doctors can perform miracles when necessary—and deserved. "ER" producer Robert Nathan says he likes to think of Dr. Mark Greene as "Saint Mark."[78] Is it any wonder people hold physicians up to standards of perfection?

To be sure, today's TV doctors possess human frailties and inadequacies. Yet even with these human flaws, the good doctors triumph and possess an unlimited capacity to heal. Despite a few mishaps and occasional deaths in recent series, dramatic programming in the medical genre on commercial TV capitalizes on death and disease, the aura of science and technology, and the ideal of human compassion and service.

A mythic theme that appears in these programs is David verses Goliath—only in this case, the conflict is between doctors and representatives of HMOs (Health Maintenance Organizations). HMO providers are usually cast as corrupt, devious, and self-serving. Medical programs offer hope that these forces can be overcome, and that order will be restored.

In one episode of "Chicago Hope," gifted neurosurgeon Dr. Aaron Shutt (Adam Arkin) takes on Rayfield HMO's Senior Vice President Jonathan

Saunders (Ken Lerner), who refuses to allow Shutt to remove a woman's massive frontal lobe (brain) tumor. Even though Dr. Shutt is more qualified and offers to reduce his fee, Saunders refuses because his HMO holds a contract with another hospital. The confrontation between Mr. Saunders and Dr. Shutt begins in the hospital corridor. The camera follows the two men as they begin their discussion while walking down the corridor. The gravity of the issue is reinforced with the absence of background music, and visually, as the characters are dressed to convey their respective roles. Shutt, dressed in white, stands for good, and Saunders, donned in black suit and fire red tie, represents evil.

Shutt then recruits the hospital's attorney, Alan Birch (Peter MacNicol), to assist him in persuading Saunders to allow him to perform the complicated surgery. During the meeting, the HMO surgeon admits to inexperience, and Birch, affectionately known as "the Eel" because of his ability to wriggle out of any legal situation, tells Saunders to, "look at your boy and tell me he's qualified." As the cameras cut to a close-up of the HMO neurosurgeon, he assumes a sheepish and ill-confident demeanor. Birch then tells Saunders that he promises to help the patient mount a lawsuit against Rayfield. Understanding the pecuniary consequences, Saunders consents to let Shutt perform the surgery.

A striking contrast is the real-life drama of New York cardiologist Allan Schwartz who is not as lucky:

> When I used to encounter an aneurysm, I would send the patient to the best aneurysm surgeon I knew. It would be where you'd want your mother to go. Now I have to look at a list of surgeons who are in an HMO's network. I do my best to identify someone in the network who is OK. But it isn't someone of the caliber that I could get otherwise.[79]

In another "Chicago Hope" scene taking place in Saunders's office, Saunders speaks to gentle, caring head of surgery Dr. Phillip Watters (Hector Elizondo). Phillip, like the Greek god of medicine, is framed standing in front of a picture window. The building outside the window bears a striking resemblance to the healing Temple of Aesculapius. Saunders, seated behind his desk, remarks that Rayfield (the nation's third largest HMO provider) will be signing contracts with two other hospitals for all their obstetrics, bypass surgery, and burn cases. Phillip objects saying, "neither of these hospitals has the personnel, the facilities or the equipment we can offer. "Chicago Hope" is the best. You know that."

A striking image in this scene is Saunders's preoccupation with butterflies. He remains seated at his desk and responds to Watters. While he speaks, the camera cuts to tight close-up of Saunders peering through a magnifying glass. This intimate, distorted close-up of the left "evil eye" and orbital region—a cinematic device—produces an emotional revulsion for the character who appears preoccupied with "crucifying" a dead butterfly specimen on a board.

The significance of this mythic image is reinforced by Saunders's lecture about change in the way health care is practiced. Saunders tells Phillip, "We here at Rayfield want to be in business with doctors who understand there needs to be a change in medicine—a *drastic* change."

Symbolically, butterflies signify change and, in some cultures, the transitory nature of happiness. As its Greek name (psyche) indicates, the butterfly is also analogous to the soul. When Saunders stands and continues his speech, we see a framed collection of butterfly specimens hanging on the wall. Ironically, it appears as though HMOs are not only changing, but systematically crucifying the soul of the American health care system. Patients now must choose doctors from HMO lists of preferred providers, and doctors must seek prior HMO approval for ordering most tests and procedures—a "drastic" change indeed.

In another segment from this episode, Dr. William Kronk (Peter Berg) performs a life-saving operative procedure that the HMO did not approve. After hearing about the operation, Saunders cancels the woman's insurance coverage and threatens to rescind the hospital's remaining contracts, which account for one-fifth of "Chicago Hope's" income. Kronk meets with Saunders in his office to plead the hospital's and the woman's case. Here again we see Saunders in an unflattering cinematic position, which capitalizes on the cultural tensions surrounding health care. The low-lit scene darkens even further when Saunders eclipses the light by closing the drapes of his office. Saunders's style of delivery conveys a subversive ideology or menacing omen denying the publics' right to health care. He launches into an emotional diatribe, "You don't get it, Dr. Kronk, do you?" He then informs Kronk that Americans must assume more responsibility for keeping themselves healthy in the future. Running to the doctor for every little ache, pain, and bout of constipation, Saunders blathers, is no longer permissible. "We train a nation of sick people," he shouts, "to keep the medical community alive." Saunders pounds his hand on his desk adding, "and it must stop." The long-shot of Saunders allows him the freedom to physically act out the subtext of his script. The combination of both script and images convincingly portrays Saunders as the satanic "Prince of Darkness." In fact, Kronk makes a point of asking him why he is closing the drapes and, at the end of Saunders's speech, Kronk, with a dumbfounded expression remarks, "You are a freaky, freaky man."

Thus, "ER" and "Chicago Hope" reinforce the myth of medicine and doctors. More than mere entertainment, these popular programs provide viewers with hope of deliverance, reassurance, and salvation in the face of uncertain times in the health care industry.

Conclusion

In conclusion, several points of clarification need to be made in considering the mythic approach to media.

I. A distinction must be drawn between form and content. Not all media content qualifies as myth. The media, however, may serve as a modern conveyer of myth. Consequently, a first step in a mythic analysis is to identify media programs that contain mythic elements.

The question of intention also must be considered: Are media communicators consciously drawing upon myth for inspiration? And are they committed to conveying mythic tales? Perhaps. At other times, they simply are trying to entertain—or make a profit. Media storytellers tap into a universal mythic wellspring for their inspiration, so that in telling stories about themselves and their immediate world, they subconsciously give voice to universal mythic concerns. Ultimately, though, the question of artistic intention is irrelevant. Much depends, instead, on the audience's response to the content. Rollo May notes that in the absence of traditional sources of myth telling, people desperately strive to discover meaning in other arenas:

> In such directionless states as we find ourselves near the end of the twentieth century, it is not surprising that frantic people flock to the new cults, or resurrect the old ones, seeking answers to their anxiety and longing for relief from their guilt or depression to something to fill the vacuum of their lives.

In this vacuum, people often look to the media for mythic explanation, which the media communicator may or may not have intended.

Finally, there is a possibility that some readers might regard this discussion of mythology as an attack on their personal belief systems. While it is easy to remain detached in a discussion of ancient Babylonian mythology, a discussion of Christianity or Buddhism as myth may be another matter entirely. In the definition of myth, the authors declare that a myth may or may not be true; and we recognize that it is beyond the scope of this chapter to make this distinction. Instead, this approach can be employed to gain some perspective into media content.

II. A mythic approach can help make media content accessible in the following ways:

A. Identifying the mythic functions of media programming.
B. Providing perspective on media content as a retelling of traditional myths.
C. Discovering mythic elements in media programs (and the universal meanings behind these elements), thus providing insight into the narrative.
D. Examining media programs as modern cultural myths that furnish insight into contemporary life.

III. A useful methodological framework for mythic analysis is as follows:

A. Does the media presentation fulfill any of the functions of myth? What does this reveal about media content?
B. What is the role of the media in the mythologizing process?
    1. In what ways do the media mythologize people, events?
    2. In what ways do the media de-mythologize people, events?
C. Does the media presentation transmit classical myths?
    1. Direct transmission of myths:
        a. Why has this myth been re-presented at this time?
        b. In what ways has this adaptation been altered from the original?
        c. What do these adaptations signify with regard to cultural attitudes, beliefs, values, and preoccupations?
    2. Is the media presentation a modification of a classical myth? Explain.
        a. Does this reconfiguration furnish perspective into cultural attitudes, beliefs, values, and preoccupations? Explain.
D. Does the media presentation contain any *mythic themes* cited in the chapter? What insights does an understanding of these mythic elements provide into the text?
E. Does the media presentation feature any *mythic figures* cited in the chapter? What insights does an understanding of these mythic figures provide into the text?
F. Does the media presentation contain any of the following *mythic elements*? What insights does an understanding of these mythic elements provide into the text?
    1. *Mythic plots*
    2. *Mythic motifs*
    3. *Mythic symbols*

G. Identify any *mythic heroines* appearing in media presentations:
  1. Heroines found in classical myths.
  2. Heroines found in cultural myths.
Discuss these heroines within the context of the functions of myth.
H. Does the media presentation reflect cultural myths cited in the chapter?
  1. What do these cultural myths reveal about the predominant values, concerns, and preoccupations within the culture?
  2. Does an understanding of the cultural myth provide insight into the media presentation? Explain.
  3. What do the cultural myths reveal about shifts within the culture?
  4. Are new cultural myths being created and conveyed through the media? Explain.
  5. Does the media presentation contain any of the following:
    a. Cultural mythic themes?
    b. Cultural mythic figures?
    c. Cultural mythic symbols?

IV. The mythic elements identified in the chapter are not a complete listing but merely present some examples. Identify other instances of the following:

  a. Mythic images
  b. Cultural mythic heroes
  c. Mythic motifs

CHAPTER 5

ANALYSIS OF
PRODUCTION ELEMENTS

Overview

Production elements refer to the *style* and aesthetic quality of a media presentation. An awareness of stylistic elements such as *editing, composition, point of view, angle, connotation, graphics, color, lighting, shape, movement, scale, sound,* and *special effects* contributes to our appreciation of media content and provides insight into media messages. Production values are roughly analogous to grammar in print, in that these elements influence:

- the way in which the audience receives the information;
- the emphasis or interpretation placed on the information by the media communicator;
- the reaction of the audience to the information.

Production elements touch the audience on an affective (or emotional) level, creating a mood that reinforces manifest messages or themes. Through production elements, the media communicator creates an environment that enables the audience to experience (as opposed to merely understand) the messages. For example, horror films generate feelings of fear in audience members, which enables them to identify with the experiences of the characters on-screen.

Media communicators strive to create seamless, self-contained productions that conceal the process of designing and assembling the presentation. Because many of these production choices slip past conscious awareness, they predispose viewers to think about the presentation from the point of view of the media communicator. During the production process, the media communicator actively selects, manipulates, and coordinates various technical elements which support media messages. For instance, when producing horror films, media communicators manipulate lighting, music, and screen space to arouse intense feelings of terror in the audience. Stylistic elements may also convey independent messages, such as the glamour associated with screen violence.

The analysis of media production elements has several objectives: (1) This approach enables individuals to understand how production elements are utilized to construct meaning in media presentations; (2) Examining production elements offers an excellent way to identify messages and themes within a media text; (3) This approach can increase an individual's awareness of the ways in which production elements affect him/her personally, as well as the wider audience.

Editing

Editing refers to the selection and arrangement of information. Editing is a process in which many elements are pieced together to give meaning to a presentation. Editing decisions can send a wide range of messages regarding media content.

Inclusion and Omission

Given the time and space limitations, critical editing decisions involve both what to *include* and what to *omit* from a media presentation. These decisions have been made before the presentation reaches the public; as a result, the audience is not in a position to make a critical judgment about the selection process. To illustrate, printed in the upper right-hand corner of the *New York Times* is the motto, "All the News That's Fit to Print." This statement conveys the message that editing decisions have been made prior to publication, and that what is "fit to print" has been determined by the editors.

In film and television, the issue of inclusion and omission is critical. The shooting ratio in a Hollywood feature film production is approximately 10:1. That is, ten feet of film has been shot for each foot of film included in the final print. The same principle applies to television. In the news, a reporter may collect thirty minutes of interviews and background information for a story. However, he/she must compress this information within a news slot of (at best) three minutes.

One way to analyze the impact of editing is to examine a variety of newspapers or television programs appearing on the same day. The same topic may be expanded, addressed from different points of view—or omitted altogether. Consequently, questions to consider include: (1) how much information can be covered in these brief segments; (2) what important stories have been ignored or downplayed; (3) what important details are left out and why; (4) who orders the segments and to whom are they important; and (5) what is the primary purpose of most lead segments.

Another area of consideration includes which *topics* have been included or omitted. For instance, media outlets often provide extensive coverage of experimental surgeries (i.e., the baboon liver transplant in Pittsburgh in 1988), or dramatic stories of individuals in search of an organ donor or support for an expensive experimental medical treatment. However, these experimental procedures and personal tragedies usually affect only one person. Long-term processes, like poverty and lack of health care, are given minimal, if any, news coverage. Viewers and readers rarely see stories dealing with access to health care for the urban poor, an issue that effects millions.[1]

Arrangement

The order in which news segments are presented provides a subtle way of telling the audience what is important. Far from practicing an exact science, newsroom staffs exercise *news judgment* about what is newsworthy based on their personal experiences, world views, and backgrounds. As a result, the placement of news may vary dramatically between various news outlets (e.g., newspapers or television stations). An example can be found in coverage dealing with the current controversy over genetically-altered crops. Researchers are working on ways to genetically alter food plants to render them free of disease. This will increase the food supply, possibly making a difference in the quality of life in a country. However, many critics are worried that tampering with nature will upset the fragile ecology.

The *Los Angles Times* covered the controversial issues of the debate in great detail. The *Times* series received front-page coverage and extended over five days in December 1997.[2] Not surprisingly, there has been minimal coverage in the *St. Louis Post-Dispatch,* where one of the major companies involved in the debate is located. On January 15, 1998, the *Post* published an article on page seven of the news section which ignored the issue, instead focusing on whether genetic engineering should be allowed in the production of products that carry the organic label.[3]

Issues of arrangement also exist in film and television. Walter Cronkite, whose television career spanned more than thirty years, became a cultural icon and one of the most trusted men in America. During his nineteen years as "CBS Evening News" anchor, Cronkite's signature sign-off, "And that's the way it is," not only promised to present all the news; it also pledged to give us the news in its order of importance. However, this is not necessarily the case. To illustrate, in a March 1998 newscast on KMOV-TV (St. Louis, Missouri) the first three stories dealt with teenage criminals who were either on trial for murder or just apprehended for murder. A story about conflict between the United States and Iraq was presented much later in the newscast.

To demonstrate more fully how newscasts can differ in what they deem important, two 10 P.M. newscasts (one on a CBS affiliate and one on an NBC affiliate, recorded on April 8, 1998), are outlined on page 200.

Although the amount of material covered in the newscast seems substantial, the news is a fast-moving hodgepodge of sound and images lacking in-depth information from which the viewer can make an informed decision. Watching the nightly news is akin to catching history on the run.

The relationship between the articles, segments and commercials can also convey messages. To illustrate: In February 1998, three top government officials were conducting a "town meeting" at Ohio State University in hopes of gathering support for the U.S. government's decision to bomb Iraq. During the broadcast, CNN injected several commercials for the new video release of *Air Force One* (1997). The film is about President James Marshall's (played by Harrison Ford) victory over terrorists.

Theme sequencing occurs in television when linkages are established between seemingly disparate topics. For instance, weather reports (featuring stories of stormy, inclement conditions or high pollen counts) are often sponsored by cold medicines, thus sending a cumulative corporate message. The weather report triggers memories of cold or allergy symptoms, while the commercials show the viewer how to get relief. The visuals establish a chain of associations between wintry weather, cold symptoms, and relief with use of the advertised product.

Editing for Contrast

Visual media such as photographs, television, and film employ editing techniques to highlight differences between settings, locations, or characters. In the film version of Henry James's novel *The Wings of the Dove* (1997), director Iain Softley utilizes editing to dramatize the differences between

Figure 5.1. Comparative Newscasts, CBS Affiliate and NBC Affiliate

Local CBS Affiliate	Local NBC Affiliate

Rundown of news to be presented
Promo station identification

Top Story
- Family presses criminal; charges against police officer for killing son suspected of robbery
- Road rage trial
- Merger of fire districts

Other Local Briefs
- Death of state representative
- Honest citizen
- Jazz Band goes to DC

National News
- LA Hospital worker accused of killing patients
- Women arrested for selling daughter to prostitution to support drug habit
- Fight in Cincinnati courtroom when four teenagers are sentenced
- School bus accident near Houston

Legal
- Tobacco Companies reject settlement

Financial
- General Motors deal
- Animal Kingdom Probe at Disney
- Boeing Contract

World
- War criminal arrest
- Rain destroys cars in France
- Threat in Hamas
- Germany test saliva in search for criminal
- Greece Terrorism

Science /Health
- Scientists hope to use satellite pictures to detect disease
- Diabetes prevention
- Overweight children
- Gene for Parkinson's disease
- Warning baby monitor recall

Interview women whose father wrote first hand account of Titanic disaster

- weather promo
- lottery numbers
- powerball numbers

Commercial (1)

Rundown of news to be presented

Top Story
- Tow boat pilot strike
- Road rage trial
- emergency first aid for teenager in ATV vehicle accident
- Tobacco companies reject settlement offer

Face to Face -Teen Smoking
- Cancer Vaccine for Melanoma
- Airlines regulate carry on luggage
- Six Flags new roller coaster ride

Promo - what's to come
Station identification

Commercial (1) + Commercial (2)
Promo for "Tonight Show"
Commercial (3)

Nation
- Child abuse arrest in MI.
- Robbery in Kansas

World Watch
- Chernobyl aftermath possible effects
- Forest Fire in Mexico City
- Bangkok Thailand religious ritual

Weather

Cover Story - Zoo Director 35th Anniversary

Promo + Promo

Lottery numbers & PowerBall numbers

Commercial (1)
Commercial (2)
Commercial (3)
Commercial (4)

Sports

Healthy Living
- exercise
- side air bags in Ford cars

Promo + Promo
Commercial (1) + Commercial (2)

Easter Egg Hunt

Weather

Commercial (1)
Commercial with travel forecast (2)
Commercial (3) + Commercial (4)

Most affluent residential areas in America

Promo station's AM news

Commercial (1) + Commercial (2)

- Weather five day forecast
- Final episode of Sinefeld

social classes. In one sequence, Kate (Helena Bonham Carter) and her rich guardian, Aunt Maude (Charlotte Rampling), attend a wedding reception. The camera moves around the vast reception hall while the sedate, wealthy guests discuss trivial topics. The scene then dissolves to an overcrowded dimly lit pub where Kate's lover, a journalist, stands in the midst of a loud, disheveled group arguing political/social issues. This juxtaposition of scenes visually establishes Kate's conflict—securing her position of wealth, versus marrying Merton (Linus Roache), a working-class man with limited financial means.

Editing for Rhythm

Editing can be fast or slow, depending on the duration of each shot in the edited sequence. The variable combinations of edited shots can be characterized as the "music of the image." In music, a sequence of eighth notes is much faster than a cluster of whole notes. Likewise, in editing for film and television, a sequence of short shots is much faster than a grouping of shots long in duration. Individual shots can be as short as one-twenty-fourth of a second or as long as ten minutes. The rhythm has an impact on the rate at which the information is absorbed by the audience, and this, in turn, determines how much attention an audience can give to a particular aspect of the narrative.

The rhythm of editing also can influence the mood of a piece (e.g., frenetic versus tranquil). Rapidly edited shots build tension, indicate urgency, and create a rushed atmosphere. Long takes use up more time; however, when they are edited in sequence, they can create suspense. Long takes with minimal changes in the camera position and the lighting for a specific shot (setups) can also deliver the desired lyrical flow to romantic narratives and impart a feeling of stability. For example, the long wedding sequence at the opening of *Soul Food* (1997) gives the audience time to meet the characters and observe the social interaction within the context of a community ritual. The subsequent long sequences during "Big Mama's" (Irma P. Hall) weekly Sunday dinners dramatize the importance of this tradition in keeping this African-American family together.

Media communicators often employ rhythmic editing techniques for purposes of emphasis. In his gangster film *Goodfellas* (1990), director Martin Scorsese edited in freeze frames to emphasize the significance of particular events. During the opening sequence, young Henry (Christopher Serrone) is beaten by his father. Suddenly, the action is frozen—and then the father's beating resumes. As the audience watches the film, they gain insight into how this moment has shaped Henry's outlook on life. This editing technique also furnishes perspective into Henry's treatment of other characters later in the film.

In a subsequent sequence, we see Henry igniting explosives and again the frame freezes while he stands and watches. Scorsese comments, "a point was being made in his life. There is an explosion and the freeze frame, Henry frozen against it—it's hellish, a person in flames in hell. . . . It is important where the freeze frames are in that opening sequence. Certain things are embedded in the skull when you're a kid. Extract a moment in time."[4]

Spatial Editing

Spatial editing establishes connections between different characters or locations. For example, in a scene from *West Side Story* (1961), the two lovers, Tony (Richard Beymer) and Maria (Natalie Wood), are each singing "Tonight" while preparing for their date together. The film juxtaposes shots of each character getting dressed in his/her own home, giving the audience a sense of the couple's mutual excitement and anticipation.

Temporal Editing

Using flashbacks, memory shots, dream images, or flash-forwards offers an opportunity for the media communicator to comment on the subjective nature of time. In *How to Make an American Quilt* (1995), director Jocelyn Moorhouse used flashbacks to dramatize the role of the past on the present in the lives of six women. Under the guidance of master quilter Anna (Maya Angelou), six women in the small town of Grasse gather to make a wedding quilt for Finn (Winona Ryder). Finn has come to spend the summer with her grandmother Hy (Ellen Burstyn) and to sort out her feelings about her impending marriage. During the quilting sessions, flashbacks reveal the past experiences of the characters. Like a square in the quilt, these women piece generations of individual memories into a present whole. As the tapestry of lives are pieced together, Finn is finally ready to make a decision about her future.

Composition

Composition, or where a character or object appears on the screen (or page), directs the viewer's eye to the part of the page or scene intended by the media communicator. Media communicators must work within the predetermined size of the page or screen. Where the character or object is placed within the screen area determines not only the amount of attention they receive, but their relative importance as well. The most stable and prominent viewing area is center-screen. Characters or objects placed center-screen convey stability and balance within the composition.

When the elements within the picture's frame are balanced (equally distributed around the center), there is a sense of stability, thus minimizing tension in the mind of the viewer. If the interrelationship between the event or objects within the frame is unbalanced (images off-center or weighted heavily on one side), then this creates instability and heightens the sense of tension for the viewer.

The media communicator may strategically place objects and figures in one of the major sections of the frame to evoke an emotional response and convey messages. For example, when focal interest is drawn to the top of the screen, it suggests ideas dealing with power, authority, and aspiration. Generally, characters or objects positioned at the top of the screen command a greater sense of importance than other figures in the frame.

If objects at the top of the screen suggest power, then objects or characters at the bottom of the screen represent subordination, vulnerability, and weakness. Using figures of equal size, a dominant/submissive relationship between two figures can be visually displayed by placing the dominant figure at the top of the screen and the subordinate member at the bottom. Media communicators also can transmit feelings of isolation or insignificance by positioning a character to the right or left side of the frame. These feelings are intensified if the rest of the page or screen is relatively barren.

When part of the object on the screen is missing, and not in our field of vision, we mentally complete the image. This perceptual response to the phenomenon is called *gestalt*, or predisposition to order. Our minds want to fill in the spaces that we cannot actually see. This allows us to perceive the whole, even though we actually only see a portion of it. For example, in a close-up shot where the top of the forehead is out of the frame, the viewer will mentally extend the figure to complete the image so that it is automatically implied that off-screen space contains the person's unseen or "cut off" portion. The completion of the image is called *psychological closure.*

Using both the off-screen and on-screen space connects these two regions. The powerful illusion of reality inside the frame encourages the perception that a larger scene continues outside the frame. Thus, the imagined space outside the screen extends the visible space. Fundamentally, "the off screen may be defined as the collection of elements (character settings, etc.) that, while not being included in the [screened] image itself, are nonetheless connected to that visible space in imaginary fashion for the spectator."[5]

Figures placed on the edge of the frame looking at or approaching the unknown outside the frame suggest that the most important visual element resides outside the frame. This can arouse feelings of uncertainty, trepidation, or fear in the viewer. Fear of what we cannot see is synonymous with fear of the unknown. For example, in the television series "The X-Files," characters are often seen looking up toward space, looking for the unknown outside the visual frame.

Another important element of composition is the amount of white space that appears between pictures, graphics, and headlines. White space in printing takes on the significance of a pause: a visual silence. Cultural historian Walter Ong declared that white space loosens the visual authority, appears more accessible, and invites dialogue. It also serves as a guide to action, akin to turn-taking in verbal conversation. When newspaper contents are tightly arranged, however, they assume a stance of completeness and the voice of final authority. The visuals of a tightly filled newspaper present a sense of closure, which discourages argument or dispute.[6]

In September 1997, the *New York Times* revamped its layout in an effort to attract more readers. Writer James Wolcott's analysis of the changes reveals that even though the *Times* added more words (215,000 to 250,000), color photos, and sections, news coverage has decreased. Wolcott believes that these changes were designed to cater to the appetites of the "urban nester," which he defines as aging yuppies with money who need a place to shop. The lavish photos and expanded sections, he claims, serve only to stimulate our "gimme glands." The new sections such as "Dining In," "Dining Out, " "House and Home," offer a menu of desirable locations for advertisers. People now read the *Times* with a shopping cart, because the paper has assumed a new mission—to "colonize every aspect of our lives as a marketing outpost."[7] The instant success of the elaborate new "ad friendly" art, food, and furnishing sections appears to have affected the *Times*'s social conscience. Wolcott found that in the past the *Times* would address social issues and agitate for legislation; now it reports stories of social concern with only a sympathetic voice for people's plight.[8]

The composition of a production can establish a visual pattern that determines the order in which the audience receives the information. For example, in *Citizen Kane* (1941), a glass with a spoon and medicine bottle loom in the foreground. The lighting, size, and proximity of the medicine and glass attracts the attention of viewers and then guides their gaze diagonally to the background, where Charles Foster Kane (Orson

Wells) and Jedediah Leland (Joseph Cotton) suddenly barge through the door.

Advertisers who must work within the constraints of the printed page also depend on placement to direct the reader's eye to the message. One recent ad for Prozac used two full pages side by side to deliver its message. The left-hand side depicted a huge gray cloud with raindrops against a black background. The type underneath informed the viewer that "Depression hurts." The page directly opposite on the right side portrayed a bright yellow sun outlined in red against a blue background; captioned under the sun were the words "Prozac can help." Since American culture reads from left to right, the placement symbolically transports the reader from living on the dark, sinister (left) side without Prozac into the luminous world of Prozac. Attached to the sunny yellow right-hand page there is a bright yellow insert which pictures a vase of bright yellow, blue, and red flowers. The words "Here comes the sun" diagonally flow from upper right corner of the insert to the top of the flowers. The placement of the words reminds the viewer of water being poured into the vase. Metaphorically, the words represent Prozac being poured into the "body container," thus allowing the individual to blossom. A shadow of drooping flowers below the vase seems to fall off the bottom of the page diagonally to the left, signifying that a person's dark shadows will evaporate once he/she has been fed with Prozac.

Point of View

Point of view refers to the source of information—who tells the story. Point of view has an impact on:

- how a story is told;
- what information is conveyed;
- the audience's orientation and sympathies.

Point of View in Print

News stories often present information from the point of view of the reporter. Before a story appears in print, the reporter must research the topic. After gathering this information, the reporter chooses what to include, what to exclude, what is emphasized, and what is omitted. Consequently, the story is not simply recorded but is filtered trhough the perspective of the reporter.

Charlotte Ryan illustrates how a story can be written to fit a preconceived point of view:

Version 1: Rats Bite Infant

An infant left sleeping in his crib was bitten repeatedly by rats while his 16-year-old mother went to cash her welfare check. A neighbor responded to the cries of the infant and brought the child to Central Hospital where he was treated and released to his mother's custody. The mother Angela Burns of the South End, explained softly, "I was only gone five minutes. I left the door open so my neighbor would hear him if he woke up. I never thought this would happen in daylight."

Version 2: Rats Bite Infant: Landlord, Tenants Dispute Blame

An eight-month-old South End boy was treated and released from Central Hospital yesterday after being bitten by rats while he was sleeping in his crib. Tenants said that repeated requests for extermination has been ignored by the landlord, Henry Brown. Brown claimed that the problem lay with tenants' improper disposal of garbage. "I spend half my time cleaning up after them. They throw the garbage out the window into the back alley and their kids steal the garbage can covers for sliding in the snow."

Version 3: Rat Bites Rising in City's "Zone of Death"

Rats bit eight-month-old Michael Burns five times yesterday as he napped in his crib. Burns is the latest victim of a rat epidemic plaguing inner-city neighborhoods labeled the "Zone of Death." Health officials say infant mortality rates in these neighborhoods approach those in many third world countries. A Public Health Department spokesperson explained that federal and state cutbacks forced short-staffing at rat control and housing inspection programs. The result, noted Joaquin Nunez, M.D., a pediatrician at General Hospital, is a five-fold increase in rat bites. He added, "The irony is that Michael lives within walking distance of some of the world's best medical centers."

Each of these versions directs the reader to think about the subject in a different way. The issue, responsibility, and solution to the problem vary according to how the facts are framed. In the first account, the mother is responsible. In the second, the responsibility revolves around the conflict between the landlord and tenants. The third version presents the broader social context in which these problems occur. All three are the result of a subjective interpretive concept. Each account can only offer a *version* of reality.[9]

Point of View in Film and Television

In film, the point of view (POV) informs the audience who is telling the story. Point of view determines the amount of information the audience has about the characters and situation. For example, the director may choose to isolate and follow the protagonist, whose image monopolizes the screen. The camera, then, takes the vantage point of a character or narrator in the film, showing us what the character sees.

Films and television programs occasionally assume a *first-person* perspective. The first-person point of view presents the action as interpreted by one character. For instance, the film *Ponette* (1996) recounts the story from the perspective (POV) of a four-year-old. The film follows Ponette (Victoire Thivisol) as she struggles to cope with the death of her mother. Director Jacques Doillon uses close-up shots of Ponette to capture her expressions of a grief she cannot understand. This child's-eye view is powerful, both in its meaning (children feel as adults but think differently) and in its ability to evoke feelings of empathy within members of the audience.

A camera shot commonly employed in first person POV is known as the *gaze*. This shot, which frequently is used in soap operas, draws the viewer into the character's mental state. Instead of glancing at an external entity, the character subjectively glances inward. While he stares into space, his eyes glazed over, or his speech falling silent, the camera often moves to a close-up, signaling that the character's attention is focused inward. What follows may be a dream sequence, memory image, intersubjective reasoning, or flashback. The gaze, then, informs us of the character's mental state.

Another point of view found in films and television programs is the *second-person perspective*, which, according to Art Siverblatt, makes the viewer the primary participant in the story. The second-person POV, says Bruce Kawin, "tell[s] 'you' the audience what to do."[10] Obviously, the second person ("you") perspective is nearly impossible to achieve in television and film unless you actually appear on the screen. However, TV and filmmakers simulate the second-person perspective by selecting performers to represent "you." For example, advertisements that use phrases like "People like you" and "Your friends" connect the people shown in the ads with the viewer. Silverblatt suggests that advertising's "man in the street approach" casts everyday people as "stand-ins" for "you" because they theoretically reflect our values and concerns.[11]

In the *third-person* POV, the media communicator follows the thoughts and activities of one character but retains some critical distance and is therefore not responsible for the behavior of the character. The third-person POV emphasizes the "separateness and individuality of the camera." Sometimes a shot may linger on a scene that a character either has not entered or has already left. The purpose is to emphasize the environment over character and action, context over content. James Monaco says in this third-person

POV, "the camera takes on a personality all its own, separate from those of the characters."[12]

Finally, the *omniscient* point of view allows the spectator to observe points of view from several characters on the screen. This perspective offers the audience a comprehensive exposure to the people and events depicted in the work. In this POV, the audience frequently is aware of the situation on-screen—even though the characters themselves remain unaware.

Laura Mulvey looks at point of view from a cultural perspective. For Mulvey, the dominant POV in film narrative is male:

> [P]leasure in looking has been split between active/male and passive/female. The determining male gaze projects its fantasy onto the female figure, which is styled accordingly . . . women are simultaneously looked at and displayed. . . . Women displayed as sexual objects is the leitmotif or erotic spectacle: from pin up to strip-tease from Ziegfield to Busby Berkeley, she holds the look, and plays to and signifies male desire.[13]

Mulvey argues that women represented on the screen are primarily the object of the male gaze from two (male) points of view: "as erotic object for the characters within the screen story, and as erotic object for the characters within the auditorium."[14] The power and privilege of male gaze results from the fact that in most instances men control both the business and apparatus of representation. In short, the majority of television and screen writers, directors, and producers are male and productions reflect their orientation and preoccupations.

For Laura Mulvey, women in cinema appear predominately as the object of male viewing pleasure. "Women are simultaneously looked at and displayed with their appearance coded for strong visual and erotic impact so that they can be said to connote to-be-looked-at-ness."[15] For example, Iain Softley's *Wings of the Dove* (1997), Atomm Egoyan's *The Sweet Hereafter* (1997), and James Cameron's *Titanic* (1997) all feature scenes with female nudity. It can be argued that these nude scenes were not needed to understand or support the narrative. The gratuitous nudity appeared for the benefit of the male gaze—including the male actors, directors, and the audience.

Angle

Angle refers to the level at which the camera is pointed in relation to the subject: high, low, or eye level. Camera angles can be used to comment on the status of the individuals on-camera. If the position of the camera is low, then the subject appears more powerful than if the camera angle is at eye level. With a low camera angle, the spectator, seeing from the camera's perspective, must look up at the subject or event. Emotionally, the superior position of the subject confirms his or her authority. A good illustration of using a low angle to communicate power is director Barry Levinson's *Wag the Dog* (1997). This film recounts how a contemporary spin doctor and Hollywood producer manipulate public sentiment. The low-angle shots underscore the power of spin doctors and media producers have to influence both what we think and how we think about events.

In automobile ads, cars photographed at a low angle appear larger and dynamic. Filming war missiles from a low angle makes them appear more destructive, and their speed is also enhanced when shot from a low angle.

When the camera takes a superior position, above eye level, the subject seen below appears smaller, inferior, frightened, or diminished psychologically. Viewers literally see the subject as "beneath them."

Cameras adjusted for straightforward viewing at eye level put the viewer on an equal plane with the subject. In television, newscasters and commercial actors look straight into the camera. It becomes synonymous with a face-to-face interaction, whereby the communicator seems to be addressing the viewer personally. The direct address at eye level creates an intimacy with the performers, inspiring feelings of trust, confidence, and loyalty in the audience.

An eye-level angle also establishes a sense of identification between the media communicator and the subject, as well as feelings of respect and acceptance. Cheryl Endicott, a graduate student at Webster University, conducted a media literacy analysis of *Sports 'N' Spokes* magazine:

> The aim of *Sports 'N' Spokes* is to portray persons with physical disabilities as positive role models by informing their readers that life doesn't end with an injury. It is aimed at showing them how to lead an active life, so that they can continue living and achieving. . . . Photos are usually taken either at eye level or looking up at the subject, which sends a departure from the standard view (looking down) at the person in the wheelchair. This choice of angle sends positive messages about the courage and achievements of these athletes.[16]

Connotation

Connotation refers to the meaning associated with a word or image beyond its literal, dictionary definition. The effect of connotative terms is dependent on whether their associative meanings are universally understood and agreed upon. For example, the word "rose" carries the denotative meaning of a flower. But depending on the context and culture, a rose also suggests love, passion,

Figure 5.2. **Photograph of Sports 'N' Spokes**

Photographing these athletes at eye level conveys a sense of respect for the players. Photo by Chuck Solomon. Copyright 1998, Paralyzed Veterans of America, by permission of S'NS.

perfection, or sexuality. Also, the color of a rose, whether it is yellow, red, or white, adds a further dimension to its meaning. And, if the rose has thorns, the implication may be the duality of pleasure and pain.

Media communicators depend on the connotative meanings to influence our thinking and feeling not only about ourselves, but about others and the world around us. The more cultural associations an audience brings to a message, the easier it is for the communicator to inform, persuade, entertain, and so forth.

Word Choice

Words are not neutral. They are a mode of communication and a medium for representing the world. Words carry both a dictionary (denotative) meaning and a connotative meaning. For instance, the word "house" simply describes a structure. However, "home" suggests a much richer meaning—a family gathered around the hearth, children playing video games, and the smells of dinner wafting in from the kitchen.

Sociologist Dorothy Melkin claims that public perceptions about science are shaped by connotative word choice. In the reporting of science and technology, war metaphors like "battles" or "struggles" create judgmental biases that underlie public policy. Medical research finds more enthusiastic support when the media tout "revolutionary breakthroughs," which is much more inspiring than "recent findings." Consider the difference between bacteria as a germ or bacteria as the enemy, and whether we "battle" diseases with "weapons" or treat them with medicine. This choice of words, Melkin says, not only evokes powerful battle images but influences public policy decisions, promoting the belief that technological progress should not be challenged and should be allowed to proceed without being questioned or regulated. However, questions the reader might pose include: "Was interferon a 'magic bullet' or a 'research tool'? Was Chernobyl a 'disaster' or an 'event'? Was Three Mile Island an 'accident' or 'an incident'? Is dioxin a 'doomsday chemical' or a 'potential risk'?"[17]

Connotative Image

In addition to words, images carry connotative meanings that derive not from image itself, but from how society has learned to use and value the image. For example, car commercials are not just about cars. Depending on the viewer, they can connote virility, power, or freedom. If a beautiful woman is in the scene, it adds a sexual dimension to the image.

Images in beer commercials and cigarette and alcohol advertisements are full of connotative meanings that promote product use. By combining words and images, advertisers strengthen the commercial message. The combination of images act much like joining a subject and a verb to make a sentence. The combination of images convey a meaning much different than a single word or single image.

Most alcohol and cigarette advertisements position young models with their products. The models appear successful, are attractive, and are engaged in fun activities. Beyond the denotative level, the choice of images suggest that using these products brings enjoyment, friendships, attractiveness, and pleasure. The ads present a constructed image that appears as reality. Connotatively, they offer personal transformation through the use of the product. The purchaser will be desirable and happy if he/she uses the product.

When images draw the viewer into identifying with the media presentation, the inner vision of the viewer connects with the outer representation in the media. This creates a world within the imagination and mind of the viewer that extends beyond what appears on-screen. This identification with the media image makes the media presentation appear natural. It unifies the viewer with the image, and the viewer begins to think of the media image as part of the natural world. In other words, the boundaries between the viewer and the media presentation are blurred. When an image elicits a response, we may be aware of its effect on us; however, an important question to consider is: why this particular image generates a certain emotional response.

Media communicators often rely on connotative images as a dramatic device. Sometimes the use of images foreshadows events. For example, in one scene in *Titanic* (1997), a crew member standing beside the captain looks out over the motionless, dark sea and remarks that the waters are so calm they will not be able to detect any icebergs. The camera immediately cuts to a close-up of the cup of black tea in the captain's hands. The tea is dark and motionless, like the ocean. As the captain rotates the cup, the liquid "waves" back and forth, and a slice of lemon suddenly emerges. This edit is not only a visual metaphor for the difficulty of detecting icebergs at night in a calm sea, but foreshadows the future tragedy. Some additional ways to read image combinations are listed below.

Condensation. This is the process by which we combine two unrelated images to form a new image. For instance, in an ad for Mercedes-Benz, the face of Marilyn Monroe is combined with the car logo to recast the image of Mercedes as a car of beauty, sexuality, and a cultural icon

Displacement. This is the process by which we transfer meaning from one sign or image to another. Displacement images often have strong sexual associations. In an ad for Baileys Original Irish Cream, the expression on the woman's face, her closed eyes, and the intimate close-up of the couple's face all impart a strong sexual meaning. The man's finger in the woman's mouth assumes a phallic symbol.

Metaphor. This is a device whereby one thing is said or inferred to be like something else. For example, an ad for PHYS nutritional web site puts broccoli instead of ice cream in an ice cream cone. Broccoli, metaphorically, takes on the qualities of ice cream. In other words, the qualities of ice cream are transferred to broccoli. This photo visually implies that broccoli is a tasty treat.

Figure 5.3. **Baileys Irish Cream**

The finger in the woman's mouth and the Baileys Irish Cream being poured into the glass at the lower right-hand corner presents strong symbolic imagery associating drinking Baileys Irish Cream with a sexual encounter. Copyright © The Paddington Corporation. Reprinted with permission.

Figure 5.4. **Broccoli on ice cream cone**

Broccoli is portrayed visually as a healthy treat. Courtesy CondéNet.
Reprinted with permission.

Metonomy. This is a process in which an image stands for a group of attributes. For example, Marlboro ads associate smoking Marlboros with individuality, freedom, independence, heroism, and, ironically, health. In liquor and beer advertisements, the consumption of the product represents fun, friends, happiness, and attractive physical appearance.

Graphics

Although content is a distinguishing factor, the form a publication takes (all graphic elements combined) sends messages about the quality, clarity, and the authority of the publication. Graphic representation is a sign system—in essence, a language for the eye. Charts, graphs, illustrations, and maps visually display complex data, making it easier to understand and store information. Like language, these figurative images tell stories. Producers of graphic material assign meaning to each sign element before it is presented. The perception of these visual displays is a process in which the viewer considers the relationship between the signs and their predetermined meaning.

Jeremy Black asserts that, in this respect, graphics "play a major role in politics, both international and domestic, reflecting the ability of visual images and messages to contribute to the discourse of power."[18] They are symbols of belief—mental images—which guide our thinking about politics, economics, society, and medical care. Charts, graphs, and statistical analyses influence decisions such as insurance rates, interest rates, and public policy. Graphic representations categorize people, places, and things. This includes class, wealth, and social environment. These symbols, printed in newspapers and posted on television, help solidify the agenda of those in power by colonizing the belief of readers and viewers.[19]

Artist and newspaper cartoonist Bob Staake contends that in the print medium, graphic images are becoming the dominant form of expression, overwhelming the written word: "It's already obvious as we look at the newspapers on the Internet. You can't just put a bunch of words up on the screen. There has to be plenty of illustrations, graphics, and pictures. . . . Artists are going to be part of the decision process."[20]

However, graphic representation certainly cannot provide a comprehensive or realistic depiction of treality. For example, during the 1990–91 Gulf War, newspapers included maps showing the movement of American troops through Iraqi territory, as well as charts and diagrams comparing American and Iraqi military weapons. These graphic representations clearly showed America's tactical success and military superiority. However, the arrows, missiles, and other symbols of war showed nothing of the destruction, fear, pain, and suffering caused by their use. In other words, the choice of the selection and representation came from a powerful political agenda and was used as a persuasive appeal for the war and the American military complex. Journalist Victor Cohn cautions that charts and graphs displaying survey results or polls are just "snapshots of the scene at the moment." These frozen moments do not represent time over a long continuum nor do they define the quality of the studies, questionnaires, or answers, written or verbal.[21] In addition, charts showing statistical analysis can lead to a mistaken and simplistic cause and effect sensibility. For example, several statistical charts reveal that the incidence of delinquent behavior is higher in families where the father is absent. There is a correlation, but correlation does not translate to causation. What is hidden and obscured are numerous other variables such as the size of the population being studied, the socioeconomic level, and the quality of education. In other words, are there other factors that would have a significant link to the high rate of delinquency in children without fathers?

Pie charts can also be easily manipulated. For instance, percentages in the pie chart may not add up to a whole (100 percent). When looking at visual graphs, charts, and diagrams, questions of concern are:

- Who says so?
- Does the source of information have any bias?
- What is missing?
- What are the groups being represented?
- What is the purpose?
- Whose agenda does it support?
- How does the title relate to the content?
- Do the numbers make sense?

To illustrate, when newspapers print graphs showing how much the unemployment rate is down, the viewer needs to examine these graphics closely. Does the graph indicate just full-time employment or does it include those people in part-time employment receiving minimum wages and limited, if any, benefits?

The visual presentation of graphics also can distort the information being introduced. For instance, a company whose earnings rose 10 percent could make the increase appear much larger through the use of a graph. Depending on the proportional increase in number along the side of the chart, the rise in earnings can visually appear as a moderate 10 percent or a soaring 10 percent. In addition, pie charts that are tilted forward for easier viewing often make the front pieces appear larger than those behind.

Figure 5.5. **Comparative graphs**

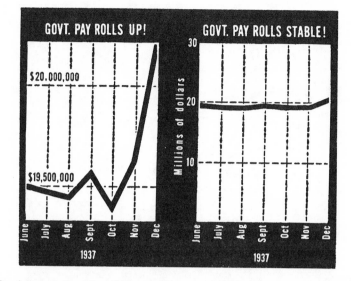

The visual presentation of graphics can affect our understanding of its message. Both graphs present identical information; however, the numerical spacing within the graph on the left makes the increase in government pay appear more dramatic than the graph on the right. From *How to Lie With Statistics*, by Darrell Huff; illustrated by Irving Geis. Copyright 1954 and renewed © 1982 by Darrell Huff and Irving Geis. Reprinted by permission of W.W. Norton & Company, Inc.

Typography

How do print publications attract and maintain their audience? The magnetic force, according to graphic designers and typographers, is in the art of typography and layout. Graphic designer Erik Spiekermann and typographer E.M. Ginger observe, "The artistry comes in offering the information in such a way that the reader doesn't get side tracked. . . . Designing . . . has to be invisible. Typefaces used for these hard working tasks are, therefore, by definition 'invisible.' "[22] However, according to Kevin Barnhurst, typography can provide a graphic representation of the content, reinforce messages, or comment on the content:

> In a sort of visual onomatopoeia, the form of typography can mimic sizes, weights, shapes and postures from the environment. Large, bold headlines are mimetic of dramatic events. In whimsical feature articles, letter forms might take the shape of ghosts, or cooking utensils. . . . Turning a word upside-down [in headline] can suggest the state of the world. When the new sense and the content of the text coincide, meaning can be reinforced or expanded.[23]

Figure 5.6. **Typefaces**

walk, (Century Bold Condensed, 24 pt.)

run, (Party Plain, 72 pt.)

jump, (La Bamba, 36 pt.)

or *dance.* (Party, 48 pt.)

Party says "Surprise" (Party, 30 pt.)

Franklin Gothic says "Urgent"
(Franklin Gothic, 18 pt.)

Randumhouse says "festive"
(Randumhouse , 24 pt.)

Treehouse says "playful" (Treehouse - Plain, 30 pt.)

Examples of how fonts can be used to express a range of emotions and feelings.

To illustrate, in the February 1, 1998 issue of the *St. Louis Post-Dispatch*, the headlines on the front page, as well as throughout the entire paper, use a variety of font sizes and type widths. The bold-type headlines grab the viewers attention first, signifying that the articles are "weighted" in importance according to the boldness of type given the headline. Two examples are: The paper included a story about the local school district and arranged it next to an article covering President Clinton's affair with Monica Lewinsky. The school headline featured a narrow, light, airy font, with a subtitle written in graceful script, while the Clinton article featured a heavy, serious, foreboding font.[24]

Typography also can communicate emotions. Spiekermann and Ginger observe that even before we read a word, its shape and thickness can trigger an opinion. Depending on the space surrounding the letters, "dark emotions call for a black typeface with sharp edges; pleasant feelings are best evoked by informal, light characters." Emotions like anger are best illustrated in black, heavy typeface with an irregular shape, which helps trigger the imagination. Typefaces that are casual and look like handwritten letters suggest surprise. Surprise needs to carry a feeling of spontaneity. Joy, on the other hand needs a "generous feel ... open forms with confident strokes and a sense of movement."[25]

Albert J. Kastl and Irvin L. Child's studies reveal that typefaces are used by advertisers to enhance certain moods. Light, ornate typefaces promote a sprightly, sparkling, dreamy or calm mood. Simple bold typefaces were rated as sad, dignified, and dramatic in mood. Typefaces are also associated with gender, race, and nationality. Roy Paul Nelson observes, "The meaning assigned to type by readers and typographers seems to spring not from some objective code but from cultural experience common to both groups."[26]

Both newspapers and magazines express their personalities through the accumulation of visual cues. Readers recognize a publication by its logotype (nameplate). One glance at a newsstand will reveal the numerous personalities vying for recognition among the cornucopia of offerings. The logotype gives the publication a personalized visual identity, which becomes a familiar symbol for the reading audience. For example, the nameplate of the *New York Times* uses narrow bold serif letters, imitating the old gothic script (textura). This type conveys the *Times*'s long-standing claim to authority and championing of progressive values rooted in nineteenth-century visionary values. In contrast, local and regional papers like the *St. Louis Post-Dispatch* and Cleveland's *Plain Dealer* sport nameplates with broad, open black letters, conveying a more accessible spirit.

Entertainment Weekly is a good example of how the power of design presents a distinctive voice to attract an audience. *Entertainment Weekly*

Figure 5.7.

GREECE
JAMAICA
Ceylon
China
M E X I C O
Tahiti
Canada
Iʀelaɴᴅ
Scotland
Denmark
Japan
pORTUGAL
BRITAIN

Over time, certain letter forms have become associated with particular countries (e.g., Greece capturing the early Greek lettering). *Source:* Nelson, Roy Paul. 1989. *Publication Design.* Dubuque: Wm. C. Brown Company, p. 79. Reprinted with permission of the McGraw-Hill Companies, Inc.

uses a consistent typography to give the readers a sense of familiarity. The magazine is organized into sections—Film, TV, Music, and so forth—each graphically identified by a color-coded tab. Each of these sections is presented in the same typographic hierarchy. The lead story is followed by shorter reviews, side bars, and graphic inserts that combine charts, illustrations, and text. To attract attention, the cover employs large pictures and introduces the lead stories with attention-grabbing gothic cover lines, which are designed differently than the rest of the magazine.

Figure 5.8. **Mastheads**

𝕿𝖍𝖊 𝕹𝖊𝖜 𝖄𝖔𝖗𝖐 𝕿𝖎𝖒𝖊𝖘

THE PLAIN DEALER

Copyright © 1998 by The New York Times Company. Reprinted by permission.

Reprinted with permission from *The Plain Dealer* © 1998. All rights reserved.

Graphic titles play a significant role in film and television, whether it be the blasting fire and neon graphics of *Casino* (1995) or the witty montage of fictional tabloid headlines in *To Die For* (1995). Like the overture to a symphony, the title sequence introduces the film's theme. Pablo Ferro, designer for *To Die For,* said the story told in the film's headlines establishes Nicole Kidman's character and clarifies the plot. Ferro wanted the audience "to find out who she was before they met her. . . ."[27]

Graphic titles lead the audience into the film, set the tone, and outline the filmmaker's intentions. Randy Balsmeyer (*Fargo, Dead Man, Kama Sutra, Naked Lunch*) says good titles "set you up emotionally for what's to follow, but also create a deep undercurrent of emotion that will color everything that comes after. . . ."[28] For example, using surveillance-type photography and kerning fonts, Kyle Cooper established Johnny Depp's outsider status in the opening credits of *Donnie Brasco* (1997), which hinted at the character's obsessions and the story of the Mafia's descent into hell.

The opening credits in *Brassed Off* (1996) represent a subtle but poignant way to foreshadow events in the film. The story takes place in Grimley, an English mining town, where the surviving pride of the community is its 100–year-old brass band. Most of the men in Grimley earn their living by working in the "pit." Not only is the pit being shut down, but many of the miners suffer from life-threatening black lung disease. In the film's opening credits, all the "P's" are bright red, foreshadowing the physical, pshychological, and economic dangers troubling this small mining community.

Logos

Logos are symbols of identity. Logos are placed on products and serve as a face, communicating the company's essence and personality. Gerry Rosentsweig says logos reflect social changes and images of American

Figures 5.9 and 5.10. **Graphic Titles,** *Donnie Brasco* (TriStar Pictures, 1997)

Graphic titles often foreshadow significant themes and events in media presentations. For example, in the opening credits of *Donnie Brasco* (1997) directed by Mike Newell, the combination of graphic titles and visuals introduces the main character's role as an FBI agent who infiltrates the mob. This graphic style is seen throughout the movie, as Brasco types his reports on mob activities and sends them to the FBI.

businesses. Today, he says, the best "new" logos are simplified in an effort to combat the years of corruption associated with business.[29] Effective logos share the following characteristics:

- original
- witty
- accessible
- mythic
- idiosyncratic
- emotive
- memorable.

Globalization necessitates that logo design are instantly recognizable and convey meaning, regardless of culture and language barriers. For example, the ubiquitous Nike "swoosh" is easily recognized throughout the world. In fact, the swoosh may be more recognizable than the name Nike itself.

Nike was the Greek Goddess of Victory. According to a Nike Consumer Affairs statement (1996), "The Nike swoosh embodies the spirit of the winged goddess who inspired the most courageous and chivalrous warriors at the dawn of civilization."[30]

The swoosh logo is a visual shorthand that embodies the company's ideology; in that regard, the swoosh may be considered the face of Nike. Its natural curved form creates a sense of perpetual motion. Nike CEO Phil Knight asserts that the swoosh logo symbolizes "never giving up . . . never slowing down . . . not being afraid to try something new. . . . It stands for passion, pride, and authenticity, innovation, and courage."[31] Nike spent $800 million in 1997 marketing its products with the swoosh logo to ensure its emotional appeal reached a worldwide audience.[32] The Nike logo has become an icon that transcends its original commercial purposes: fifty-nine easily identifiable swooshes were counted in the editorial pages of a ninety-page pro football magazine.[33]

Color

Colors evoke a wide range of emotional responses in the viewer. For example, warm colors (red, orange, and yellow) can cause an "aggressive" reaction. Psychological research has found that extroverted personality types often prefer these colors; in contrast, introverts are attracted to cooler, subtler tones such as blue, green, or purple. Warm colors (yellow, orange), also can heighten nostalgic feelings. Researchers have found that muscle reaction is measurably faster under the influence of red, whereas bubblegum pink, when used in a decoration scheme, lowers heart and pulse rates.[34]

Practically every religion, tradition, and superstition has assigned symbolic meaning to specific colors. In some cultures, red has been viewed as the vigorous color of health. For healing purposes, red wool was applied to sprains in Scotland, sore throats in Ireland, and was used to reduce fever in Macedonia. The Chinese wore brilliant red rubies to ensure long life. Conversely, red also signals blood and danger, and, for Valentine's Day enthusiasts, red symbolizes love and passion. Since the days of heraldry, yellow has been associated with gold. Religious painters have shrouded the Virgin Mary in blue. Since Roman times, purple has been symbolic of power, leadership, royalty, and respect.

The University of Basel in Switzerland compiled the following associations and responses to color from subjects in Western Europe and the United States:

- Blue—trust, sensitivity, loyalty, nurturance, piety, and sincerity.
- Brown—vitality, receptivity, and sensuality (the color of Mother Earth).
- Green—regeneration and growth, harmony, and abundance (associated with hope).
- Orange—competition, a color of excitability and activity.
- Red—impulse and intensity, blood and sexuality, youthfulness and forcefulness.
- Yellow—philosophical, intellectual (associated with anticipation).[35]

The *shade* of a color can also affect its meaning. In Western cultures, dark blue is associated with peace, security, and contentment. Violet (a variation of purple) represents magic, imagination, and romance.[36] But while each culture may ascribe its own distinctive meaning to colors, there is often considerable overlap between cultures, reflecting some level of consensus.

In media presentations, color often sets the mood and tone of a production. For example, cold blue colors with harsh edges can create an ominous futuristic environment. Subdued colors reflect conservative values; vibrant red can warn of danger and violence.

The meaning of color also will vary depending on the context in which it is presented. For instance, in *Event Horizon* (1997), a sci-fi horror film that takes place on a space ship, cinematographer Adrian Biddle used sepia brown and flashes of red coming up from the floor "to make people uncomfortable on the ship." Whereas green usually evokes feelings of calm, Biddle used a "lot" of green to produce the "nasty horrible green you get from fluorescence when it's not corrected."[37] Biddle said he wanted the viewers to feel uncomfortable and to convey the idea that something evil was lurking on the ship.

The juxtaposition of contrasting colors can produce feelings of tension. Tim Burton's *The Nightmare Before Christmas* (1993) makes strategic use of contrasting colors to evoke feelings of confusion in the audience. The story revolves around the leader of dark Halloween town, Jack Singleton, who wanders through the forest and gains renewed hope when he stumbles upon the vibrant colors and joy of Christmas town. The dark blues and grays creates a nightmarish atmosphere that corresponds to Jack's inner darkness and confusion. At the same time, the vibrant colors of Christmas in the town convey a vision of joy and hope.

Since the meaning of color varies among cultures, media communicators must be sensitive to the cultural language of color when attempting to convey a message. For instance, when an Irish beer producer aired his beer commercial in Hong Kong, sales dropped dramatically. The commercial featured the tossing of a green hat. The company quickly pulled the commercial off the air when they were informed that "wearing a green hat" was a Chinese euphemism for being cuckolded.[38]

Another example occurs in the film *Selena* (1996). Latino cinematographer Edward Lachman contrasted Selena's Anglo world from her roots in the Latino culture. Lachman explains:

> Color is very important to Latinos. It's a part of our world, one that has a more intense use of color than the Anglo world. We used color to weave the emotions of the story. Selena grew up in an Anglo neighborhood, so we used umbers and monotone colors to reflect that experience. Then she is introduced to her Latino heritage, we began to use more pastel primary colors, which are indicative of that culture. . . .[39]

Black and white (as a contrast to color) can also be used to distinguish the imagined from the real when depicting a dream or imaginary sequence. For example, in Kasi Lemmons's film *Eve's Bayou* (1997), the character Mozelle (Debbi Morgan) has a gift for telling fortunes. Mozelle's psychic visions of the future are presented in black and white, while the remainder of the narrative is presented in color.

A recent Tavist-D (antihistamine) commercial thematically uses black-and-white and color to dramatize the effects of the product. The black-and-white opening scene shows a tight close-up of a frowning women obviously in discomfort. The caption and voice-over ask, "Where do you go for help?" As she emerges from her car on a cold, rainy evening and walks into a drug store. As she reaches for the Tavist-D, color sweeps over the screen. Next, we see the same woman transformed in a bright red coat, hair coifed and makeup applied energetically run down the steps. Sporting a vibrant smile, she greets a man passing her on the steps with a cheerful "Good Morning."

Within sixty seconds Tavist-D magically changes her life both from sickness to health, as the scene changes and from drab monotony to "full-color" lively existence.

Color is often used as a narrative device to convey themes. Throughout the film adaptation of Jane Austin's novel *Sense and Sensibility* (1995), director Ang Lee displayed the constrained values of Victorian society through a muted and subdued color palate. Conversely, in *Mishima* (1985) director Paul Schrader chose three color schemes to delineate the spheres of the playwright's life. Schrader rendered Mishima's contemporary life in Technicolor, his past life in black and white, and his theatrical plays in surreal yellows, greens, reds, and blacks.

Lighting

"And God said let there be light." Light has been laden with symbolism since the remote mists of time. Importantly, in visual media those objects or people who are "in the light" attract our attention and are presumed to be the most important within the frame. Lighting composition not only directs the viewer's attention to the particular subject, but also elicits certain emotional responses to the scene.

Bright lighting used in comedies and musicals evokes a feeling of joy, security, and optimism, while film noir's harsh dark lighting drapes the world in shadows, reinforcing the genre's theme of subjective reality by making it difficult to differentiate hero from villain. "X-Files" director Rob Bowman says he creates harsh shadows to emphasize the threatening quality of reality. The signature for the television series, he maintains, is darkness: "The alien aspect is just a metaphor for the mistrust of the Government, about our isolation. The subtractive lighting isolates the viewer. There is the inevitable doom that seems to be waiting for you. You'll never figure out the conspiracy."[40]

Lighting can be hard, soft or any gradation in between. Hard lighting creates strong shadows, while soft lighting is shadowless. The type of lighting used depends on the story to be told. Lighting can be manipulated to produce a desired dramatic effect. For example, in *The Bridges of Madison County* (1995) the soft overhead lighting in Francesca's (Meryl Streep) kitchen creates a warm lush atmosphere that lends romance to the slow dance between Francesca and Kincaid (Clint Eastwood). Cinematographer Jack Green designed the lighting in the romantic scene "to be lush and warm when the characters were together and falling in love."[41]

Depending on its context, lighting can signify truth and wisdom. The television dramas "ER" and "Chicago Hope" frequently use overhead light-

Figure 5.11. *Bridges of Madison County* (Warner Brothers, 1995)

Lighting can create an atmosphere which supports themes and situations in visual communications. In this scene from *Bridges of Madison County* (1995), the soft overhead lighting creates a romantic atmosphere that helps fuel their brief impassioned affair.

ing sources to enshrine the doctors while they operate. The remainder of the cast perform in the dark background. This sends the message that the doctor is privileged with the light of divine wisdom, endowing him with the knowledge and skill to cure, while the remainder of the operating room staff works in the shadows of "dark ignorance." (In contrast, real-life operating rooms are brightly lit, so that the entire staff can see to perform their essential duties.)

Dark or harshly lit pictures can trigger feelings of fear, tension, and a sense of impending evil in the audience. *Twelve Monkeys* (1995) is a futuristic film set in 2035, a time when most of the Earth's population has been wiped out by a mysterious plague. Cole (Bruce Willis) is selected to travel from the underworld back to 1996 in hopes of identifying the source of the fatal, pandemic contagion. When Cole emerges above ground, he enters a world that director Terry Gilliam calls a "twilight area of snow, a place where there are no human beings, just animals." The exterior scenes in this "dead world" are portrayed in "cold, darkish, unfriendly light."[42]

Figure 5.12. *Chicago Hope* ("Right to Life," January 22, 1996, Producer David E. Kelly)

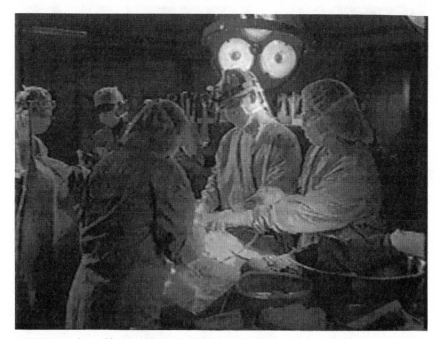

In this scene from *Chicago Hope*, the lighting behind Dr. Kronk (Peter Berg) elevates his status as a healing physician.

In *Thelma and Louise* (1991) director Ridley Scott employed lighting to foreshadow the film's thematic transition from optimism to tragedy. Coffee-shop waitress Louise (Susan Sarandon) and Thelma (Geena Davis), an abused housewife, decide to take a weekend fishing trip as a diversion from their oppressed lives. The two friends set out on their trek in bright, sunny daylight.

The lighting, mood, and situation change, however, as the two women stop at a bar for a drink. As they leave the dimly lit building, the women confront an even darker night outside. Suddenly, the situation shifts from an innocent weekend of fun and fishing as Thelma is accosted and raped in the parking lot. Louise intercedes on her friend's behalf, fatally shooting the assailant. In a panic, the two decide to flee the country. Most of their journey is brightly lit, symbolizing their hopes as they head toward a new life. But once again, the lighting switches to foreshadow their tragic end. As they drive through the New Mexico desert at night, the world is dark and silent. The car headlights bouncing off the rock formations serve as the only

Figure 5.13. *Twelve Monkeys* (Universal Entertainment, 1995)

In this scene from *Twelve Monkeys*, director Terry Gilliam manipulates lighting to create a "dead world in darkish, unfriendly light."

illumination. Once again the lighting brightens for their final "liberation," driving off a precipice to escape the armed brigade of police who are pursuing them.

Shape

Lines and shapes are major structural elements of media presentations. Vertical lines impart a sense of dignity, class, and power. Advertisers for business and financial services construct images featuring vertical lines, block graphs, and towering skyscrapers to convey a sense of power, wealth, and stability.

Horizontal lines create a relaxed, calm, quiet, serene impression. Travel and leisure advertisers design their ads with wide horizontal tranquil vistas, inviting the viewer to expand his/her horizons in a relaxed environment. In contrast, advertisements for products like cars and sports equipment usually position the products on a diagonal trajectory to evoke a sense of escape, movement, or speed.

Diagonal lines are dynamic, which suggests action. Curved lines evoke a natural feeling of warmth and humor. Converging lines add depth and perspective to a presentation.

Although individual lines have their own core meaning, they may be combined to make shapes like circles, squares, and triangles, which carry added significance. Media communicators, both literally and symbolically, use lines and shapes to construct their media productions, and their subsequent meanings.

Circle

The circle is a geometric form that represents wholeness. It has no beginning or end. Its shape reminds us of the sun and the moon, symbolizing the vital aspect of life that psychologist Carl Jung calls the ultimate wholeness of the self.[43] Hans Biederman says the circle holds important symbolic meaning in many cultures:

> For various native American peoples, the orbit of the moon, and the apparent orbits of the sun and stars, are round forms, and such forms appear in the way things grow in nature. Thus the camp, the teepee, and the seating arrangements are all based on the circle. It is not uncommon to find traditional dances following (or generating) circles. In Zen Buddhism the circle stands for enlightenment. . . . In the Chinese the symbol of Yin and Yang, duality is enclosed in the circle.[44]

In magic lore, the circle is a protected and consecrated space that keeps out evil spirits. Ancient civilizations built walls around their cities for protection against potential enemies. And in terms of interpersonal interactions, "social circles" exclude by setting people apart.

The circle has a particular significance in modern times as well. According to Jung, the "visionary rumor of flying saucers (or UFOs), is an attempt by the unconscious collective psyche to heal the 'split' of man's lost soul. The soul is separated from its roots and things spiritual."[45] Lovable characters like the Smurfs, Care Bears, and the Pillsbury Dough Boy have a round, soft, benign, and nurturing quality, Conversely, villainous characters like the Horde Troopers and Darth Vader have a hard, angular appearance, signifying power and triggering feelings of fear and aversion in the audience.

Square

The square represents the material world. In contrast to the circle, the square is associated with four spatial orientations of horizontal and vertical directions. Navigation around the square's perimeter symbolizes the need to find one's way in a chaotic world. The right angle symbolizes justice and the true law. The right angle formed by the square also signifies the ideal balance between body and spirit.[46] Psychologically, its form gives the impression of firmness and stability, which explains its frequent use in symbols of corporate organizations.

In his treatise on democracy, Aristotle suggested that each town establish an *agora*. Agora is the Greek name for marketplace, a consecrated open space which became the center of commercial, political, and religious activity. As time progressed, these agoras became known as public *squares*. People assembled in locations such as the town hall, coffee house, and taverns for open and robust political debates and action.

Significantly, the television screen itself is square. The engaged viewer symbolically enters the square and vicariously participates in the exchange of ideas. Since the square represents stability and order, the multitude of visual squares in television news presentations psychologically sends a message of order and stability in the world.

The electronic display of squares in television presentations has become the modern counterpart of the public square. When on-site reporters converse with off-site guests, the off-site guests are framed in squares. Within these squares, dialogues occur, ideas are expressed and, sometimes, heated words are exchanged. These visual icons evoke images of democracy where political discussions and community action take place.

However, at times the concept of the town square is merely an illusion. On February 18, 1998, CNN taped three top policy officials in a town hall format. This meeting was set up to discuss the administration's declared intent to bomb Iraq, in the face of violations of the UN treaty agreement reached in the Gulf War. Defense Secretary William Cohen, Secretary of State Madeline Albright, and National Security Adviser Samuel Berger met with students, faculty, and guests at Ohio State University. Seated in the midst of the University's basketball arena, the three officials were supposed to provide information and answer questions regarding the administration's policy decision.

But instead of a town hall (square) meeting, the session presented a closed circle. Aristotle's idea of the public square as a matrix of democratizing politics had been reconfigured into a closed circle within a private square for purposes of publicity and image. Defense Secretary Cohen responded to the first question with another question. When asked as to whether the United States had the moral right to attack the Iraqi nation, Cohen replied, "The question is also, does Saddam Hussein have the moral right to use weapons of mass destruction against his people"?

Madeline Albright seemed adept at deflecting skeptical questions as well. One audience member repeatedly questioned why the United States singled out Iraq when other countries had committed similar violations. After giving evasive answers, Ms. Albright patronizingly responded, "I suggest, sir, that you study carefully what American foreign policy is. . . ."[47]

What should have been a "celebration of democracy" turned into what Representative John Boehner (R-Ohio) called an "unmitigated disaster."[48] Questions were asked, but answers never came, an exchange of ideas never occurred.

Triangle

The triangle carries a wide variety of interpretations. In pre-Christian times the philosopher Xenocrates viewed the equilateral triangle as "divine," and the isosceles as "demonic."[49] The Greek letter delta, triangular in form, was a symbol of cosmic birth. Early Christians used the triangle as a symbol of the Trinity, signifying the Father, the Son, and the Holy Ghost.

When triangles began to appear on ceramics, those pointing downward were interpreted as water symbols, suggesting falling rain. Those pointing upward were seen as fire symbols, upward being the direction of flames.

These triadic structures with three angles and three sides are recognizable patterns that help organize the visual world around us, producing a sense of psychological closure. Accordingly, Harry Remde says, man is a triadic creature and his unity and sense of wholeness depend on the balance of shapes like the triad.[50] The triangle exemplifies the intricate intertwining of the head that thinks, the body that performs, the feeling that unites. Claude Bragdon explains, "Three is preeminently the number of architecture, because it is the number of our space, which is three-dimensional, and, of all the arts, architecture is most concerned with the expression of spatial relations. The division of a composition into three related parts is so universal that it would seem to be the result of an instinctive action of the human mind."[51]

The laws of polarity, which is the tension of two opposites, are never static. The dynamic interaction of two parts react upon one another to produce a third, hence the law of the Trinity. Translated into metaphysical terms, the human conscience can be viewed as the third principle, the duality and tension between good and evil within each individual.[52] The conflicting images of the triangle's opposing sides (horizontal and vertical) are conjured up in such phrases as the Oedipal triangle, the love triangle, and Bermuda triangle.

Media communicators effectively utilize the tensions created by triangular relationships in their presentations to comment on the dynamics of human relationships. For example, the film adaptation of Henry James's novel *The Wings of the Dove* (1997) effectively illustrates the psychological tensions within the characters themselves and the dynamic tensions of a

Figure 5.14. **Two Triangles**

triangular relationship. Kate Croy (Helena Bonham Carter) is enmeshed in a passionate love affair with working-class journalist Merton Densher (Linus Roache). Survival for Kate dictates that she marry the shiftless Lord Mark (Alex Jennings) or be disinherited by her Aunt Maude (Charlotte Rampling). Therefore, marriage for Kate and Merton is out of the question.

Kate befriends American heiress Milly Theale (Alison Elliot). When she discovers that Milly is dying, Kate devises a scheme whereby Merton will seduce Milly. Her plan is that Milly, who is already attracted to Merton, will leave her fortune to him upon her death, so that he can marry Kate. The tensions revolve around love, avarice, and deception. This sordid plan results from the conflictual decision that confronts Kate—to live a loveless life as defined by her guardian or suffer destitution.

Outside the narrative format, talk shows like "Jerry Springer" often capitalize on the dramatic tensions created by triangular relationships. Either the host, acting as a third party, will provoke the tension, or a third party who is involved with the couple will serve as the catalyst.

The media themselves are structured on an active triangular relationship revolving around the media communicator, the production, and the audience. Several interactive tensions regulate the flow of this relationship. First, the relationship between the communicator and his/her production depends on economic, political, and technical factors. Second, the production must attract an audience, which implies that there is a relationship between the work and the audience. The production must in some way respond to the needs of the audience or it would not be produced or realize wide distribution. This leads to a third relationship between the communicator and the audience. The communicator must balance the tension between his own creative expression, economic viability, and meeting the needs of the audience. The communicator's work must attract an audience to ensure continued production of his/her work.

Movement

Motion is a unique characteristic of television and film. Movement has a dramatic impact on the spectator's viewing position. Art Silverblatt observes, "The principle of movement reduces the distance between illusion and reality, and, in the process, also narrows the distinction between media and reality."[53] One category of movement commonly employed in film and television is *camera speed*. The variable speed of the camera allows the filmmaker to alter the rate at which events are depicted on-screen in order to send a desired message to the viewer. Slow motion stretches time, revealing details of motion that would not be perceptible in real time. Media communicators sometimes use slow motion to create a romantic or poetic mood. Time lapse photography shows the subtle nuances of changes over a period of time: the metamorphosis of a caterpillar, or the opening of a flower can be condensed into a few seconds of screen time. Fast motion speeds up and condenses time. Fast motion is also frequently used for comedic effect, making normal actions look absurd. All these techniques allow us to comprehend events that happen too quickly or too slowly under normal time.

Camera movements establish the relationship between the camera, the subject, and the viewer:

- In a *pan shot,* the camera rotates on its axis, giving a panoramic view of the screen and situating the viewer within the scene's environment. A pan shot can also be used to follow the movement of characters across the screen.
- *Tilting* moves the camera up and down to follow the movement of the screen subject.
- In *tracking shots,* the camera moves on the ground in a vertical line, horizontal line, or a vector.
- *Crane shots* are taken by cameras mounted on a "cherrypicker," which allows shots to be taken from several directions. In both tracking and crane shots, the subject within the frame can be moving while the camera moves along with the subject, or the camera can move while the subject remains still.

The various combinations of these mechanical movements provide opportunities for the media communicator to reinforce themes and convey messages. Television's medical drama "ER" uses a fast careening steadicam that grabs viewers' attention, pulling them into the scene and engaging them in the journey as the camera swoops through crowded corridors and zooms in and out of trauma rooms. The rapid-pulsed camera movement evokes a feeling of vitality and flux that captures the tension and chaos of the emergency room.

Character movement constitutes a third type of motion employed in film and television. Because the audience's frame of reference is the camera, a character's movement toward or away from the camera triggers an emotional response in the viewer. The meaning behind a particular movement often is defined by the context of the situation. If the character is a villain, his movement toward the camera can seem aggressive, hostile, or threatening. The same action by an attractive character will feel friendly, inviting, or seductive. In general, forward movements by both types of characters are strong and confident. In contrast, movement away from the camera lens (audience) lessens the intensity of feeling, diminishes the threat of a villainous character, or signals abandonment.

Movement from top to bottom of the screen often has a negative connotation, suggesting a transgression, failure, or unhappiness. A pivotal scene in *Raging Bull* (1980) is a brutal boxing match between Jake La Motta and Sugar Ray Robinson. At the end of the scene, there is a close-up of the rope that surrounds the boxing ring. The rope encompasses the entire screen. On the right side of the rope (screen), we see La Motta's blood transmitting a visceral resonance as we watch the blood's rhythmic descent from the top of the screen to the bottom (drip, drip, drip).

Similarly, lateral movement can carry significant meaning. In Western cultures, movement from left to right is considered more "natural," legitimate, and appropriate (in part because of the direction in which we read). Conversely, movement from right to left goes against the natural flow and signals awkwardness, abnormality, or contrivance. For example, in *The Wings of the Dove* (1997), Merton (Linus Roache) is disappointed after waiting several hours for Kate (Helena Bonham Carter) to meet him. Director Iain Softley exploits Merton's psychological state of rejection by having Merton rise from the park bench and sluggishly straggle off to the left of the screen.

Automobile commercials frequently rely on movement to dramatize the performance of the advertised vehicles. For example, the use of movement in a recent ad for Cadillac Catera equates the movement of the automobile with speed, power, excitement, freedom, and risk-taking. The ad shows the car suddenly swerving into the oncoming lane, crossing a double yellow line to pass a BMW and a Lexus. This pass takes place while the car is going uphill on a two-lane road. An approaching vehicle coming over the hill would have difficulty slowing down or avoiding a head-on collision with the Catera.[54] The movement of the automobile offers a sense of rebirth—suggesting that owning the car is a regenerative experience. The slogan for the ad—"Born to be alive"—reinforces this nonverbal cue.

The commercial also equates the movement of the vehicle with a sense of purpose, direction, and progress. This visual message reinforces the voice-over, which announces that people who drive a Catera are "born to lead." However, in order to be a leader, the ad visually shows that you must

Figure 5.15. *Raging Bull* (United Artists, 1980)

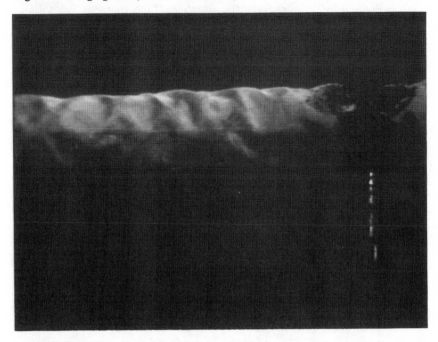

Movement from top to bottom of the screen often has a negative connotation. This scene from Martin Scorsese's *Raging Bull* features a close-up of blood dripping from the rope surrounding the ring. This movement symbolizes the brutality of the sport and its terrible cost to the two boxers.

break the rules—the car is speeding and moving beyond the yellow lines. Drivers in these types of commercials seem to be exempt from the law, since they are never apprehended by the police for speeding. Indeed, the risky driving style (accelerating rapidly, swerving around curves, etc.) appears normal, safe, and commonplace in the ad.

Scale

Scale refers to the relative size of two objects on a page or screen. Scale determines how the audience responds to the people and objects depicted and influences our perception of the events portrayed.

Epic films utilize scale to illustrate the adventures of heroic or legendary heroes and themes. Grand epic films like *The Ten Commandments* (1956), *Star Wars* (1977), *Gandhi* (1982), and *Dances with Wolves* (1990) contain striking contrasts between mortals and the vast landscape, enabling the viewer to experience the magnitude of grand themes such as humans' relationship with God and nature and the conflict between good and evil. The relative size of objects on screen can also reveal cultural dynamics. Zang Zimou's *Raise the Red Lantern* (1991) presents a confined world, as the camera repeatedly looks down on an enclosed courtyard. On either side of the courtyard, houses are adorned with red lanterns where the master's four wives live. The master resides in a large house situated at the end of the long courtyard. Throughout the film, the four wives of the master are seen through the confining frames of doorways and archways.

Occasionally we get a glimpse of an open vista from the rooftop, which is lit in cold twilight grays. Any sense of freedom quickly vanishes when the camera shifts to the secret tower on the roof. Murmurings suggest that the tower holds previous wives who did not submit to the master's whims. The scale speaks powerfully to the stifled emotions both of the women and of the larger Chinese population who are confined under the "master" government.

Paul Verhoven's *Starship Troopers* (1997), uses giant, large "scale," insects as symbols of cultural angst. "X-Files" screenwriter Chris Brancato says "it's millennium paranoia: people are very nervous about what'll happen."[55] The plethora of insect films in the late 1990s reflects our fear, says horror filmmaker Wes Craven: "As we move toward the end of the century we wonder if nature will take revenge. . . . Insects are symbols of corruption, and filth. They share our space, and we know they can really hurt us. They stand for an element of nature that's voracious and ultimately sees us as food. . . ."[56]

Many fears also arise from the recent scientific news about cloning, biological engineering, and possible discoveries of life on other planets. These new scientific breakthroughs threaten our sense of the familiar. The larger-than-life insects are metaphors for the larger-than-life fear of the unknown.

Scale also refers to shot selection in photography, film, and television. Alfred Hitchcock insisted that shot scale is "the single most important element within the director's arsenal for manipulating the audience's identification with a character." Jacques Aumont explains:

> It is hardly by chance that the label for various shot scales—close-up, medium shot, medium-long shot, long-shot—were established in reference to the actor's body within the frame. As we know, the very idea of editing a scene in different shot scales was born from the desire to make the spectator grasp the actors' facial expressions, underline their gestures, and mark their dramatic function, all by the inclusion of the close-up.[57]

For instance, the close-up brings the camera (and audience) in close proximity with the characters. Consequently, the close-up establishes an intimate relationship between the character and the spectator. For example,

Figure 5.16. *Raise the Red Lantern* (Orion Classics, 1991)

In *Raise the Red Lantern*, director Zang Zimou uses space to reinforce the feeling of confinement and tension.

in *Twelve Monkeys* (1995) when Cole (Bruce Willis) moves through a thirty-foot-long dark chimney cell, the camera maintains a tight close-up of Cole's face. Cinematographer Roger Pratt, wanted "to capture the look of a man in some kind of internal torment."[58] The tight close-up links the spectator face-to-face with Cole's disordered, drugged expression. Eye-to-eye, the spectator experiences Cole's paranoid state as he travels through the dark, tight quarters of the tube.

The degree of attention, shared emotion, and viewer identification with a character depends on the relative size of the actors on screen and the varying proximity of the camera's eye to each character. Depending on the type of shot, viewers may focus total attention on one character or see the character as merely one figure within a larger context.

Sound

Sound occurs in three different forms in media productions: dialogue, background sound, and music. Dialogue is written material that is intended to sound like conversation. A script may contain a great deal of information and complex layers of meaning. This material is presented very rapidly, like speech, so that the audience must pay attention to the messages being delivered.

Background sound consists of the noises that normally are expected within a given setting (e.g., crowd noise at a baseball game). Frequently natural sound is added to the audio tracks of media presentations to add a feeling of realism. *Literal sounds* are directly connected to the visuals on the screen. For example, when you see an actor talking, you hear him at the same time. Because these events occur within the same space, time, and sound environment, literal sounds lend authenticity and furnish essential information to the narrative.

Nonliteral sounds are not source-connected but instead support the image by adding meaning and emotional energy to the on-screen event. To illustrate, loud frightening noises may act as a cue, anticipating an action on-screen. Romantic music adds atmosphere to a love scene. A cartoon character's actions will be punctuated by "bangs," "pows," and "whams." Car chases, space battles, and martial arts fights are frequently energized by sound effects.

When media communicators construct images, they carefully select the right sounds to fit the predetermined visual patterns. Herbert Zettl declares, "The sound rhythm acts like a clothesline on which you can hang shots of various length without sacrificing rhythmic continuity."[59] For example, quick edits may be hung on a line of staccato beats. Hanging a slow edit sequence on fast rhythm or a fast edit sequence on a slow rhythm will add not only add interest and texture to the montage but will influence our emotional responses.

Sound may also provide clues about characters' internal states of consciousness. Dissonant sounds can inform the audience of inner tensions stirring within a character, while melodic music can indicate tranquility. Music can also dramatize the visuals by punctuating the action. Curtis Hanson, director and co-screenwriter of *L.A. Confidential* (1997), observes, "A movie is made up of many, many details, and nothing is more important than the music. In picking the music [for *L.A. Confidential*], my goal was to help delineate the characters and also provide counterpoint for the individual scenes that they're caught up in."[60]

By unlocking emotions, music can set a romantic mood, cue tension, and heighten suspense. In that sense, musical cues tell viewers how to feel about what they are watching. Music is also a way for media communicators to establish cultural, ethnic, or historical contexts in association with the images projected on-screen. For instance, Terence Blanchard, who composed the film score for *Eve's Bayou* (1997), combined jazz and regional folk into a traditional classical orchestration to capture the romantic epic life of the story's southern black family living in the gothic bayou country of Louisiana.

However, when image and sound do not harmonize, the viewer must make an effort to reconcile this tension or ambiguity. Famed Russian film director Sergei Eisenstein designed many of his montages around what he called a "collision of opposites." He reversed the usual pattern of matching image with music by placing jarring music under placid images or vice versa.

Film director Martin Scorsese has a clearly defined purpose for each musical selection performed in his productions. He combines the music and dialogue to create a distinct mood in his films. In *Casino* (1995), which is the story of the rise and fall of Mafioso kingmakers, Scorsese wanted music that reinforced the theme of finding Paradise, only to lose it through pride and greed. Scorsese observes that the film opens with Bach's monumental musical score *St. Matthew Passion* in order to convey the "splendor of destruction of this sin city":

> I guess for me it's the sense of something grand that's been lost. . . . There was a sense of an empire that had been lost, and the music needed to be worthy of that. The destruction of a city has to have the grandeur of Lucifer being expelled from heaven. . . . The viewer of the film should be moved by the music. Even though you may not like the people and what they did, they're still human beings and it's a tragedy. . . . [61]

Raging Bull (1980) is another Scorsese film that combines music and image to construct a thematic message. The opening sequence features Jake La Motta (Robert De Niro) in the boxing ring. Wearing boxing gloves and a hooded robe, La Motta is shown practicing his boxing footwork in slow motion to the intermezzo from the opera *Cavalleria Rusticana*. The graceful foot movements are in sync with the music, reinforcing the connection between the tragic opera and the life of Jake La Motta, which is defined by brutality, betrayal, and self-destruction. These elements also set up the thematic juxtaposition between the beauty and brutality of life.

Special Effects

Special effects encompass a wide variety of techniques that can create almost whatever can be conjured up in the imagination. Essentially, the art of special effects originates from three principal premises.

- Although film runs continuously, each frame of film can be photographed separately.

- Paintings, artwork, and miniature models can be filmed in a way that makes them appear real.
- Images and elements can be composited.[62]

At the turn of the century, Hollywood filmmakers discovered they could build miniature models and make them appear real if they "overcranked" the camera at faster than normal speeds. George Melies, credited as the father of special effects film making, combined stop-action with miniature models to create his famed image of a rocket ship in *A Trip to the Moon* (1902). Films like Fritz Lang's *Metropolis* (1926) presented its gothic futuristic city with filmed models. The Emerald City and seventy other models were constructed and painted to perfect *The Wizard of Oz* (1939). Even in *King Kong* (1933), the mammoth gorilla, who stood towering over of the Empire State Building in the film, was a mere eighteen-inch model.

Another notable special effect was rear screen projection, in which a film is projected onto a screen behind the actors. Many a Hollywood car ride with scenic routes or city streets was made of scenes projected onto a matte screen, while actors sat "wheeling" a stationary car in the studio. Eventually, matte, blue, and split-screen shots allowed separate images to be composited into a single shot. For example, *Jurassic Park* (1993) managed to keep the massive dinosaur in the same frame with the characters rather than cutting from a shot of a dinosaur to a separate shot showing the actors' reactions.

Motion-controlled photography was a significant development in special effects technology. Rather than keeping the camera stable and manipulating the model (set, figures, etc.), the camera moves through a stationary model. The use of this technique enabled the audience of *Star Wars* (1977) to travel with the characters through the star fields, planets, and laser bursts.

Today, computers composite many elements in the same frame, giving animators the ability to create (and destroy) entire cities. Various elements (e.g., insects, space ships, planets, and people) can be inserted into a film without loss to the picture quality. For example, matte painter Mark Sullivan and his coworkers created twenty-three digital matte painting shots for the film *Starship Troopers* (1997). One particular matte painting was of a Mormon settlement. Using the painting as a backdrop, the special effects team composed photographic elements such as blowing dust, miniature windmills, rock formations, and live-action humans to create a realistic world.[63]

Through composite imaging, natural and supernatural elements can be *personified,* assuming human attributes and motivations. Through special effects, nature seemingly possesses rational thoughts and can direct her demonic energies at will. For example, the tornado in *Twister* (1996) maintained the role of the antagonist throughout the entire film.

Over the past few years special effects not only have delivered the message; they have become the message. Audiences attend big budget, special effects films in part because these films offer an alternative experience. For instance, people attended *Titanic* (1997), in large part, for the experience of being on the ship and vicariously experiencing the tragedy. However, the model ship never saw water. It sat in a parking lot with mountains in the background. The ocean, the glitter on the water, the illusion of a floating ship, were all computer-generated. The people and their shadows, the smoke stacks, and smoke were all created through the computer. The suspension of disbelief remains fixed, so that seeing is believing, and the boundaries between reality and fiction are obliterated.

Ultimately, special effects are contemporary elements that deliver the same themes common to narratives since the beginning of time. These effects are woven into stories that recount how people navigate obstacles, overcome fears (real or imagined), conquer demons (personal or political), and triumph over adversity.

Media Literacy Analysis: Production Elements

R.T. Radanovic, a graduate student in media communications at Webster University, focused on production values in his media literacy analysis of Disney's *The Lion King* film.

Plot Summary

From Walt Disney Pictures comes an epic story, a coming-of-age saga, about a proud ruler Mufasa and his young son Simba, who "Can't Wait to be King." Underlining the *circle of life* theme, the story begins with a presentation of newly born Simba, the future king, to the animals. Unfortunately, while still a cub, Simba's careless days are over when his envious Uncle Scar, with his hyena henchmen, concocts a scheme in which Mufasa dies while saving his son from a stampede. Afraid and ashamed by what he believes he has caused, Simba runs away, leaving the crown to his cruel uncle. Befriended by the warmhearted warthog Pumbaa and his meercat companion Timon, Simba forgets his responsibilities and grows up in the carefree lifestyle of "Hakuna Matata" (don't worry). However, a wise baboon, Rafiki, Mufasa's old friend and adviser, finds Simba and helps him understand and accept his predestined role as ruler of lion's land. Upon his return home, Simba finds his once prosperous country desolate and barren;

the hyenas have sucked the last drop of life out of it. In a fight with his foxy Uncle Scar, Simba finds out that Scar was responsible for his father's death. In a rage, Simba sends his uncle to live in exile. However, the hyenas, whom Scar has betrayed, make Scar their last meal in lion country. When life returns to the valley, a new son of Simba and Nala, and the future king, is presented to the animals. The circle of life continues.

Media Analysis

Combining magnificent cinematic animation and an evocative score, Disney's *The Lion King* has become "The Greatest Wonder of All" (*Los Angeles Times*). From the musical opening over breathtaking African savannas to the emotionally charged climax, the animated feature combines an innovative camera approach, and skillful use of visual images to create an absorbing world view that engages its audience, both young and old.

The Lion King sets itself apart from other Disney's cartoons with the look the directors Roger Allers and Rob Minkoff used to appeal to the audience. In order to make it more "alive," he simply relied on what audience is accustomed to seeing in contemporary films: a dynamic camera. Unlike previous cartoons, *The Lion King* does not use flat two-dimensional backdrops that focuses only on the foreground area. Instead, it was drawn to appear as if the sets were real, giving them depth and three-dimensionality by applying drawings that simulate traditional camera techniques such as rack focus, crane movements, aerial, and tracking shots. This style is present from the very first scene, when the establishing shots reveal the African vista at daybreak. As the sun rises and life is awakening, the aerial view reveals nature on the move. Occasional "lens flare" and "foreclosure" effects on the flying birds fool the audience into believing that a camera is used to create the scene. Another effective camera move is used when Simba is faced with the danger of being stampeded by buffaloes. To show his internal state of alarm, the so-called "Vertigo shot" (camera technique first time used in film *Vertigo*) is applied. By simultaneously dollying the camera toward, and zooming away from the subject, the subject stays in place while the surroundings stretch, expressing Simba's growing internal tension. While simple cuts are mostly used to put the scenes together, occasional dissolves help express mood as well as transitions in time and space.

Skillfully applying the connotative meanings of colors and light, the director offers insight into the minds of specific characters. Scenes filled with happiness, optimism and life are painted in bright, saturated colors, using hi-key lighting techniques (no deep shadows). Life-threatening situations, fear, and pessimism are presented through contrast lighting and cold hues. For example, when Simba plays with his friend Nala in the safe zone, the scene is painted in sunny reds, yellows, and greens, revealing their carefree, cheerful mood. However, as they stray into the elephant grave-yard, the dangerous and forbidden territory of the hyena's land, the scene suddenly turns dark, foggy, and overcast, and the colors change into grays, cold greens, and blues, giving an overall impression that something is about to go wrong.

Throughout the cartoon, shapes and forms help communicate connota-tive meanings even further. In the wonderfully designed scene where Scar establishes himself as the leader of hyenas, he sits on top of a boulder while the hyenas underneath goose-step in a perfect formation. As they are lit from below by numerous active geysers occasionally shooting fire in the air, the hyenas cast huge shadows on the surrounding rocks. Although there is no sign pointing to Nazi Germany, this picture has a very clear message about how we should see Scar as he gathers his army to take over the kingdom. When compared with documentary footage from World War II, almost exact camera angles can be seen in photographs of Hitler and his army marching. The perfect formation of his troops represents order, while the leader's figure looking down onto the soldiers indicates his power and control.

The director also used the power of scale to connote strength: After Mufasa saves Simba and Nala from the nasty hyenas, he calls Simba to give him a lecture. As Simba fearfully approaches his father, he accidentally steps into an impression of Mufasa's paw. A close-up of the small Simba's paw in the ten times bigger impression says everything that needs to be said about Mufasa's strength in comparison to Simba's. Further, the shot has thematic implications, showing how much Simba must grow before he can realize his potential.

Much of the cartoon's success can be attributed to outstanding casting decisions. Through actors' voices, the drawn animals have assumed charm-ing characters. Moreover, the cartoonists somehow succeeded in embedding facial traits of the actors into the faces of the animals. For instance, Shanzy, a hyena portrayed by Whoopi Goldberg, has facial expressions identical to those of the actress. Because Goldberg is associated with the likable and comical characters she usually plays, the audience immediately reacts posi-tively toward her character.

What the cartoon could not have achieved through the visuals, it accom-plished through its sound. The dialogue relies on the stereotypes of certain social groups with which the audience can identify. For instance, the lan-guage hyenas use to communicate among themselves is an impression of the slang used in a street gang. On a few occasions the script cleverly employs commonly used expressions in conjunction with their literal meanings. In one scene, after stuffing himself with food, Pumbaa, the warthog, exclaims "I ate like a pig!" Much of the effectiveness of the film can be credited to the music. The songs combine African ethnic melos and rhythms with western production standards and meaningful lyrics to complement the plot and create a memorable, everlasting soundtrack. The editors put together these production pieces in such a way so they leave a lasting impact on the audience, making watching the cartoon an enjoyable and satisfying experience.

The stylistic elements of *The Lion King* enable the audience to quickly and effectively suspend their disbelief and immerse themselves in the imaginary world created by the cartoonists. The visual and aural elements in the cartoon are strong so that both the young and adult audiences can fully appreciate them.[65]

Conclusion

The following categories summarize the important elements to be analyzed in media productions.

I.   Editing

    A. Examine a variety of newspapers or television programs appearing on the same day.
       1. How much information can be covered in these brief segments?
       2. What important stories have been ignored or downplayed?
       3. What important details are left out and why?
       4. Who orders the segments and to whom are they important?
       5. What is the primary purpose of most lead segments?
    B. Which *topics* have been included or omitted from a program?
       1. Are the segments informative or are they sensationalized?
    C. When looking at film or television, how are shots are pieced together (edited) to convey the story being told?
       1. Emphasis—are there any individual shots inserted to convey messages that are independent of the story being presented?
       2. Contrast—how does a sequence of shots relate to the sequence connected to it?
       3. Editing for rhythm—what is the duration of each shot in the edited sequence?
          a. What effect does the duration of the shot have on the viewer?

    4. Spatial rhythm—how does the content of each shot differ?

    5. Temporal and spatial continuity—what do the juxtaposed images say about chronological time, physical space, relationship with people, places, and events, past or present?

  D. Arrangement

    1. In what order are the news segments arranged?

    2. Are lead stories of national, international, or local importance?

II. Composition

This refers to how the elements are placed within the frame.

  A. Where are the images placed within the screen or page?

  B. What is your emotional response to the image(s)?

  C. Where does the article appear on the page?

  D. How does the composition direct our viewing?

  E. Is the composition set up to help us envision what is outside the frame?

III. Colors

Colors convey symbolic meaning that evokes a wide range of emotional responses.

A. How does color set the mood and tone of a production?

  B. What feelings do the colors evoke?

  C. Do the colors convey meanings that correlate with or contrast with the content of the production?

IV. Lines

Lines are basic structures employed in media productions to convey meaning.

  A. What lines are used?

  B. How do they support the message given by the media communicator?

  C. What is the purpose of the vertical lines in the production?

    1. Horizontal lines

    2. Diagonal—movement

    3. Curved—natural

    4. Converging—depth perspective

V.   Shapes

Shapes carry symbolic meanings that support the overall message of the production.

A. What are the major shapes employed in the production?
B. Do the shapes emotionally support the message of the media communicator?

VI.   Lighting

The style of lighting sets the tone and helps focus our attention. It supports moods and themes in the production and impacts of our emotions.

A. What types of lighting are used: dim, bright, hard, or soft?
B. How does the lighting support the mood and theme of the production?
C. Does the lighting cast shadows?
D. What do the shadows represent?

VII.   Scale

Scale refers to the relative size of two sets of dimensions.

A. How does the size of the production relate to the theme being communicated?
B. How does the relationship between objects in a scene/shot relate to the overall theme?

VIII. Angle

Angle refers to the position the camera takes in viewing the object or subject on the screen.
A. Does the use of angles reinforce themes in the presentation? Explain.

IX.   Movement

Movement is a unique characteristic of televison and film.

A. Camera speed refers to the ability of the camera to alter the rate at which events are depicted on-screen.
   1. Is the production fast, slow, or time-lapse motion?

B. Camera movements establish the relationship between the camera, the subject, and the viewer.
1. How does the camera follow the subject/object on the screen?
2. What is the movement of the camera—up or down, side to side?
C. Character movement refers to how a character moves in relation to the camera's lens.
1. In which direction does the character move in relation to the lens?
2. How does the character's/object's movement effect our emotions?

X. Point of View

Points of view refer to the source conveying the information.
A. Who is telling the story?
B. What information is being conveyed?
C. How does it orient us to the story?
D. How does it effect our sympathies?
E. Whose view is missing and is it important?

XI. Sound and Music

This refers to the sounds either directly related to or supporting the visuals on the screen.

A. What information do the sounds convey?
B. Are the sounds directly related to the screen images?
C. Do the sounds signal an off-screen event?
D. How do the sounds and music cue our emotions?
E. Does the music correspond with the image on the screen or is it directly opposite to what is being presented?

XII. Graphics

Graphics refers to the figurative images used to illustrate the text.
A. Graphic Representations
1. What is the source of this information?
2. Does the source of information have any bias?
3. What is the function of the graphic representation?
4. Do the visuals accurately present the information?

     5. Does the graphic representation leave out significant details? Explain.

B. Typography

  1. Is the type plain or decorative—heavy or light?

  2. What meaning does the typeface convey?

  3. Does the typeface evoke particular emotions?

  4. What is the significance or the spacing between the type?

  5. Are the headlines in lower-case or upper-case letters? What does this signify?

  6. Does the typeface in the headline comment on the story?

  7. How are the headlines arranged?

XIII. Connotation

A. Connotative words refer to the meaning associated with a word beyond its literal, denotative definition.

  1. What associated meanings are attached to the word?

  2. What cultural associations are attached to the word?

B. Connotative image refers to the meanings given to the image through its use in the society.

  1. What associated meanings are attached to the image?

  2. What cultural associations are attached to the image?

  3. Does the image evoke an emotional response? Explain.

  4. Are the combination of images change the meaning? How?

XIV. Special Effects

Special effects are technical activities that are manipulated and combined to deliver images.

A. Why does the media communicator use special effects in the program?

B. What emotions do the special effects evoke?

C. What is the role of special effects in the film?

D. What is the relationship between the created world of special effects and the real world?

NOTES

Notes to Chapter 1

1. Raymond Williams, *Keywords: A Vocabulary of Culture and Society* (London: Oxford University Press, 1995), p. 118.
2. Linda Holtzman, interview by Art Silverblatt, St. Louis, Missouri, January 23, 1998.
3. Nikolai Zlobin, interview by Art Silverblatt, St. Louis, Missouri, December 2, 1997.
4. Roland Barthes, *Mythologies* (New York: Hill and Wang, 1957).
5. Len Masterman, "Shifting the Power, Addressing the Ideology." *Mediacy* 13, no. 2 (Spring 1991): 1–6.
6. Len Masterman, *Teaching the Media* (New York: Routledge, 1985), p. 195.
7. Ben Bagdikian, *The Media Monopoly,* 5th ed. (Boston: Beacon Press, 1997).
8. Ibid., pp. 47–48.
9. *Newsweek,* September 15, 1996, p. 16.
10. Warren Hoge, "Murdoch's HarperCollins Won't Publish Book that Criticizes China," February 28, 1998, http://www.stlnet.com.
11. Ibid.
12. Bagdikian, *The Media Monopoly,* p. 85.
13. Frank Rich, "The Price Is Right," *New York Times,* January 10, 1988, p. A25.
14. Wally Bowen, "News Tie-ins to Made for TV Movies." media-la-l@nmsu.edu au 12. 1997.
15. Rick Desloge, "KMOX Given Ultimatum: Double Profits," *St. Louis Business Journal,* February 26–March 3, 1996, p. 1A.
16. Jeremy Iggers, "Get Me Rewrite!" *The Utne Reader,* September 1, 1997, p. 46.
17. Ibid.
18. Ronald Collins, *Dictating Content; How Advertising Pressure Can Corrupt a Free Press* (Washington, DC: Center for the Study of Commercialism, 1992), p. 25.
19. Bob Herbert, "Fashion Statement," *New York Times,* February 15, 1998, http://www.stlnet.com.

20. Julie Grippo, interview by Art Silverblatt, St. Louis, Missouri, December 5, 1997.

21. Michito Kakutani, "Portrait of the Artist as a Focus Group," *New York Times Magazine*, March 1, 1998, p. 26.

22. Tripp Frohlichstein, interview by Art Silverblatt, St. Louis, Missouri, March 10, 1998.

23. Ibid.

24. Vernon Stone, "Minorities and Women in Television News," University of Missouri, jourvs@showme.missouri.edu, 1995 and 1996.

25. Editorial, *St. Louis Post-Dispatch,* December 17, 1997, p. B6.

26. Kim Gordon, interview by Art Silverblatt, St. Louis, Missouri, December 8, 1997.

27. Joe Baltake, "On Internet, Everyone Is a Critic," *St. Louis Post-Dispatch,* July 4, 1997, p. E1.

28. Kim Gordon, interview by Art Silverblatt, St. Louis, Missouri, December 8, 1997.

29. Jasper Becker, "Good News! You're Fired," *South China Morning Post,* October 15, 1997. In *World Press Review,* February 1998, p. 31.

30. Max Frankel, "The Next Great Story," *New York Times Magazine,* March 15, 1998, p. 30.

31. *St. Louis Post-Dispatch,* August 31, 1997.

32. "Car Crash Kills Princess Diana," *St. Louis Post-Dispatch,* August 31, 1997, p. A1.

33. Peter Hernon, "Beyond Photos: Paparazzi Hunt Celebrity Subjects," *St. Louis Post-Dispatch,* September 1, 1997, p. 1A.

34. Seth Faison, "In China, Better Unread than Read," *New York Times,* September 7, 1997, sec. 4, p. 5.

35. Kim Gordon, interview by Art Silverblatt, St. Louis, Missouri, December 8, 1997.

36. Harold D. Laswell, *Power and Personality* (New York: W.W. Norton, 1948), chapter 6.

37. John C. Merrill, John Lee, and Jonathan J. Friedlander, *Modern Mass Media* (New York: Harper and Row, 1990), p. 428.

38. Michito Kakutani, "Taking Out the Trash," *New York Times Magazine,* June 8, 1997, p. 39.

39. Josef Joffe, "America the Inescapable," *New York Times Magazine,* June 8, 1997, p. 43.

40. Ibid, p. 38.

41. Panrawee Pantumchinda, "*Cosmopolitan* Magazine in Thailand," unpublished paper, Webster University, March 5, 1998, p. 8.

42. Joffe, "America the Inescapable," p. 43.

43. Art Silverblatt, *Media Literacy: Keys to Interpreting Media Messages* (Westport, CT: Praeger, 1995).

44. Sut Jhally and Justin Lewis, *Enlightened Racism: "The Cosby Show," Audiences, and the Myth of the American Dream* (Boulder, CO: Westview Press, 1992).

45. Edson Yoder, "Clinton's Call for Civility Reflects a Belief in Power of Reason," *St. Louis Post-Dispatch,* July 13, 1995, p. 7B.

46. Richard Cohen, "Clock Already Ticking on Clinton Honeymoon," *St. Louis Post-Dispatch,* November 6, 1992, p. 3C.

47. William Safire, "In Office Since '81, GOP Just Went Sour," *St. Louis Post-Dispatch,* November 9, 1992, p. 3B.

48. Associated Press, "Yeltsin Questions the Cost the People of Russia Are Paying for Materialism," *St. Louis Post-Dispatch,* December 27, 1997, p. 21.

49. Adam Zagorin, "The Mall the Merrier," *Time Magazine,* November 24, 1997.

50. Scott Simon, "Affluenza," KETC/PBS, September 19, 1997.

51. Ibid.

52. Ibid.

53. Ibid.

54. Stuart Ewan in "The Public Mind: All Consuming Images," Public Broadcasting Service, November 8, 1989.

55. Simon, "Affluenza.".

56. Robin Anderson, *Consumer Culture and TV Programming* (Boulder, CO: Westview Press, 1995), p. 15.

57. Michael Schaller, "Godzilla, Present and Past," *New York Times,* May 16, 1998, p. A27.

58. Ibid.

59. Ibid.

60. Michael Parenti, *Make Believe Media* (New York: St. Martin's Press, 1992), p. 60.

61. Roger Silverstone, "Television Myth and Culture," in *Media, Myths, and Narratives,* ed. James W. Carey (Newbury Park, CA: Sage, 1988), p. 34.

62. William Lutz, *The New Doublespeak: Why No One Knows What Anyone Is Saying Anymore* (New York: HarperCollins, 1996), pp. 6, 7, 176, 241, 258, 190.

63. Jim Drinkard, "Lobbying Groups Play Distracting Name Game," Associated Press, *St. Louis Post-Dispatch,* December 23, 1997, p. B1.

64. Molly Ivins, "Who Is Funding Those Who Are Debating Global Warming?" *St. Louis Post-Dispatch,* December 16, 1997, p. B7.

65. Drinkard, "Lobbying Groups Play Distracting Name Game," p. B1.

66. Alison Mitchell, "G.O.P. Hopes Climate Fight Echoes Health Care Outcome," *New York Times,* December 13, 1997, p. A1.

67. George Lakoff and Mark Johnson, *Metaphors We Live By* (Chicago: University of Chicago Press, 1981), p. 5.

68. Ibid, pp. 7–8.

69. "Ariane Doublespeak," http://drycas.club.cc.cmu.edu.

70. Christopher Goodwin, "Ku Klux Klan Cleans Up Image," *London Sunday Times,* August 18, 1996.

71. Mitchell, "G.O.P. Hopes Climate Fight Echoes Health Care Outcome," p. A1.

72. Ibid.

73. Fredrick McKissack, Jr., "Nike Memo Details Abuses in Asian Factory," *St. Louis Post-Dispatch,* November 21, 1997, p. C19.

74. Molly Ivins, "A Fuddy-duddy's View of Free Trade," *St. Louis Post-Dispatch,* November 20, 1997, p. B7.

75. James Melvin Washington, ed., *A Testament of Hope: The Essential Writings of Martin Luther King, Jr.* (San Francisco: Harper and Row, 1986), p. 286.

76. Joseph Schuster, interview by Art Silverblatt, St. Louis, Missouri, December 9, 1997.

77. Nikolai Zlobin, interview by Art Silverblatt, St. Louis, Missouri, February 3, 1998.

78. Internet Movie Database.

79. Daniel Chandler, *Semiotics for Beginners,* http://www.aber.ac.uk/dgc/semiotic.html.

80. Henry A. Murray, "The Possible Nature of a 'Mythology' to Come," in *Myth and Mythmaking,* ed. Henry A. Murray (New York: George Braziller, 1960), p. 338.

81. Chandler, http://www.aber.ac.uk/dgc/semiotic.html.

82. John Cawelti, "Myth, Symbol, and Formula," *Journal of Popular Culture* 8 (Summer 1974): 1–10.

83. Stephan Brookfield, "Media Power and the Development of Media Literacy: An Adult Educational Interpretation," *Harvard Educational Review* 56, no. 2 (May 1986): 151–170.

84. Douglas Kellner, "TV, Ideology, and Emancipatory Popular Culture," *Socialist Review* 9, no. 3 (1979): 13–53.

85. James M. Collins, "The Musical," in *Handbook of American Film Genres,* ed. Wes D. Gering (New York: Greenwood Press, 1988), p. 274.

86. Ibid., p. 175.

87. Ibid.

88. Darlene Diel, unpublished paper, Webster University, 1997.

89. Lakoff and Johnson, *Metaphors We Live By,* pp. 14–15.

90. Angela Rollins, "Tommy Hilfiger and the American Ideal," unpublished paper, Webster University, March 2, 1998.

91. Jane Caputi, "Charting the Flow: The Construction of Meaning through Juxtaposition in Media Texts," *Journal of Communication Inquiry* 15, no. 2 (Summer 1991): 34.

92. Gary Schwitzer, "Doctoring the News: Miracle Cures, Video Press Releases, and TV Medical Reporting," *Quill* (November–December 1992): 19–21.

93. Bill Nichols, *Ideology and the Image* (Bloomington: Indiana University Press, 1981), pp. 3–5.

94. Bob Herbert, "Fashion Statement," *New York Times,* February 15, 1998, sec. 4, p. 13.

95. Anonymous, "The Story Behind Dracula," Internet.

96. Linda G. Rich, Joan Clark Netherwood, and Elinor B. Cahn, *Neighborhood: A State of Mind* (Baltimore: Johns Hopkins University Press, 1981).

97. "Marketers Partner with New James Bond Movie," *Mining Company Guide to Advertising Industry,* December 7, 1997, http://advertising.tqn.com/library/weekly/aa120797.htm.

98. Jeff Daniel, "Melrose Placements," *St. Louis Post-Dispatch,* February 16, 1998, p. E4.

99. Ibid.

100. Frank J. Prial, "We'll Have the Chateau Cuervo," *New York Times,* March 15, 1998, sec. 4, p. 2.

101. Nichols, *Ideology and the Image,* p. 290.

102. Kay Quinn, KSDK, January 11–12, 1993. "Hepatitis Feature," 10 O'Clock News.

103. David J. Garrow, "Letting the Public Decide about Assisted Suicide," *New York Times,* June 29, 1997, sec. E, p. 4.

Notes to Chapter 2

1. Michael Lewis, *Trail Fever* (New York: Alfred A. Knopf, 1997).

2. Ibid.

3. Jean Seligmann, Barbara Kantrowitz, and Rick Marin, "Blood Ties or Blood Feud," *Newsweek,* August 11, 1997, p. 53.

4. *Mediacy* (Winter 1990): 10.

5. Nancy Kruh, "State of the Unions," *St. Louis Post-Dispatch,* July 15, 1997, p. D1.

6. Byron Reeves, "Children's Understanding of Television People," in *Children Communicating,* ed. E. Wartella (Newbury Park, CA: Sage, 1979), p. 132.

7. Diane Toroian, "The Impact of Pop Lyrics Depend on Who's Listening," *St. Louis Post-Dispatch,* January 22, 1998, p. D1.

8. Charles W. Turner, Bradford W. Hesse, and Sonja Peterson-Lewis, "Naturalistic Studies of the Long-Term Effects of Television Violence," *Journal of Social Issues* 42 (1986): 51–73.

9. Richard Frost and John Stoffer, "The Effects of Social Class, Gender, and Personality on Psychological Responses to Filmed Violence," *Journal of Communication* 37 (Spring 1987): 29–46.

10. David Buckingham, *Moving Images: Understanding Children's Emotional Responses to Television* (Manchester and New York: Manchester University Press, 1996) p. 213.

11. Barry Gunter, *Dimensions of Television Violence* (New York: St. Martin's Press, 1985).

12. Byron Reeves, "Children's Understanding of Television People," in *Children Communicating,* ed. E. Wartella (Newbury Park, CA: Sage, 1979), p. 143.

13. Ibid., p. 133.

14. Frost and Stoffer, "Responses to Filmed Violence," p. 30.

15. W. Andrew Collins, "Children's Comprehension of Television Content," in *Children Communicating,* ed. E. Wartella (Newbury Park, CA: Sage, 1979), pp. 72–73.

16. Ibid., pp. 71–72.

17. Ibid., pp. 76–77.

18. Buckingham, *Moving Images,* p. 3.

19. Ibid., p. 145.

20. Ibid., p. 150.

21. Ibid., p. 150.

22. Ibid., pp. 110–12.

23. Len Masterman, *Teaching the Media* (New York: Routledge, 1988), p. 239.

24. Ibid., p. 239.

25. Douglas Kellner, *Media Culture: Cultural Studies, Identity and Politics Between the Modern and the Postmodern* (London and New York: Routledge, 1995), p. 32.

26. Masterman, *Teaching the Media,* p. 839.

27. Gloria Johnson Powell, "The Impact of Television on the Self Concept Development of Minority Group Children," in *Television and the Socialization of the Minority Child,* eds. Gordon L. Berry and Claudia Mitchell-Kernan (New York: Academic Press, 1982), p. 107.

28. Esther B. Fein, "The End of 'Seinfeld' Has Hit Show's Fans Grieving," *New York Times,* December 27, 1997, p. A28.

29. Ibid., p. A28.

30. David Buckingham, *Children Talking Television: The Making of Television Literacy,* (London: Falmer Press, 1993), p. 185.

31. Buckingham, *Moving Images,* p. 161.

32. Aimee Dorr, "Television and Its Socializing Influences in Minority Children," in *Television and the Socialization of the Minority Child,* eds. Gordon L. Berry and Claudia Mitchell-Kernan, (New York: Academic Press, 1982), p. 27.

33. Ibid., p. 27.

34. Judy McMillan, interview by Art Silverblatt, St. Louis, February 26, 1998.

35. Robin Anderson, *Consumer Culture and TV Programming* (Boulder, CO: Westview Press, 1995) p. 35.

36. Jane Sumner, "Isabella Rossellini—Without Makeup," *St. Louis Post-Dispatch,* July 16, 1997, p. 3E.

37. Alison Byrne Fields, interview by Art Silverblatt, March 5, 1998.

38. *-ISM (N.) Curricular and Faculty Development Project*, 1997–98 (Campus Application, 1997), p. 4.

39. Ibid., p. 11.

40. Martha Chono-Helsley, "VIDKIDCO/Long Beach Museum of Art," in *L.A. Freewaves Catalog of Southern California Youth Media Programs*, ed. by Gina Lamb (Los Angeles: L.A. Freewaves, 1994), pp. 38–39.

41. *Video Data Bank*, promotional materials (Chicago).

42. Ellen Schneider, " 'E.C.U.': Home for Video Diarists," *Current*, March 6, 1995, p. 2.

43. jesikah maria ross and Barbara Osborne, "Media Literacy and Public Access TV Training," *Strategies for Media Literacy* 6 (Summer/Fall 1993).

44. Ty Burr, "When Will Oscar Really Know the Score?" *New York Times*, March 1, 1998, p. B13.

45. Aspen Institute, National Leadership Conference on Media LIteracy, Queenstown, MD, December 7–9, 1992.

46. Elizabeth Thoman, "Blueprint for Responsive-Ability," *Media & Values* 35 (Spring 1986): 12–14.

47. Jeffrey A. Chester and Anthony Wright, "A Twelve Step Program for Media Democracy," *The Nation*, June 3, 1996, pp. 9–15.

48. Len Masterman, *Teaching the Media.* pp. 31–32.

49. Barry Duncan, "Media Literacy at the Crossroads: Some Issues, Probes and Questions," *The History and Social Science Teacher* 24, no. 4 (Summer 1989).

50. Cary Bazalgette, and David Buckingham, "Introduction: The Invisible Audience," in *In Front of the Children: Screen Entertainment and Young Audiences* (London: BFI, 1995), pp. 4–14.

Notes to Chapter 3

1. Vespereny, Cynthia, "Remember the three 'E's' when making a speech," *St. Louis Business Journal*, November 2–8, 1998, p. 37.

2. Dale G. Leathers, *Successful Nonverbal Communication: Principles and Applications*, 3rd ed. (Boston: Allyn and Bacon, 1997), p. 6.

3. "I Never Told Anybody to Lie," News Services, *St. Louis Post-Dispatch*, January 27, 1998, Postnet.

4. James Bennet, "Clintons Present Their Act to an Admiring Argentina," *New York Times*, October 17, 1997, p. A1.

5. Tony Capaccio, "The Kelly Flinn Spin Patrol," American Journalism Review (September 1997): 12–13.

6. Joshua Meyrowitz, *No Sense of Place* (New York and London: Oxford University Press, 1985).

7. Erving Goffman, "Gender Advertisements," *Studies in the Anthropology of Visual Communication* 3, no. 2 (1976): 100.

8. Ibid., p. 102.

9. Ibid., p. 105.

10. Ibid., p. 121.

11. Ibid., p. 123.

12. Jane Bruns, interview by Art Silverblatt, St. Louis, March 17, 1998.

13. Richard E. Porter and Larry A. Samovar, *Communication Between Cultures*, 2d ed. (Belmont, CA: Wadsworth, 1995) p. 180.

14. Judy Pearson, Richard West, and Lynn Turner, *Gender Communication,* 3rd ed. (DuBuque, IA: Brown and Benchmark, 1995), p. 122.

15. Tripp Frohlichstein, *Media Training Handbook* (St. Louis: MediaMasters, 1991), p. 31.

16. Jan Hargrave, *Let Me See Your Body Talk* (Dubuque, IA: Kendall/Hunt, 1995), p. 209.

17. Goffman, "Gender Advertisements," p. 116.

18. Desmond Morris, *Bodytalk* (New York: Crown Trade Paperbacks, 1994), p. 189.

19. Peter E. Bull, *Posture and Gesture,* International Series in Experimental Social Psychology, series ed. Michael Argyle (New York: Pergamon Press, 1987), pp. 122–141.

20. "What's A-O.K. in the U.S.A. Is Lewd and Worthless Beyond," *New York Times,* August 18, 1996, sec. 4, p. 7.

21. Pearson, West, and Turner, *Gender Communication,* p. 119.

22. Leathers, *Successful Nonverbal Communication,* p. 87.

23. Ibid., p. 403.

24. Porter and Samovar, *Communication Between Cultures,* p. 203.

25. Mattias Thuresson, mattias.thuresson@mbox300.swipnet.se.

26. Porter and Samovar, *Communication Between Cultures,* p. 203.

27. Pamela Cooper, *Speech Communication for the Classroom Teacher,* 3rd ed. (Scottsdale, AZ: Gorsuch Scarisbrick, 1988).

28. Leathers, *Successful Nonverbal Communication,* p. 122.

29. Ibid., p. 145.

30. Kathryn Perkins, "Study: Sex, Age, Work Against Women." *Sacramento Bee,* November 30, 1996.

31. Eugene Rosow, *"Born to Lose": The Gangster Film in America* (Oxford: Oxford University Press, 1978), p. 185.

32. Farid Chehoune, *A History of Men's Fashion,* tr. Richard Martin (Paris: Flammarion, 1993), p.196.

33. Harriet Woroby, interview by Art Silverblatt, St. Louis, October 10, 1997.

34. Cheri Bank, interview by Art Silverblatt, WCAU-TV, Philadelphia, November 3, 1997.

35. "Read or Listen, But Don't Look; Eyes Will Lie, Says TV Researcher," *St. Louis Post-Dispatch,* February 2, 1995, p. 2A.

36. Leathers, *Successful Nonverbal Communication,* p. 161.

37. Frohlichstein, *Media Training Handbook,* p. 33.

38. "Read or Listen, But Don't Look," p. 2A.

39. Clyde Taylor, "New U.S. Black Cinema," in *Movies and Mass Culture,* ed. Clyde Taylor.

40. Ibid., p. 40.

41. Phil Wilson, interview by Jane Ferry, May 1997. Wilson is an international performer and lecturer on jazz currently at Berklee College of Music, Boston, MA.

42. Terry Corpal, interview by Art Silverblatt, October 1, 1997.

43. Deputy Tom O'Connor, interview by Art Silverblatt, St. Louis, December 8, 1997.

44. Ibid.

45. Ibid.

46. Allan Pease, *Signals* (Toronto: Bantam Books, 1981), p. 69.

47. Morris, *Bodytalk,* p. 182.

48. Deputy Tom O'Connor, interview by Art Silverblatt, St. Louis, MO, December 8, 1997.

49. Pease, *Signals,* p. 130.

50. Hargrave, *Let Me See Your Body Talk,* p. 72.

51. Morris, *Bodytalk,* p. 152.

52. Ibid., p. 152.

53. Hargrave, *Let Me See Your Body Talk,* p. 73.

54. Morris, *Bodytalk,* p. 154.

55. Samantha L. King, "Magazine Advetisements: What Do They Tell Us About Gender?" unpublished paper, Webster University, October 15, 1997.

56. Pease, *Signals,* p. 156.

57. Ibid., p. 159.

58. Ibid., p. 75.

59. Ibid., pp.157–158.

60. Richard Klein, "After the Preaching, the Lure of the Taboo," *New York Times,* August 24, 1997, sec. 2, p. 1.

61. "Tobacco Use Among High School Students/United States, 1997," MMWR (Morbidity Mortality Weekly Report), Center for Disease Control and Prevention, United States Department of Health and Human Services, Atlanta, GA, April 3, 1998, vol. 47, no. 12.

62. William DeJong, Charles K. Atkin, and Lawrence Wallack, "A Critical Analysis of Moderation Advertising Sponsored by the Beer Industry: Are 'Responsible Drinking' Commercials Done Responsibly?" *The Milbank Quarterly* 70, no. 4 (1992); personal interview with DeJong.

63. Ibid.

Notes to Chapter 4

1. Max Mueller, *The Philosophy of Mythology, the Science of Religion* (London, 1873), pp. 353–355.

2. Mircea Eliade, *The Sacred and the Profane,* trans. Willard R. Trask (New York: Harper and Brothers, 1957), p. 205.

3. Gilbert Highet, *The Classical Tradition: Greek and Roman Influences on Western Literature* (New York: Oxford University Press, Galaxy Books, 1957), p. 540.

4. Rollo May, *The Cry for Myth* (New York: W.W. Norton, 1991), p. 27.

5. Roland Barthes, *Mythologies* (New York: Hill and Wang, 1957), p. 129.

6. May, *The Cry for Myth,* p. 282.

7. Jerome S. Bruner, "Myth and Identity," in *Myth and Mythmaking,* ed. Henry A. Murray (New York: George Braziller, 1960), p. 280.

8. Harry Levins, "Original Sin Sells," *St. Louis Post-Dispatch,* February 1, 1998, p. A2.

9. Dan O'Neill, "He's Ba-a-a-ck: Tiger Woods Is Talk of Texas," *St. Louis Post-Dispatch,* May 14, 1997 p. 6D.

10. Ibid., p. 6D.

11. May, *The Cry for Myth,* pp. 50–51.

12. Henry A. Murray, "The Possible Nature of a 'Mythology' to Come," in *Myth and Mythmaking,* ed. Henry A. Murray (New York: George Braziller, 1960), p. 337.

13. Joseph Schuster, interview by Art Silverblatt, Webster University, December 20, 1997.

14. Murray, "The Possible Nature of a 'Mythology' to Come," p. 338.

15. Ibid., p. 338.

16. D'Auaires' *Book of Greek Myths* (New York: Doubleday, 1962), pp. 14–15.

17. Rayshawn Campbell, "The Story of Jim," unpublished, 1998.

18. Deborah Peterman, " 'Hercules' Is One Hades of a Movie," *St. Louis Post-Dispatch,* June 29, 1997, p. E3.

19. Deborah Peterman, "The Sharper Image," *St. Louis Post-Dispatch,* June 29, 1997, pp. E1, E5.

20. Murray, "The Possible Nature of a 'Mythology' to Come," p. 324.

21. Ibid., pp. 316–317.

22. Edith Hamilton, *Mythology* (Boston: Mentor Books, 1963), p. 72.

23. Stephanie Coontz, *The Way We Never Were* (New York: Basic Books, 1992), p. 176.

24. May, *The Cry for Myth,* p. 294.

25. Carl Jung, *The Archetypes and the Collective Unconscious,* trans. R.F. C. Hull (Bollingen Series XX, Pantheon Books, 1959), p. 260.

26. Joseph Campbell, "The Historical Development of Mythology" in *Myth and Mythmaking,* ed. Henry A. Murray (New York: George Braziller, 1960), p. 148.

27. Northrup Frye, "Archetypal Criticism: Theory of Myths," *Anatomy of Criticism: Four Essays* (Princeton: Princeton University Press, 1957), pp. 187–188.

28. Jung, *The Archetype and the Collective Unconscious,* p. 262.

29. Ibid., p. 262.

30. Christopher Vogler, *The Writer's Journey* (California: Michael Wiese Productions, 1992), p. 21.

31. Ibid., p. 34.

32. Darryl Sharpe, "C.G. Jung, Analytical Psychology and Culture: Glossery of Jungian Terms," http://www.cgjung.com/glossary.html.

33. Jung, *The Archetype and the Collective Unconscious,* p. 69.

34. Ibid., p. 70.

35. Ibid., p. 71.

36. Vogler, *The Writer's Journey,* p. 64.

37. Ibid., p. 69.

38. Vogler, *The Writer's Journey,* p. 70.

39. Steven F. Walker, *Jung and the Jungians on Myth* (New York and London, 1995), p. 63.

40. Vogler, *The Writer's Journey,* p. 75.

41. Ibid., p. 77.

42. http://webserver.maclab.comp.uvic.ca/writersguide/Pages/LTTheme.html.

43. Ronald B. Tobias, *20 Master Plots* (Cincinnati: Writer's Digest Books, 1993), p. 57.

44. Joseph Campbell, *The Hero with a Thousand Faces* (Princeton, NJ: Princeton University Press, 1949), p. 22.

45. Linda Seger, *Creating Unforgettable Characters* (New York: Henry Holt, 1990), p. 185.

46. Campbell, *The Hero with a Thousand Faces,* p. 146.

47. Tobias, *20 Master Plots,* pp. 138–139.

48. "36 Plots" is based on a classroom handout, the source of which is unknown. All efforts to track the original or author have proven unsuccessful.

49. Tobias, *20 Master Plots,* p. 99.

50. Sir James George Frazer, *The New Golden Bough,* ed. with notes and foreword by Theodor H. Gaster (New York: S.G. Phillips, 1959), p. 284.

51. Richard Cavendish, ed., *Man, Myth, and Magic* (Wichita, KS: McCormick-Armstrong, 1962), p. 66.

52. Eva C. Hangen, *Symbols: Our Universal Language* (Wichita, KS: McCormick-Armstrong, 1962), p. 72.

53. Foster R. McCurley, "American Myths and the Bible," *Word & World* 8, no. 3: 226–227.

54. Frederick Jackson Turner, *Encyclopedia Brittanica,* vol. 22 (Chicago: William Benton, 1983), p. 625.

55. May, *The Cry for Myth,* p. 101.

56. Ibid., pp. 105–106.

57. Reverend Andrew Greeley, "Myths, Symbols, and Rituals in the Modern World." *The Critic* 22, no. 3 (December–January 1962): 20–21.

58. Vladimir Propp, *The Morophology of the Folktale,* 2d ed. (Austin: University of Texas Press, 1968).

59. Amy Harmon, "For UFO Buffs, 50 Years of Hazy History," *New York Times,* June 14, 1997, pp. 1, 6.

60. Ibid., p. 6.

61. Ibid.

62. May, *The Cry for Myth,* 108.

63. Dennis McLellan, "New Book Takes Shot at Myth of John Wayne," *St. Louis Post-Dispatch,* April 3, 1997, p. 3G.

64. Seger, *Creating Unforgettable Characters,* pp. 186–187.

65. May, *The Cry for Myth,* p. 112.

66. Ibid., p. 99.

67. Ibid., p. 100.

68. Steven F. Walker, *Jung and the Jungians on Myth* (New York: Garland, 1995), p. 82.

69. Greeley, "Myths, Symbols, and Rituals in the Modern World," p. 19.

70. Hal Himmelstein, *Television, Myth and the American Mind,* 2d ed. (Westport, CT: Praeger, 1994), pp. 123–124.

71. Greeley, "Myths, Symbols, and Rituals in the Modern World," pp. 25–26.

72. Kimberly Althege, "Twister," unpublished paper, Webster University, 1997.

73. John O'Connor, "The Operation Was a Success: E.R. Lives," *New York Times,* October 23, 1994, p. H37.

74. Evelyn Barkin, *Are These Our Doctors?* (New York: Sell, 1952), pp. 171–172.

75. Mircea Eliade, *The Sacred and the Profane,* p. 21.

76. Michael Crichton, *Current Biography Yearbook 1993,* ed. Judith Graham (New York: H.W. Wilson, 1993), p. 143.

77. Steven Poole, "Whoa! I Gotta Pumper!" *Times Literary Suupplement,* February 1, 1996.

78. Rick Marin and Mark Miller, "S*M*A*S*H," *Newsweek,* October 31, 1994, sec. Life/Style, p. 46.

79. George Anders, *Health Against Wealth: HMOs and the Breakdown of Medical Trust* (New York: Houghton Mifflin, 1996).

80. Allan Schwartz, quoted in George Anders, *Health Against Wealth: HMOs and the Breakdown of Medical Trust* (New York: Houghton Mifflin, 1996), p. 81.

Notes to Chapter 5

1. Dr. Arthur Caplan, cited in Gary J. Schwitzer, "Doctoring the News: Miracle Cures, Video Press Releases, and TV Medical Reporting," *Quill* (November–December 1997).

2. Rone Tempest, Martha Groves, and John Daniszewski, "FAR FROM PLENTY," *Los Angeles Times,* December 22–26, 1997, sec. A, p. 1+.

3. Bill Lambrecht, "What Food Is Organic? Federal Rules Decide," *St. Louis Post-Dispatch*, January 15, 1998, sec. A, p. 7.

4. Kathleen Murphy, "Made Men," interview with Martin Scorsese, *Film Comment* (September–October 1990): 30.

5. Jacques Aumont, Alain Bergala, Michel Marie, and Marc Vernet, *Aesthetics in Film*, trans. Richard Neupert (Austin: University of Texas Press, 1992), p. 13.

6. Walter J. Ong, *Orality and Literacy: The Technologizing of the Word* (New York: Routledge, 1996), pp. 127–132.

7. James Wolcott, "Paper Monster," *Vanity Fair*, February 1998, p. 48.

8. Ibid., pp. 46–52.

9. Charlotte Ryan, *Prime Time Activism* (Boston: South End Press, 1991), pp. 53–56.

10. Bruce Kawin, *Mindscreen: Bergman, Godard, and First-Person Film* (Princeton: Princeton University Press, 1978), quoted in Edward Brannigan, *Point of View in the Cinema* (Berlin, New York: Mouton, 1984), p. 221.

11. Art Silverblatt, *Media Literacy: Keys to Interpreting Media Messages* (Westport, CT: Praeger, 1995), p. 111.

12. James Monaco, *How to Read Film* (New York: Oxford University Press, 1981), p. 173.

13. Laura Mulvey, *Visual and Other Pleasures* (Bloomington: Indiana University Press, 1989), p. 19.

14. Ibid.

15. Ibid.

16. Cheryl Endicott, "Journalism Analysis: *Sports 'N' Spokes* Magazine," unpublished paper, Webster University, March 1998.

17. Dorothy Nelkin, *Selling Science* (New York: W.H. Freeman, 1987).

18. Jeremy Black, *Maps and Politics* (London: Reaktion Books, 1997).

19. Victor Cohn, *News & Numbers* (Ames: Iowa State University Press, 1989).

20. Don Corrigan, "Future of Newspapers Belongs to Visual Artists," *St. Louis Journalism Review* 28, no. 206 (May 1998): 1.

21. Cohn, *News & Numbers*, p. 45.

22. Erik Spiekermann and E.M. Ginger, *Stop Stealing Sheep & Find Out How Type Works* (Mountain View, CA: Adobe Press, 1993), p. 15.

23. Kevin Barnhurst, *Seeing the Newspaper* (New York: St. Martin's Press, 1994), p. 156.

24. *St. Louis Post-Dispatch*, February 1, 1998.

25. Speikermann and Ginger, *Stop Stealing Sheep*, pp. 47–48.

26. Roy Paul Nelson, *Publication Design*, 3rd ed. (Dubuque: WM. C. Brown, 1989), p. 79.

27. Pablo Ferro, quoted in Tim Purtell "Credits Where Credit Is Due," *Entertainment Weekly* (1996), accessed January 1998 available from http://www.cgi.pathfinder.com; internet.

28. Kyle Cooper, quoted in David Geffner, "First Things First," *Filmmaker* 6, no. 1 (Fall 1997): 14.

29. Gerry Rosentswieg, *The New American Logo* (New York: Madison Square Press, 1994), intro.

30. Nike Consumer Affairs, 1996; author unknown, "Content/Conditions in Which Propaganda Occurs," accessed March 1998, available http://www.hq.simplenet.com/nike/info/prop.htm internet.

31. M. DeMartini, "The Great God Nike: Good or Evil," *Sporting Goods Dealer* (March 1997): 36.

32. M. Ellis, "Designers putting their best foot forward," July 16, 1997, Reuters.

33. Author unknown, "Content/Conditions in Which Propaganda Occurs."

34. Rosemary Sadex Friedman, "Psychological Aspects of Color Choices in House," *St. Louis Post-Dispatch,* May 2, 1998, p. L-15.

35. Ibid.

36. Ibid.

37. *St. Louis Post-Dispatch,* February 1, 1998.

38. Kyle Cooper, quoted in David Geffer, "First Things First," *Filmmaker* 6, no. 1 (Fall 1997): 14.

39. Author unknown, "Content/Conditions in Which Propaganda Occurs.".

40. Jerome Sterngold, "X-Files: An Adventure for Directors," *New York Times,* interview with Rob Bowman, March 10, 1998, sec. B, p. 1+.

41. Jack Green, quoted in Stephen Pizello, "A Rural Romance That Bridges Eras," *American Cinematographer* (August 1995): 54–55.

42. Stephen Pizello, "Twelve Monkeys: A Dystopian Trip Through Time," *American Cinematographer* (May 1996): 53.

43. Carl G. Jung, *Man and His Symbols* (New York: Doubleday, 1964), pp. 240–252.

44. Hans Biederman, *Dictionary of Symbolism: Cultural Icons and the Meanings Behind Them* (New York: Meridian, 1994).

45. Jung, *Man and His Symbols,* p. 249.

46. Biederman, *Dictionary of Symbolism,* pp. 70–71.

47. James Bennet, "Bad Vibes from the Heartland Launch Fleet of Finger-Pointers," *New York Times,* February 19, 1998, p. A9.

48. Ibid.

49. Biederman, *Dictionary of Symbolism..*

50. Harry Remde, "Inner Surface," *Parabola* 14, no. 4 (1989): 15, pp. 70–71.

51. Claude Bragdon, "An Architecture of Changless Change," *Parabola* 14, no. 4 (1989): 38–39.

52. Remde, "Inner Surface," pp. 14–15.

53. Art Silverblatt, *Media Literacy,* p. 108.

54. 13th Annual Harlan Hubbard Lemon Awards (Washington, DC: Center for Science and Public Interest, 1997).

55. Bernard Weintraub, "Hollywood Is Bitten by the Bugs," *New York Times,* June 24, 1997, sec. B, p. 11.

56. Ibid., sec. B, p. 4.

57. Aumont et. al., *Aesthetics in Film,* p. 229.

58. Roger Pratt, quoted in Stephen Pizello, "Twelve Monkeys: A Dystopian Trip Through Time," *American Cinematographer* (January 1996): 41.

59. Herbert Zettl, *Sight, Sound and Motion: Applied Media Aesthetics,* 2nd ed. (Belmont, CA: Wadsworth, 1990), p. 335.

60. Curtis Hanson, *LA Confidential,* Video Quote.

61. Jan Christe, "Martin Scorsese's Testament," interview with Martin Scorsese, *Sight and Sound* (January 1996): 11.

62. Monaco, *How to Read Film,* p. 106.

63. Mark Sullivan, interviewed by Todd Vaziri, Visual Effects Headquarters accessed April 1998 available from http://www.vfxhq.com; internet.

64. R.T. Radanovic, "Media Literacy Analysis: Production Elements," unpublished paper, Webster University, April 1998.

Bibliography

Althage, Kimberly. "Twister." Unpublished paper, School of Communications, Webster University, St. Louis, Mo., 1997.

Anders, George. *Health Against Wealth: HMOs and the Breakdown of Medical Trust*. New York: Houghton Mifflin, 1996.

Anderson, Robin. *Consumer Culture and TV Programming*. Boulder, Co.: Westview Press, 1995.

anonymous. ???? . Available from http://webserver.maclab.comp.uvic. ca/writersguide/pages/LTTTheme.html.

Associated Press,. 1997. "Yeltsin Questions The Cost The People of Russia Are Paying For Materialism." *St. Louis Post-Dispatch*, 27 December, sec.? p. 21.

Aumont, Jacques, Marc Vernet, Alain Bergala, and Michel Marie. *Aesthetics in Film*, Trans. Richard Neupert. Austin: University of Texas Press, 1992.

Bagdikian, Ben. *Media Monopoly*. 5th ed. Boston: Beacon, 1997.

Baltake, Joe. "On Internet, Everyone Is a Critic." *St. Louis Post-Dispatch*, July 4, 1997, sec. E, p. 1.

Barkin, Evelyn. *Are These Our Doctors?* New York: Sell, 1952.

Barthes, Roland. *Mythologies*. Trans. Annette Lavers. New York: Hill and Wang, 1957.

Becker, Jasper. 1997. "Good News! You're Fired." *South China Post*, October 15, 1997, Reprinted in *World Press Review*, February 1998, p. 31.

Bennet, James. "Bad Vibes from the Heartland Launch Fleet of Finger-Pointers." *New York Times*, February 19, 1998, sec. A, p. 9.

———. "Clintons Present Their Act to an Admiring Argentina," *New York Times*, October 17, 1997, sec. A p. 1.

Berger, John. *Ways of Seeing*. New York: Penguin Books, 1972.

Biederman, Hans. *Dictionary of Symbolism: Cultural Icons and the Meanings Behind Them*. Trans. James Hulbert. New York: Meridan, 1994.

Black, Jeremy. *Maps and Politics*. London: Reaktion Books, 1997.

Bowen, Wally. *News Tie-ins to Be Made for TV Movies*, Accessed August 12, 1997. Available from http://www.media-1a-1@nmsu.edu.

Bragdon, Claude. 1989. "An Architecture of Changless Change." *Parabola* 14 (4): 38–41.

Branhurst, Kevin. *Seeing the Newspaper*. New York: St. Martins Press, 1994.

Brookfield, Stephen. "Media Power and the Development of Media Literacy: An Adult Educational Interpretation." *Harvard Educational Review* 56 (2): May 1986, 151–170.

Bruner, Jerome. *Actual Minds, Possible Worlds*. Cambridge, Mass.: Harvard University Press, 1986.

———. "Myth and Identity." In *Myth and Mythmaking*, ed. H. A. Murray. New York: George Braziller, 1960, p. 280.

Buckingham, David. *Children Talking Television: The Making of Television Literacy*. London: Falmer Press, 1993.

———. *Moving Images: Understanding Children's Emotional Responses to Television*. Manchester and New York: Manchester University Press, 1996.

Bull, Peter E. *Posture and Gesture*. In *International Series in Experimental Social Psychology*, ed. M. Argyle, New York: Pergamon Press, 1987, pp. 122–141.

Burr, Ty. "When Will Oscar Really Know the Score?" *New York Times*, March 1, 1998, sec. 2, p.13.

Campbell, Joseph. *The Hero with a Thousand Faces, Bollingen Series, vol. 17*. New York: Pantheon Books, 1949.

———. "The Historical Development of Mythology." In *Myth and Myth making*, ed. H. A. Murray. New York: George Braziller, 1960, pp. 000–000.

Campbell, Rayshawn. "The Story of Jim." Unpublished paper, St. Louis, Mo., 1998.

Capaccio, Tony. "The Kelly Flinn Spin Patro." *American Journalism Review*, September 1997, pp. 12–13.

Caputi, Jane. "Charting the Flow; The Construction of Meaning Through Juxtaposition in Media Texts." *Journal of Communication Inquiry* 15 (2): Summer 1991, 32–47.

Cawelti, John. "Myth Symbol, and Formula." *Journal of Popular Culture* 8 (Summer): 1–10, 1974.

Chandler, Daniel. 1997. *Semiotics for Beginners*. Available from http://www.aber. ac.uk/dgc/semiotic.html.

Chenoune, Farid. *A History of Men's Fashion*. Trans. Richard Martin. Paris: Flammarion, 1993.

Chester, Jeffrey A., and Anthony Wright. "A Twelve Step Program for Media Democracy." *The Nation*, June 3, 1996, pp. 9–15.

Chono-Helsley, Martha. 1994. " VIDKIDCO/Long Beach Museum of Art." In *L.A. Freewaves Catalog of Southern California Youth Media Programs*, ed. G. Lamb. Los Angeles: Freewaves, pp. 38–39.

Christie, Ian. "Martin Scorcese's Testament."*Sight and Sound* 6 (1): 7–11, 1996.

Cohen, Richard. "Clock Already Ticking on Clinton Honeymoon." *St. Louis Post-Dispatch*, November 6, 1992, sec. C, p. 3.

Cohn, Victor. *News and Numbers*. Ames: Iowa State University Press, 1989.

Collins, Andrew W. "Children's Comprehension of Television Content." In *Children Communicating*, ed. E. Wartella. Beverly Hills, Calif.: Sage Publications, 1979, pp. 72–73.

Collins, James M. 1988. "The Musical." In *Handbook of American Film Genres*, ed. W. D. Gering. New York: Greenwood Press, 1988, p. 268.

Collins, Ronald. *Dictating Content: How Advertising Pressure Can Corrupt a Free Press*. Washington. D.C.: Center for Study of Commercialism, 1992.

"Content/Conditions in Which Propraganda Occurs." 1996. Accessed March, 1998. Available from http://www.hq.simplenet.com/nike/info/prop.htm.

Coontz, Stephanie. *The Way We Never Were*. New York: Basic Books, 1992.

Cooper, Mike. 1998. "Study: More U.S. High School Students Smoking." Atlanta, Ga.: Reuters, Center for Disease Control, 1998.

Cooper, Pamela. *Speech Communication for the Classroom Teacher*, 3d ed. Scottsdale, Ariz.: Goruch Scarisbrick, 1988.

Corrigan, Don. "Future of Newspapers Belongs to Visual Arts." *St. Louis Journalism Review*, May 1998, p. 1.

Crichton, Michael. *Current Biography Yearbook*. ed. Judith Graham. New York: H.W. Wilson, 1993.

D'Aulaire, Edgar Parin. *Ingri and Edgar Parin d'Aulaire's Book of Greek Myths*. New York: Doubleday, 1962.

Daniel, Jeff. "Melrose Placements.." *St. Louis Post-Dispatch*, February 16, 1998, sec. E, p. 4.

De Jong, William, Charles Atkin, and Lawrence Wallack. *The Influence of Responsible Drinking TV Spots and Automobile Commercials on Young Drivers*. Washington, D.C.: American Automobile Association Foundation for Traffic Safety, 1992.

DeMartini, M. "The Great God Nike: Good or Evil?" *Sporting Goods Dealer*, March, 1997, p. 36.

Deslodge, Rick. "KMOX Given Ultimatum: Double Profits." *St. Louis Business Journal*, February 26–March 3, 1996, sec. A, p.1.

Dorr, Aimee. "Television and Its Socializing Influences in Minority Children." In *Television and the Socialization of the Minority Child*, ed. G. L. Berry and C. Mitchell-Kerman. New York: Academic Press, 1982, p. 27.

Drinkard, Jim. "Lobbying Groups Play Distracting Name Game." Associated Press. *St. Louis Post-Dispatch*, December 23, 1997, sec. B, p. 1.

Eliade, Mircea. 1957. *The Sacred and The Profane : The Nature of Religion*. Trans. Willard R. Trask. New York, London: Harcourt Brace, 1957.

Ellis, M. 1997. "Designers Putting Their Best Foot Forward." *Reuters*, July 16, 1997.

Endicott, Cheryl. "Journalism Analysis: Sports N' Spokes Magazine." Unpublished paper, School of Communications, Webster University, St. Louis, Mo., 1998.

Faison, Seth. "In China, Better Unread than Read." *New York Times*, September 7, 1997, sec. 4, p. 5.

Fein, Esther B. "The End of 'Seinfeld' Has Hit Show's Fans Grieving." *New York Times*, December 27, 1997, sec. A, p. 28.

Frankel, Max. "The Next Great Story." *New York Times Magazine*, March 15, 1998, pp. 30.

Friedman, Rosemary Sadex. "Psychological Aspects of Color Choices in House. *St. Louis Post-Dispatch*, May 2, 1998, sec. L, p. 15.

Frolichstein, Tripp. *Media Training Handbook*. St. Louis, Mo.: MediaMasters, 1991.

Frost, Richard, and John Stoffer. "The Effects of Social Class, Gender, and Personality on Psychological Responses to Filmed Violence." *Journal of Communication* 37 (Spring 1987): 29–46.

Frye, Northrup. "Archetypal Criticism: Theory of Myths." In *Anatomy of Criticism: Four Essays*. Princeton, N.J.: Princeton University Press, 1957, pp. 187–188.

Gavindish, Richard, ed. *Man, Myth, and Magic*. Wichita, Kans.: McCormick-Armstrong, 1962.

Geffner, David. "First Things First." *Filmmaker*, Fall 1997, pp. 14–17 ff.

Giannetti, Louis. *Understanding Movies*. 7th ed. Englewood Cliffs, N.J.: Prentice Hall, 1996.

Goffman, Erving. "Gender Advertisements." *Studies in The Anthropology of Visual Communication* 3 (2), 1976, pp. 69–152.

Goodwin, Christopher. "Ku Klux Klan Cleans Up Image." *London Sunday Times*, August 18, 1997.

Grazer, Sir James George. *The Golden Bough.* Ed. T. H. Gaster. New York: S.G. Phillips, 1959.

Greely, Rev. Andrew. "Myths, Symbols and Rituals in the Modern World." *Critic,* December–January 1961–1962, pp. 18–25.

Gunter, Barries. *Dimensions of Television Violence.* New York: St. Martin's Press, 1985.

Hamilton, Edith. *Mythology.* Boston: Mentor Books, 1963.

Hangen, Eva. *Symbols: Our Universal Language.* Wichita, Kans.: McCormick-Armstrong, 1962.

Hanson, Curtis. *LA Confidential.*

Hargrave, Jan. *Let Me See Your Body Talk.* Iowa: Kendall Hunt, 1995.

Harmon, Amy. "For UFO Buffs, 50 Years of Hazy History." *New York Times,* June 14, 1997.

Harms, Samantha L. "Magazine Advertisements: What Do They Tell Us About Gender?" Unpublished paper, School of Communications, Webster University, St. Louis, Mo., October 15, 1997.

Herbert, Bob. "Fashion Statement." *New York Times.* February 15, 1998. Available from http://www.stlnet.com.

Highet, Gilbert. *The Classical Tradition and Roman Influences on Western Literature.* New York: Oxford University Press/Galaxy Books, 1957.

Himmelstein, Hal. *Television Myth and the American Mind,* 2d ed. Wesport, Conn.: Praeger, 1994.

Hoge, Warren. *"Murdoch's Harper Collins Won't Publish Book That Criticizes China".* Accessed on February 28, 1954. Available from http://www.stlnet.com.

Huff, Darrell. *How To Lie With Statistics.* New York: W.W. Norton, 1954.

"I Never Told Anybody to Lie." *St. Louis Post-Dispatch,* January 27, 1998. Available from http://www.Postnet.com.

Iggers, Jeremy. "Get Me Rewrite!" *Utne Reader,* September/October, 1997, pp. 46–48.

International Movie Data Base. http://www.imdb.com

Ivins, Molly. "A Fuddy-Duddy's View of Free Trade." *St. Louis Post-Dispatch,* November 29, 1997, sec. B, p. 7.

———. "Who Is Funding Those Who Are Debating Global Warming?" *St. Louis Post-Dispatch,* December 16, 1997, sec. B, p. 7.

Jhally, Sut, and Justin Lewis. "Enlightened Racism: The Cosby Show." In *Audiences and the Myth of the American Dream.* Boulder, Col.: Westview Press, 1992.

Joffee, Joseph. "America the Inescapable.." *New York Times Magazine,* June 8, 1997, pp. 38–43.

Jung, Carl G. *Man and His Symbols.* New York: Doubleday, 1964.

Kakutani, Michiko. "Taking Out the Trash." *New York Times Magazine,* June 8, 1997, pp. 30–34.

———. 1998. "Portrait of the Artist as a Focus Group." *New York Times Magazine,* March 1, 1998, p. 26.

Kawin, Bruce. *Mindscreen: Bergman, Godard, and First Person.* Film. Princeton, N.J.: Princeton University Press, 1979, p. 338.

Kellner, Douglas. "TV, Ideology, and Emancipatory Popular Culture." *Socialist Review* 9 (3), 1979.

———. *Media Culture-Cultural Studies, Identity and Politics Between the Modern and the Postmodern.* London and New York: Routledge, 1995.

Klein, Richard. "After Teaching, the Lure of the Taboo". *New York Times,* August 24, 1997, sec. 2, p. 1.

Kruh, Nancy. "State of the Unions." *St. Louis Post-Dispatch*, July 15, 1997, sec. D, p.1.

Kwain, Bruce. *Mindscreen: Bergman, Godard, and First Perso- Film*. Princeton, N.J.: Princeton University Press, 1978.

Lakeoff, George, and Mark Johnson. *Metaphors We Live By*. Chicago, London: University of Chicago Press, 1981.

Lambrecht, Bill. "What Food is Organic? Federal Rules Decide." *St. Louis Post-Dispatch*, January 15, 1998, sec. A, p.7.

Laswell, Harold D. *Power and Personality*. New York: W.W. Norton, 1948.

Leathers, Dale G. *Successful Nonverbal Communication: Principles and Applications*. 3d ed. Boston: Allyn and Bacon, 1997.

Levins, Harry. "Original Sin Sells." *St. Louis Post-Dispatch*, February 1, 1998, sec. A, p. 2.

Lewis, Michael. *Trail Fever*. New York: Alfred A. Knopf, 1997.

Lutz, William. *The New Doublespeak: Why No One Knows What Anyone is Saying Anymore*. New York: HarperCollins, 1996.

McCurley, Foster R. "American Myths and the Bible." *Word and World* 8 (Summer 1988): pp. 226–233.

McKissack, Fredrick, Jr. "Nike Memo Details Abuses in Asian Factory." *St. Louis Post-Dispatch*, November 21, 1997, sec. C, p. 19.

McLellan, Dennis. "New Book Takes Shot at Myth of John Wayne." *St. Louis Post-Dispatch*, April 3, 1997, sec. G, p.3.

Martin, Rick, and Mark Miller. "*S*M*A*S*H*." *Newsweek*, October 31, 1994, sec. Life/Style, p. 46.

Masterman, Len. *Teaching the Media*. Vol. ? Routledge. New York, 1985

———. "Shifting the Power, Addressing the Ideology." *Mediacy* 13 (2): Summer 1991, pp. 1–6.

May, Rollo. *The Cry for Myth*. New York, London: W.W. Norton, 1991.

"Marketer's Partner with New James Bond Movie." In *Mining Company Guide to Advertising Industry*. 1997. Available from http://advertising.tqn. com/library/weekly/aa120797.htm.

Mediacy. 10 Ontario, Canada, (Winter 1990).

Merrill, John C, John Lee, and Jonathan J. Friedlander *Modern Mass Media*. New York: Harper and Row, 1990.

Meyrowitz, Joshua. *No Sense of Place: The Impact of Electronic Media on Social Behavior*. New York, Oxford: Oxford University Press, 1985.

Mitchell, Allison. "G.O.P. Hopes Climate Fight Echoes Health Care Outcome." *New York Times*, December 13, 1997, sec. A, p. 1.

Monoco, James. *How To Read Film*. Oxford: Oxford University Press, 1981.

Morris, Desmond. *Body Talk*. New York: Crown Trade Paperbacks, 1994.

Muller, Max. *The Philosophy of Mythology, The Science of Religion*. London, 1873.

Mulvey, Laura. *Visual and Other Pleasures*. Bloomington: Indiana University Press, 1989.

Murphy, Kathleen. "Made Men." *Film Comment*, September/October 1990, pp. 25–27.

Murray, Henry A. "The Possible Nature of a 'Mythology' to Come." In *Myth and Mythmaking*, ed. H. A. Murray. New York: George Braziller, 1960, p. 338.

Nelkin, Dorothy. *Selling Science: How the Press Covers Science and Technology*. New York: W.H. Freeman, 1987.

Nelson, Roy Paul. *Publication Design*. Dubuque, Iowa: WM. C. Brown, 1989.

Nichols, Bill. *Ideology and the Image: Social Representation in Cinema and Other Media*. Bloomington: Indiana University Press, 1981.

O'Connor, John. "The Operation Was a Success: E.R. Lives." *New York Times*, October 23, 1994, sec. H, p.37.

O'Neill, Dan. "He's Ba-a-a-ck: Tiger Woods Is Talk of Texas." *St. Louis Post-Dispatch.* May 14, 1997, sec. D, p. 6.

Ong, Walter. *Orality and Literacy: The Technologizing of the Word.* New York: Routledge, 1996.

Pantumchinda, Panrawee. "Cosmopolitan Magazine in Thailand." Unpublished paper, School of Communications, Webster University, St. Louis, Mo., 1998.

Parenti, Michael. *Make Believe Media.* New York: St. Martin's Press, 1992.

Pearson, Judy, Richard West, and and Lynn Turner. *Gender Communication.* 3d ed. Du Buque, Iowa: Brown and Benchmark, 1995.

Pease, Allan. *Signals.* Toronto: Bantam, 1981.

Perkins, Kathryn. "Study: Sex, Age, Work Against Women." *The Scramento Bee,* November 30, 1996, http://www.sacbee.com.

Peterman, Deborah. "Hercules' Is One Hades Of A Movie." *St. Louis Post-Dispatch,* January 29, 1997, sec. E, p. 3.

———. "The Sharper Image." *St. Louis Post-Dispatch,* 1997, sec. E, p. 1ff.

Pizzello, Stephen. "A Rural Romance That Bridges Eras." *American Cinematographer,* August 1995, pp. 52–56.

———. "Twelve Monkeys: A Dystopian Trip Through Time." *American Cinematographer,* January 1996, pp. 36–43.

Poole, Steven. "Whoa! I Gotta Pumper!" *Times Literary Supplement,* February 1, 1996, p. 18.

Porter, Richard E., and Larry A. Samovar. *Communication Between Two Cultures.* 2d ed. Belmont, Wash.: Wadsworth, 1995.

Powell, Gloria Johnson. "The Impact of Television on the Self-Concept Development of Minority Group Children." In *Television and the Socialization of the Minority Child,* ed. G. L. Berry and C. Mitchell-Kerman. New York: Academic Press, 1982, p. 107.

Prial, Frank. 1998. "We'll Have the Chateau Cuervo." *New York Times,* March 15, 1998, Sec. 4, p. 2.

Propp, Vladmir. *The Morpohology of the Folktale.* 2d ed. Austin, London: University of Texas Press, 1968.

Purtell, Tim. "Credits Where Credit Is Due." *Entertainment Weekly,* 1996. Accessed January 1998. Available from http://www.cgi. pathfinder.com.

Quinn, Kay. *Hepatitis A Feature*: KSDK (a National Broadcasting Company [NBC] affiliate) Broadcast January 11–12, 1993.

Radonovic, R.T. "Media Literacy Analysis: Production Elements." Unpublished paper, School of Communications, Webster University, St. Louis, Mo., 1998.

Reeves, Byron. "Children's Understanding of Television People." In *Children Communicating,* ed. E. Wartella. Beverly Hills, Calif.: Sage Publications, 1979.

Reference, Myth cite # 48? .

Remde, Harry. "Inner Surface." *Parabola* 14 (4): 14–16, 1989.

Rich, Frank. "The Price is Right." *New York Times,* January 10, 1988, sec. A, p. 25.

Rich, Linda G., Joan Clark Netherwood, and Elinor B. Cahn. *Neighboorhood: A State of Mind.* Baltimore: Johns Hopkins University Press, 1981.

RJ-(rj@tezcat.com). "Arianne Doublespeak." Available from http://drycas.club.cmu.edu /-tina/humor/ariane.html.

Rollins, Angela. "Tommy Hilfiger and the American Ideal." Unpublished paper, School of Communications, Webster University, St. Louis, Mo., 1998.

Rosentswieg, Gerry. *The New American Logo.* New York: Madison Square, 1994.

Rosow, Eugene. *Born to Lose: The Gangster Film in America.* Oxford: Oxford University Press, 1978.

ross, jesikah maria, and Barbara Osborne. "Media Literacy and Public Access TV Training." *Strategies for Media Literacy* 6 (Summer/Fall 1993). Available from http://www.interact.uoregon.edu\medialit\fo\in\articlefolder.t

Ryan, Charlotte. *Prime Time Activism*. Boston: South End Press, 1991.

Safire, William. "In Office Since '81, GOP Just Went Sour." *St. Louis Post-Dispatch*, November 9, 1992, sec. B, p. 3.

Schneider, Ellen. " 'E.C.U.': Home for Video Diarists." *Current* March 6, 1995, p. 2.

Schwitzer, Gary. "Doctoring the News: Miracle Cures, Video Press Releases, and TV Medical Reporting." *Quill* November/Decembe 1992, 19–21.

Seger, Linda. *Creating Unforgettable Characters*. New York: Henry Holt, 1990.

Seligmann, Jean, Barbara Kantrowitz, and Rick Martin. "Blood Ties or Blood Feud?" *Newsweek*, (date?) 1997, p. 53.

Sharpe, Daryl. "C. G. Jung, Analytical Psychology and Culture: Glossary of Jungian Terms." Accessed January 1998. Available from http://www.cgjung.com./glossary.html.

Silverblatt, Arthur. *Media Literacy: Keys to Interpreting Media Messages*. Westport, Conn.: Praeger, 1995.

Silverstone, Roger. "Television Myth and Culture." In *Media, Myths, and Narratives*, ed. J. W. Carey. Newbury Park, Calif.: Sage Publications, 1988, p. 34.

Simon, Scott. *Affluenza*: KETC/PBS. Produced by KCTS/Seattle and Oregon Public Broadcasting. Broadcast September 19, 1997.

Smith, Gavin, "Interview with Martin Scorsese." *Film Comment*. September/October 1990, pp. 27–29.

Spiekermann, Erik, and E.M. Ginger. *Stop Stealing Sheep and Find Out How Type Works*. California: Adobe Press, 1993.

Sterngold, James. "X-Files: An Adventure for Directors." *New York Times*, March 10, 1998, sec. B, p.1 ff.

Stone, Vernon. "Minorities and Women in Television News." University of Missouri, 1995, 1996. Available from jourvs@showne.missouri.edu.

Stuart, Ewan. *The Public Mind: All Consuming Images*: Public Broadcasting System. November 8, 1989.

Sumner, Jane. "Isabella Rosellini—Without Makeup." *St. Louis Post-Dispatch*, July 16, 1997, sec. E, p. 3.

Taylor, Clyde. "New U.S. Black Cinema." In *Movies and Mass Culture*. ed. J. Belton. New Brunswick, N.J.: Rutgers University Press, 1996, p. 238.

Tempest, Rone, Martha Groves, and John Daniszewski. "Far From Plenty." *Los Angeles Times*, December 22–26, 1997, sec. A, p.1 ff.

Thoman, Elizabeth. "Blueprint for Responsive-Ability." *Media &Values* 35 (Spring 1986): 21–14.

Thuresson, Mattias F. (mattias.thuresson@mbox300.swipnet.se).

Tobias, Ronald B. *20 Master Plots*. Cincinatti, Ohio: Writer's Digest Books, 1993.

Toroian, Diane. "The Impact of Pop Lyrics Depend On Who's Listening." *St. Louis Post-Dispatch*, January 22, 1998, sec. D, p. 1.

Turner, Charles W., Bradford W. Hesse, and Sonja Peterson-Lewis. "Naturalistic Studies of the Long-term Effects of Television Violence." *Journal of Social Issues* 42: 51–73, 1986.

Turner, Fredrick Jackson. In *Encyclopedia Brittanica*. Chicago: William Benton, 1983.

U.S. Department of Health and Human Services. "Tobacco Use Among High School Students—1997." *MMWR (Morbidity and Mortality Weekly Report)* 47, no. 10, Atlanta, Ga.: CDC (month? 1998), p. 625.

Vaziri, Todd. *Visual Effects Headquarters*. Accessed April 1998. Available from http://www.vfxhq.com.

Vogler, Christopher. *The Writer's Journey*. Calif.: Michael Wiese, 1992.

Walcott, James. "Paper Monster." *Vanity Fair*, February 1998, pp. 46–52.

Walker, Steven F. *Jung and the Jungians on Myth*. New York and London: Garland Publishing, 1995.

Washington, James Melvin, ed. *A Testament of Hope: The Essential Writings of Martin Luther King, Jr.* San Francisco: Harper and Row, 1986.

Weintraub, Bernard. "Hollywood Is Bitten by Bugs." *New York Times*, June 24, 1997, sec. B, p. 11.

Williams, Raymond K. *Keywords: A Vocabulary of Culture and Society*. London: Oxford University Press, 1995, p. 251.

"Yeltsin Questions the Cost the People of Russia Are Paying for Materialism," (Associated Press). *St. Louis Post-Dispatch*, December 27, 1997, sec. B, p. 21.

Yoder, Edson. "Clinton's Call for Civility Reflects A Belief in Power of Reason." *St. Louis Post-Dispatch*, July 13, 1995, sec. B, p. 7.

Zagorian, Adam. "The Mall the Merrier." *Time Magazine*, November 24, 1997.

Zettl, Herbert. *Sight Sound and Motion: Applied Media Asthetics*. 2d ed. Belmont, Wash.: Wadsworth, 1990.

INDEX

ABOUT THE AUTHORS

Art Silverblatt is a professor of communications in the School of Communications at Webster University. He is author of *Media Literacy: Keys to Interpreting Media Messages* and co-author of the *Dictionary of Media Literacy.*

Jane Ferry is an adjunct professor in the School of Communications at Webster University.

Barbara Finan is an academic advisor and the program coordinator of the School of Communications at Webster University.